100 Places After

A Journey to Honor My Mom's Final Wish

Scott C. Hall

This is a work of nonfiction based on the author's personal experiences, memories, and interpretations. Events, conversations, and locations are recounted to the best of the author's recollection. Some names, personal details, and identifying characteristics have been changed to respect privacy or to preserve anonymity.

The views and opinions expressed in this book are solely those of the author and do not represent the views of any city, country, organization, brand, or institution mentioned. The author is not affiliated with, endorsed by, or sponsored by any landmarks, governments, companies, or entities referenced throughout the text.

This book contains references to medical conditions and treatments. These descriptions are based on personal experience and should not be considered medical advice. Readers should consult qualified professionals regarding any medical concerns.

ISBN: 979-8-9909201-0-1 (Paperback)

ISBN: 979-8-9909201-3-2 (Hardcover)

ISBN: 979-8-9909201-5-6 (eBook)

For inquiries, contact the author at www.scottchall.com

instagram.com/scott_c_hall/

facebook.com/hallscottc/

For Mom

CONTENTS

About the Book

I lost my mom, Joanne, to stomach cancer in September 2012. To honor her final wish, I had her body cremated and embarked on a journey to carry her memory to one hundred unforgettable places. This book is one hundred stories about my pursuit of those places, why I chose them, and the struggles she endured that motivated me to keep going.

Sometimes, I searched for a moment; other times, I searched for weeks. I sought places that offered adventure, breathtaking beauty, or where she dreamed of visiting. Interspersed are those with historical, political, and religious significance. I'm not a historian, politician, theologian, or anything else ending in *-ian*. I'm just a traveler sharing what I saw, felt, and learned along the way.

In some cases, the story might feel like a list of facts, almost entirely about the place itself, with little of my own involvement. As much as I tried to avoid such situations, each place had a purpose, and I would have done you a disservice if I had said, "This is where the tragedy happened," or "This is where someone influential is buried," or "This is where the world changed," without explaining why. If I have made any factual errors, they were unintentional.

I never intended for this book to delve into deeper topics, but the more I saw of the world, the more my views of it changed. Travel transformed me in ways I couldn't have predicted. I was a different person by the end of 100 Places After. Please forgive me if any of my opinions offend you.

Finally, throughout these pages, you will see this symbol (M), marking the place I deemed worthy of Mom's wish.

THE STRUGGLE AND THE WISH

It began with abdominal discomfort and nausea. A month later, on New Year's Eve, Mom vomited blood. The following week, she received the life-altering diagnosis—cancer in her stomach, pancreas, liver, and a lymph node in her neck. She had beaten cancer before and was ready again for the fight of all fights.

Chemotherapy struck first. Four rounds of epirubicin, cisplatin, and fluorouracil were administered every three weeks, with each infusion lasting a day. The first two rounds cleared her liver and pancreas, improved her lymph node, and shrank the stomach tumor. Her spirits soared. But with each subsequent round—accompanied by steroids, iron infusions, blood infusions, and antihistamines—she weakened. The nausea and fatigue worsened, the stomach lesion bled, her blood sugar spiked, rashes erupted, her taste buds morphed until only aluminum remained, and the diarrhea became depressive.

Tired of seeing her coveted hair fall out in clumps, one tearful evening, she cut off what remained and replaced it with a wig she named Kailani—Hawaiian for sea and sky. When the final round ended, she welcomed the break.

Besides the treatment, the worst part was the waiting. After weeks of mystery, despite the initial progress, the stomach tumor stopped shrinking and appeared brighter, more active, on the PET scan. The spot on her lymph node remained. That night, she cried herself to sleep.

With her morale bruised but not broken, the next weapon was external beam radiation therapy. Nearly every day for six weeks, she spent her lunches undergoing the painful procedure before returning to work. Side effects included fatigue, high blood sugar, and radiation burns akin to a bad sunburn, worsened by more sun. But compared to chemo, it was a dream. Her energy and taste buds returned, her nausea subsided, and her head sprouted peach fuzz. To amuse the radiation technicians, she taped a sign to her stomach that read "Radioactive—Danger."

Waiting for the results again, she occupied her mind as a Clinical Study Manager for a Phase I pharmaceutical research company, responsible for administering clinical trials involving healthy subjects to determine the safety and efficacy of pharmaceuticals that could potentially reach the market. A workaholic and a shirker of pity, she never fell behind, vowing not to let cancer strip her pride.

A month later, the PET scan showed the stomach tumor had shrunk but hadn't gone away. The spot on her lymph node stayed the same. Two additional lymph nodes lit up, as did part of her thyroid.

The next attempt to destroy the stomach tumor was surgery. The best-case scenario was a partial gastrectomy to amputate part of the stomach. If necessary, a total gastrectomy would remove all of it. The surgeon would connect whatever remained to the esophagus or small intestine. The procedure required recovery in the ICU, a feeding tube, a bladder catheter, needle sticks, a scar from the belly button to the breastbone, months of healing, and a lifestyle change. Nervous and scared, she was willing to endure the pain and bought new pajamas for her hospital stay.

Before going under the knife, another scan showed no change in the stomach or thyroid, but a new spot appeared on the liver, and its surrounding lymph nodes had become active. Surgery was no longer an option. She felt relieved to have avoided the debilitating procedure, only to discover the metastases later. On the bright side, she could enjoy her favorite restaurants. Or so she thought.

Another regimen of chemo ensued. This time, it was a combination of docetaxel and carboplatin, which she incorrectly assumed would produce side effects similar to before. Vomiting and dehydration were accompanied by severe nausea and abdominal pain. She lost eight pounds in the first week and was prescribed dronabinol, a synthetic form of cannabis, to treat her appetite loss. But all she could eat was soup, soup, and soup. Occasionally, it overpowered the aluminum.

The chemo decimated her bone marrow and plummeted her white blood cell count. She avoided restaurants, movie theaters, friends, and outdoor activities. She missed a day of work for the first time since it all began. Her absenteeism worsened as she left early to take naps. If she made it through the day, she was in bed by 9 p.m. To boost her energy, she took methylphenidate, a central nervous system stimulant used to treat ADHD and narcolepsy.

After ten days of misery, her vitality and appetite returned. She then spent the next ten days catching up on work. Once she felt better, the chemo was re-administered, and the clock restarted. Thus began the cycle of ten bad days and ten good days. However, after four rounds, her liver cleared up, and her stomach improved. So effective, much to Mom's dismay, she underwent a fifth round. If it worked, it was worth it.

We entered the holiday season. During Thanksgiving, those who hadn't seen her recently did their best to feign surprise. One friend went behind closed doors to cry. Christmas was more subdued, celebrated with Mom, her boyfriend, and me. With no chemo for a month and multiple blood transfusions, she had regained much of her strength just in time for another form of chemo.

Next came the weekly doses of gemcitabine. Supposedly easier on nausea and vomiting, she tolerated it well after two treatments. As a bonus, she didn't taste metal. The main concern was the devastation of blood platelets, a component critical to clotting. Fearing an infection, she worked from home, where her color returned, her energy stabilized, and her outlook improved.

A month later, the stunning results arrived. Every trace of cancer except the original stomach lesion had vanished. Wanting to keep her foot on the gas, she arranged for a second opinion at an internationally renowned cancer center in Boston, Massachusetts. She faxed them 137 pages of medical records.

Nothing groundbreaking emerged. The Department of Gastrointestinal Oncology Chairman agreed with the local oncologist's treatment plan and was satisfied with the use of gemcitabine. If it ceased to be effective, he recommended switching to another chemotherapy, irinotecan. Conversely, surgery was no longer an option due to the belief that irremovable cancer seeds were present. Her condition was chronic. As much as the operation frightened her, she was tired of treatment, wanting a cure, not care.

So began another cycle of chemo, transfusions, and medications. Five months later, a scan showed the stomach cancer had grown and become more aggressive. It had spawned a tumor in the lower abdomen the size of a grapefruit, accompanied by an ascites, an abnormal buildup of fluid in the abdomen that pressed against her bladder. Extra fluid had accumulated around the heart, causing shortness of breath with any exertion. Mom was running out of options.

A nurse practitioner (NP) laid it all out. Continuing the gemcitabine might offer little benefit. Alternatively, an interferon treatment could start, named so because it "interferes" with viruses to stop their proliferation. At this point, the side effects would have been excruciating. The NP said the pain probably wasn't worth it and brought up palliative care. Mom said, "We're not there yet." Recognizing we were, the NP provided a timeline—maybe one more Christmas, but not two. It was August.

They hugged, cried, and discussed the ascites. Unable to eliminate it, to relieve the discomfort, Mom could undergo a paracentesis—a procedure to remove the fluid with a needle. She scheduled an appointment for a few days later. (When an ascites develops, the typical life expectancy is four to twelve months. The NP's timeline made sense.)

Knowing her medical options were limited, Mom sought salvation elsewhere. She had grown up in a Catholic family outside of Detroit, Michigan. No longer a churchgoer, her faith in God never waned, as she praised Him for the good news and prayed for help with the bad. In utter desperation, she searched for a miracle.

Without a church of her own, a friend suggested a local minister. I took her to meet him one afternoon after work. The short-statured, well-dressed man with jet-black hair and thin-rimmed glasses offered comforting words that surmised life is like high school and that our suffering is a prelude to college, our entry into Heaven. She nodded as her eyes welled up. Aided by two parishioners, she slunk down, and he anointed her fluffy hair with oil. Despite longing for a magical cure, she knew it wouldn't happen. If nothing else, she had attained a modicum of solace and came to grips with reality.

On the way home, for the first time, we broached what would happen after she was gone. Foremost was her body. I'm unsure when or why, but she had decided on cremation. Fearful of fire, the thought of burning to death scared her more than cancer. Having endured so much trauma, turning her body to ash represented a new beginning.

The conversation shifted to my plans. I hadn't thought much about them, but she had envisioned my future. We both loved to travel, often visiting family in Massachusetts, Florida, and California. Every few years, we would go to Mexico or Hawaii. I had recently left North America for the first time and returned with an unanticipated zeal. Knowing what my heart desired, she gave me a vague yet simple request that changed my life. Her final wish was for me to travel the world and spread her memory.

I tossed out a few suggestions: the Greek Isles, Australia, and Hawaii. For the first time in a long while, our spirits eased as I had found a purpose, and she had found hope. Nearly home, we kept the list short.

Starting Small

1 ♦ Las Vegas, Nevada

It's been one month since Mom took her last breath. One month since I clutched her hospital gown and erupted into tears. One month since I noted her time of death. One month since I no longer had any parents. One month since I had lost my confidant, adviser, best friend, and the person who loved me most.

I lived in a fog and cried for no reason. I drank to feel anything other than pain. Filled with confusion and emptiness, I just had to go somewhere. Anywhere.

Having exhausted my vacation days, I could only muster a weekend in Las Vegas, a three-hour flight west of my Kansas home. This oasis in the Mojave Desert shouldn't exist, but it does so due to its pandering of vices. Mom had contributed through cheap slot machines. I used to donate via low-limit poker but grew tired of losing the equivalent of my electric bill. Notwithstanding my dislike of gambling, a free hotel room made the decision easier.

Mom's downward spiral caught me off guard. Standing in the hospital hallway, with only hours of life remaining, a doctor asked where to send her body. I couldn't answer, so I took a friend's recommendation of a local funeral home.

The next day, I met with the director to discuss options. The first decision was between burial or cremation, before drilling down to the type of container, memorial package, flowers, urn, obituary, and death certificates. Along with the celebration of life luau, I spent seven thousand dollars. After that, I welcomed anything gratis.

On a Saturday night in mid-October, some friends and I strolled along the city's main thoroughfare, Las Vegas Boulevard. Multi-thousand-room hotels and pedestrians carrying open alcohol containers flanked eight lanes of pavement, filled with taxis advertising anything a person desired.

I stopped at a high-end behemoth Mom frequented to watch the fountain show. I approached an alcove with an unobstructed view of the artificial lake (M) as a purple hue spread across the hotel's exterior, and nozzles poked through the water's surface. Hundreds of streams danced an aquatic ballet of twisting, crisscrossing, and corkscrewing, complemented by thousands of pulsing lights. All elements synchronized to a tune I had heard ad nauseam as a child.

We spent most evenings of my youth at the dinner table. I did homework, and Mom worked a second job to pay for our travels. Music often played in the background. Her favorite was the soundtrack to *A Chorus Line*, the 1985 film about dancers auditioning for a Broadway musical. I grew so tired of the main track, *One*, that I begged to listen to something different every time it played. I would have given anything to hear it with her once more.

When the melody of my childhood faded, a singular sensation overcame me—a quiet realization that I had taken the first small step in fulfilling her wish.

The first small step

2 ♦ Cancun, Mexico

I have played it safe my entire life. I was a good student, stayed away from drugs, captained my high school soccer team, avoided open-air vehicles, frequented the dentist, and never pet stray dogs. Besides getting caught with alcohol at a party when I was 18 and a speeding ticket the same year, I have avoided trouble. I had a fine house, an average car, and many friends.

I worked as a Proposal Analyst at the same pharmaceutical research company as Mom, a desirable job for some, where I provided cost estimates for drug studies based on size, scope, and duration. Every Monday through Friday morning, I arrived at the clean, climate-controlled office and completed most of my deliverables before lunch. I often gazed out the window of my cubicle in the afternoon. Just before 6 p.m., I took the same route home, exercised, ate dinner, watched TV, and went to bed. Living the life many would gladly have, I had nothing to complain about. Repetition offers comfort. But I sought more than routine. I wanted to see the world.

The genesis of my obsession began when I was 29, dreaming of visiting Europe for longer than I could remember, but never failing to generate excuses—money, vacation days, fear, and telling myself I would do it later. After long talks with a friend, we garnered the courage to book a two-week trip to Italy and Greece. A few months later, Mom received her diagnosis, but adamantly insisted I didn't cancel.

Within hours of arriving in Rome, I was captivated by the timeless structures—the Colosseum, the Trevi Fountain, the Pantheon, the Roman Forum, and Piazza Navona. After that day, I traveled for the places. My insatiable lust grew as I glided down the Amalfi Coast, Greek Island-hopped, and ended in Athens. In the cab to the airport, I felt demoralized to return home. Looking out my cubicle window, I thought, "Where's next?"

I earned five weeks of vacation annually, an unheard-of amount in America. But with no time in the bank after dealing with Mom, I had limited travel opportunities. With an indeterminable timeframe to chip away at the wish, I could take weekend trips or hoard for a few longer outings. Deep down, I longed for the unthinkable—resign, pack a bag, and go.

The idea revealed a myriad of questions. Who would take care of my house? What would I do about the gap on my resume? What about health insurance? Where would I travel? How long could I travel? How long would I want to travel? All of these would figure themselves out, depending on the most important question: what about money?

As a consummate saver, I had reserves to dip into. But they wouldn't get me where I wanted to go. I thought about selling everything and becoming another internet cliché, but I didn't have the desire or guts to go full nomad. I liked the idea of having a base, somewhere to return to. Once again, Mom came through.

It's heartbreaking when someone knows they will die young. She suffered arthritis, psoriasis, osteopenia, vascular disease, hypertension, hyperlipidemia, a dysfunctional gallbladder, broken bones, and thyroid cancer at the age of 37. The rub is she never smoked and rarely drank. Her diet wasn't great, and exercise was rare. But that didn't merit the raw deal. Knowing she wouldn't live to old age, she had the foresight to buy a robust life insurance policy. Never remarrying after my father, everything went to me.

Despite my newly swollen bank account, as the saying goes, "Money can't buy happiness." I had never felt such misery. What money provided was the opportunity to pursue what I thought would make me happy. After all, isn't happiness the goal? Everything we do is in pursuit of it—the material possessions we buy, the food we eat, the hobbies we take up, the people we help, the relationships we enter, and the places we go. In the past, I was hell-bent on the car and the house, my version of the American Dream. I enjoyed them as much as possible, but neither brought the bliss of my time in Europe.

One week after Vegas, I resigned, eager to see the world. But with the holiday season nearing, I didn't venture far. A few weeks before Christmas, I flew three hours south to Cancun, Mexico, a popular destination on the country's southeast coast dominated by beachfront hotels lining a stretch of pristine sand in the Caribbean Sea. I had visited there a few times during my adolescence with Mom, who never tired of the crashing waves or sunsets.

I spent my days on the Mexican sand, buried in a self-help book advocating a work-less, live-more lifestyle. A gift from a work colleague during my final days of employment, the inner cover bore the inscription:

> Scott,
>
> Always remember to work to live!
>
> Good Luck!
>
> Mike

The work aspect didn't apply, but living had never been more important. Envious of the author's exploits, I craved similar stories but was cautiously hopeful I could achieve them. After a week of soul-searching, just before my flight home, I went back to the beach where I had found some clarity at Mom's happy place (M). Now, I needed to find my own.

Mom's happy place

Running Away

3 ♦ Franz Josef, New Zealand

A few weeks after Mexico, I faced the Christmas that Mom never made it to. Like every celebration, this became the new normal. With the arrival of the New Year, I put in motion where to go next. For some reason, I chose New Zealand. I didn't know much about the country but had heard good things. What intrigued me was its location on the other side of the planet.

In February 2013, I packed a bag, grabbed my one-way ticket, and set off on what I thought would be a once-in-a-lifetime adventure. (Unaware there would be loftier ones in the years ahead, this was my favorite. If I could relive any part of my life, it would be my time in New Zealand.) A four-hour flight to Los Angeles was followed by thirteen more to the capital city of Auckland. Combined with crossing the international dateline, I encountered the phenomenon of departing on Tuesday and arriving on Thursday. I would get the day back whenever I went home.

New Zealand is a playground for the adventurous. If it can be climbed, hiked, skied, floated, jumped, or biked, it happens here. Besides parasailing as a teenager, I had avoided adventure sports because of the "what ifs." "What if I got hurt?" or, more consequentially, "What if I died?" Like most people, I have a healthy fear of death. But this fear wasn't stopping me. It was my fear of dying before Mom. While her passing tore my heart out, I cherished that the natural order remained intact. Children are supposed to bury their parents. But with her gone, my fear of a premature demise vanished.

As a 31-year-old man with no wife, no kids, and nobody to care for, I had unlimited risk-taking freedom. I booked a three-week tour of the North and South Islands, where I sailed the Tasman Sea, went blackwater rafting in Waitomo, whitewater rafting in Rotorua, and zorbed down green hills. Each experience was more exhilarating than a hotel fountain or a beach, but I wanted to kick off my first big trip with something grand.

A whirring helicopter waited in the South Island's Westland Tai Poutini National Park. Six of us instinctively ducked our heads, strapped in, and put on headsets. The pilot lifted the collective lever, pitched the nose forward, and performed a series of acrobatic turns that pressed my body into the seat as he whisked us to Fox Glacier, a sloping thirteen-kilometer (8 mi) wall of ice. He dropped us on a patch of black stones shaped like an X halfway up the cascading frozen river, sandwiched between dirt peaks and dense foliage.

Two guides greeted us and handed out crampons, metal spikes that attached to our shoes. We trudged upward, avoiding cracks and crevasses with no visible bottoms. I had the lofty aspiration of reaching the top, a foolish notion. Over the course of two hours, we climbed one hundred vertical meters (330 ft), and the rock X had slightly shrunk. As I looked up, the ice seemed endless. Nature had taught me humility.

I grabbed a seat on a boulder (M). Peering down, I saw a group of older travelers who had just arrived aboard the same flying chariot that had chauffeured us. Moving slower than my youthful group, I credited the seasoned veterans of life. There is no way Mom would have attempted this.

Watching these silver-haired thrill-seekers reminded me of my favorite film, *The Curious Case of Benjamin Button*, a fictional story about a man born elderly who ages in reverse. I felt connected to the protagonist in a way. I was living backward by entering my golden travel years while healthy and mildly wealthy, postponing my primary employment for when my body crumbled.

Maybe I could have hiked a glacier decades later. There's no guarantee I would get the chance. Time, not money, is our greatest commodity. More valuable than gold, silver, oil, corn, cocoa, coffee, or cotton, it's the only thing we can't create more of. Some get a little. Others get a lot. I wasn't going to waste mine.

Fox Glacier

4 ♦ Queenstown, New Zealand

Having removed my fear of dying before Mom, I replaced it with a fear of regrets. To minimize my lost chances, I signed up for everything possible during my three days in Queenstown, the adrenaline capital. First up—skydiving.

After weighing, I received a jumpsuit, goggles, harness, and an introduction to my tandem jumpmaster before boarding a fixed-wheel twin-engine turboprop with a squircle-shaped fuselage. My initial stoicism withered as the plane gained altitude, and I perspired where I didn't think possible. After half an hour, at twelve thousand feet (3,660 m), the sectional door rolled up, and my standard fear response of a clenched backside kicked in.

My new friends, Elliott and Tammy, went first. I watched as they sat at the edge before vanishing in a blink. I wondered what it would feel like—a minor car accident, a punch in the face, or nothing at all. I scooted toward the door. Feet dangling, I looked over the edge for what felt like an eternity. In one smooth motion, the earth gave way to the sky, and the plane's underside receded. Unsure if it was psychological or physiological, my stomach sank.

We had exited backward, and I thought something had gone wrong. My jumpmaster, who had done this a few thousand times, righted us within seconds and deployed the drogue chute. The wind stripped the spit from my agape mouth, my eyes bulged, and my chest hammered as we screamed downward at 200 kph (124 mph).

Forty-five seconds later, the parachute cracked open. Aside from a gusty whisper, there was silence. The stranger behind me pulled the cords above his head, turning us left and right. I surveyed the pristine dark blue sky, which was only outshone by the mountain-encased sapphire water of Lake Wakatipu.

After five minutes of silent gliding, we approached the drop zone. He yanked the cords, we flared, leveled out, and I raised my feet before sliding on the soft grass. When asked how it was, I mumbled incoherently.

I spotted Elliott and Tammy. We ran toward each other and embraced in a group hug. He smiled, she wept tears of joy, and I fell somewhere in between. I returned my gear and sat at a picnic table by a wooden fence (M) to watch more of my new friends land. Whether she wanted to or not, Mom had joined me on the most exhilarating ride of my life.

The drop zone

5 ♦ Queenstown, New Zealand

In 1979, wearing a top hat and tails, holding a glass of champagne, David Kirke executed the first modern bungy jump from the 250-foot-high (76 m) Clifton Suspension Bridge in Bristol, England. Soon after, his friend Simon Keeling followed suit. They were arrested and promised not to do it again. As members of the Oxford University Dangerous Sports Club, they had been inspired by "land diving," a ritual performed by men in Vanuatu, jumping off platforms with vines tied to their legs.

Their daring actions planted the seed for A.J. Hackett, a New Zealander who, in 1986, bungy jumped from the Greenhithe Bridge in Auckland and, a year later, leapt off the Eiffel Tower without permission, gaining international attention. In 1988, Hackett opened the world's first commercial bungy site at the Kawarau Bridge near Queenstown. By 1999, he launched the Nevis Highwire Bungy, a 134-meter (440 ft) drop that would become my next challenge, the second highest in the Southern Hemisphere and the fourteenth highest worldwide.

I climbed into a trashcan-sized open-air cable car that carried me to a narrow metal walkway suspended by wires over a deep gorge. At the end sat the planet's only purpose-built bungy gondola. The now-familiar terror sweats kicked in when the thick, stretchy cord was attached. Feigning conviction, I shuffled to the edge, avoided looking down, and waited for the one-word command. "GO!"

I spread my arms and pushed off with everything I had. A thin river slicing through the empty canyon replaced the horizon. My body tensed up, my stomach became weightless, and my backside clenched as I plummeted earthwards.

Eight seconds later, the cord tightened, halting my freefall and snapping me upward before gravity reclaimed me for another plunge. I reached up and pulled the leg release, transitioning from vertical to horizontal, and attached the ascent cable that reeled me in like a fish (M)—another unimagined adventure sport in the books.

The Nevis Bungy. Photo by Elliott Rouse.

6 ♦ Queenstown, New Zealand

There's a difference between meeting people while traveling and traveling with people you meet. The former creates acquaintances, whereas the latter forges paths to lifelong friendships. While hiking a glacier, jumping from an airplane, and trusting my life to a giant rubber band invigorated me, the people made this my most incredible trip.

Spending nearly every waking moment with them for three weeks, they became closer than friends I had known for decades. These former strangers served as my temporary family, affecting my life more than they could ever realize. They mended my broken heart. But in doing so, a new crack emerged.

When the trip abruptly ended days later in Christchurch, making my rounds of hugs, I had the sobering insight that this would be the last time I would be with most of them. To leave the door open should they reenter my life, I adopted the mantra of "see ya' later" instead of "goodbye." I had said goodbye months earlier in a hospital room. I didn't want to do it again unless it was necessary.

I found that the best way to handle loss is to keep busy. Without a ticket home, I teamed up with two sisters from the tour, and we had no hesitation about the six-hour drive back to Queenstown. Due to our large suitcases, I requested a full-size car and received a tragedy of an automobile. From the crank windows to the tape deck to the hamster-powered engine to the pedestrian styling, it was the worst car I had ever driven. At least it was cheap and only had to survive the thousand-kilometer (620 mi) round trip.

Regardless of our solemn moods, we were optimistic about returning to the place that had given us a lifetime of beautiful memories, doubtless that more would come. But from the moment we arrived, the wind left our sails. We tried catching a breeze with more adventure sports during the day and the bars at night. It wasn't the same. We missed our friends.

Near the end of the week, I was stir-crazy and despondent. To clear my head, I jumped in the poor excuse for an automobile destined for Glenorchy, forty-six kilometers (29 mi) away. With my right arm out the window and the breeze blowing through what hair I had, I cruised the mountain highway with music from my phone reverberating in the cup holder. For a brief moment, I wasn't sad.

I repeatedly stopped to admire the scenery, each view more mesmerizing than the previous. What should have taken forty-five minutes ended up taking two hours to reach the five-hundred-person town. I motored on, but gave up after a few kilometers when the pavement turned to gravel. I didn't think the crap car was up for it.

Halfway back to Queenstown, I sensed Mom's presence. I pulled off, climbed over the guardrail, and hiked up a dirt hill to the cliff's edge. The blinding sun ricocheted off the lake and illuminated wispy clouds. Vegetated conical mountains in the foreground gave way to snow-capped peaks. Blessed with nature's poetry but nobody to share it with, the moment felt bittersweet (M).

I had insulated myself from loneliness over the past few weeks. But being separated from both old and new friends, I had never felt so alone. While Mom was with me in spirit, she couldn't replace flesh and blood. I so wished to share this with someone. I didn't know where my future travels would take me. The one certainty is that there would be similar days.

Bittersweet

7 ♦ Manly, Australia

I had gone to the other side of the world to escape my problems. Unwilling to face them, I needed to figure out my next move. The answer came from Hallie, whom I met in Europe the year before. She had followed my escapades on social media and invited me to stay with her family in Sydney, Australia.

After a three-hour flight from Christchurch, she picked me up at the airport and drove to the city center, a metropolis of modest high-rises. We went to a pub and met her friend, Bill, with whom I bonded over a love of beer. We remained the Three Musketeers for the next week, going to the beach during the day and out every night. I had found a reprieve from solitude.

On a Thursday afternoon in March, we took a ferry across the bay to Manly, grabbed some beers, and went to the beach next to the port. There was nothing special about the place. A few boats were anchored in the harbor, and buoys demarcated a swimming area. We threw the frisbee and balanced on pylons driven into the sand. Remembering how I felt in New Zealand, I was glad to be with friends (M).

Manly Beach

8 ♦ Victoria, Australia

I caught a ninety-minute flight to Melbourne. The rental car company was out of standalone navigation units, so they upgraded me to a luxury car with one built-in. I welcomed a proper ride after Queenstown.

Before quitting my job, my longest trip lasted three weeks. Having traveled for twice that, I had reached my wanderlust limits. I stopped taking pictures, watched movies, and slept. I was ready to go home. Hoping to find one more place before leaving, Bethany, a friend from my New Zealand trip, would join me on a short road trip. I once again welcomed the company.

There were several ways to reach our objective—the quicker and less scenic interior routes or the longer, more picturesque coastal option. We chose the latter due to its name, the *Great Ocean Road.*

Four hours of winding past forests, cliffs, and beaches brought us to a coach-filled parking lot and a visitor center. We walked through a tunnel beneath the road to a bluff lined with sturdy handrails (M). Off the coast rose the Twelve Apostles—soft limestone stacks, broad at the base and tapering toward the top, each rising fifty meters (160 ft) above the surf. Formed by ocean erosion ten to twenty million years ago, oddly, there were never actually twelve. Nine existed at the turn of the century. After collapses in 2005 and 2009, only seven remained.

The exposed rock layers told the story of the eons—bands of dark and light, smooth and rough. The undulating cliffs of the mainland stayed just out of reach of the crashing waves. A constant breeze kept the heat at bay.

As dusk approached, we took the inland highway back, and the high-performance car cruised over the well-paved roads. We made it home in under three hours. I dropped Bethany off, hugged her, and said, "See ya' later."

♦♦♦

Two days later, I boarded my flight to Kansas. It took two weeks to recover from the jet lag. At that time, a ticket for 282 AUD ($295) accompanied a letter from the State of Victoria. Returning from the Twelve Apostles, a camera recorded me doing 113 kph in a 100 kph zone (70 mph in a 62 mph zone). The rental car company added a 38 AUD ($40) administrative fee. I considered not paying it but relented, thinking I would return to Australia the next year. I never made that trip.

The Twelve Apostles

THE SEARCH BEGINS

9 ♦ Ely, England

I'd buried my mom. I'd seen a different corner of the world. I'd conquered fears. I'd made lifelong friendships. The 31st year of my life had been the most formative of my adulthood. The problem was I didn't know it.

When I got back home, I asked my lifelong friends, "What's new?" The common answer was, "Nothing." I didn't understand. What had they been doing? Why hadn't their outlooks changed? Why didn't they want to travel like I did? Why didn't they see things the way I do? Why didn't they want to live life to the fullest?

I faulted their apathy, simple-mindedness, and ability to thrive in mediocrity. I was angry with them. It took time to realize there was no reason for them to be different. Their lives stayed the same from when I left to when I returned. It was as if I had done it in a vacuum. I needed to step back and consider their worlds, not the other way around. A traumatic event made me reevaluate everything. Without similar motivation, they had no reason to change.

Regardless of my new lease on life, I suffered from mild depression being home. The conversations were repetitive. The scenery was dull. The nights out were insipid. I was bored out of my mind and missed my new friends. To make matters worse, I was annoyed at myself for feeling this way. I had accomplished more in six weeks than most do in a lifetime and was dealing with ludicrous First World problems. (I had yet to see the Second or Third Worlds to put things into perspective.)

The one person I related to was Jeff, whom I met years earlier at a destination wedding in Mexico. At 32, he worked as an attorney. Fed up with his situation, he left his employer (who was later disbarred) and spent six weeks in Spain before returning to start his own law practice. Now in his mid-50s, he had become my mentor/older brother figure.

We discussed New Zealand and Australia over dinner. Unsure of my next steps, he threw out the idea of taking Mom to one hundred places and writing a book. He even helped with part of the title. It was the “aha” moment I needed. Instead of wandering the Earth endlessly, I now had direction and a clear goal. Ten, twenty, or fifty places seemed too few. Two hundred, five hundred, or a thousand felt like too many. Like Goldilocks, one hundred was just right. From that night on, I officially began searching for 100 Places After.

I flew to London in the summer of 2013, grabbed my rental car, and drove two hours northeast to Ely, where small roads converged into the small-town home of Stacey, my best friend from New Zealand. We didn’t do any adventure sports together. Our friendship grew on the long bus rides. Being half a decade younger, we had nothing in common besides taking jokes too far. I missed her the most.

Knowing her address would be hard to find on GPS, she suggested meeting at a pub. Seeing each other for the first time in three months felt peculiar. No longer in a fairytale, the real world lacked exhilaration. Unlike me, she had adjusted back to normal life. Her hair was closer to its natural auburn color, though she had kept some blonde streaks. A diamond ring showed her engagement to her long-time boyfriend.

With pints in hand, surrounded by dark wood from floor to ceiling, she admitted to also suffering from depression following New Zealand. I felt comforted knowing I was on the same page as someone.

I followed Stacey to her parents’ house, where her mum and younger sister welcomed me with hugs, and her dad supplied a firm handshake. Spending most of my childhood in a single-parent home, I had little experience with a nuclear setting. I wouldn’t trade my upbringing, but at times I envied those with two parents and siblings.

I tolerated my 32nd birthday the next day. A few months after Mom's cancer diagnosis, she threw me a surprise 30th at Jeff's. Her declining health limited my 31st. Like Christmas, I struggled on this first occasion without her. While Mom always made a bigger deal than I did, not having a homemade cake or going to dinner with her felt strange. Ever so gracious, Stacey provided both.

Having enjoyed my time in England and knowing about Mom's wish, Stacey offered her favorite spot. She drove me to the city's eastern edge and guided me on a twenty-minute walk along a wooded path to a cluster of trees and thick bushes. Insects chirped, and water lapped against the shoreline of the artificial lake (M). The squared silhouette of Ely Cathedral created the sole interruption of the organic outline.

We sat in reticence until Stacey said she was grateful to be part of this, wishing she could have met Mom. I wanted the same. The irony is that if Mom hadn't died, I wouldn't have gone to New Zealand and would never have met Stacey. I often questioned how the catch-22 of the worst moment of my life catalyzed the best moments.

The outline of the Ely Cathedral

10 ♦ Berlin, Germany

I fell in love with Berlin, Germany, a year earlier. From the food to the people to the nightlife to the history, I had never found anywhere like it. I could have justified writing *100 Places After in Berlin*.

My adoration materialized when I walked up the stairs from the *Brandenburger Tor* metro station and laid eyes on the Brandenburg Gate, Germany's most iconic landmark. The patina-green quadriga of four muscular horses pulling a chariot came into view. The twelve sandstone Doric columns grew taller with each step up to street level. Unassuming from afar, its size became intimidating as I approached. A chill ran down my spine when I passed through the central archway.

The Gate's origins date back to 1788 when King Frederick Wilhelm II commissioned it at the start of the road from Berlin to Brandenburg an der Havel. Modeled after the Propylaea, the gateway to the Acropolis in Athens, the quadriga, installed in 1793, was driven by Eirene, the Greek goddess of peace.

Napoleon captured Berlin in 1806, used the Gate for a victory procession, and sent the quadriga to Paris. The French general had risen to power during the Revolution, declaring himself Emperor in 1804 and building an empire that stretched across much of Europe before his downfall a decade later. After his defeat in the Parisian outskirts in 1814, the quadriga returned to Berlin, and Eirene was replaced by Victoria, the goddess of victory. Salting the French wound, the square where the Gate resides was named *Pariser Platz* (Paris Square).

The Gate remained relatively innocuous until the rise of the Nazis, who used it to celebrate Adolf Hitler's rise to power in 1933, marking the first of many propaganda events there. After Germany's defeat in World War II, the victorious allies carved up the ruined country. The U.S., Britain, and France took the western part, while the Soviet Union received the eastern part, including the damaged Gate. The opposing governments worked together to patch the holes.

Foot traffic and vehicles moved freely through it until 1961, when East German police and military closed the border between East and West Berlin. The proximity of the Berlin Wall led to decades of neglect. When the Wall fell in 1989, thousands gathered at the Gate to celebrate the country's reopening. A year later, it hosted the official reunification ceremony, adorned with the black, red, and gold national flag. The renovated Gate reopened on October 3, 2002, marking the twelfth anniversary of the reunited nation.

After a quick flight from London, I returned to *Pariser Platz*, my favorite place in my most beloved city. The cobblestone pedestrian area was exactly as I remembered it. The line at Starbucks stretched out the door. Across the street was the hotel where, in 2002, Michael Jackson dangled his baby over the balcony. The American and French flags fluttered in front of their embassies. The Gate stood at the far end, where U.S. President Barack Obama had spoken about nuclear arms reduction just a week earlier. As I passed through the central archway for the second time, a chill ran down my spine again (M). It felt good to be back.

The Brandenburg Gate

11 ♦ Prague, Czech Republic

In this sense, the theory of the Communists may be summed up in the single sentence: Abolition of private property.

...

The Communists are further reproached with desiring to abolish countries and nationality.

— Karl Marx and Friedrich Engels, *Manifesto of the Communist Party* (1848)

A week after Mom's death, I canceled a trip to Eastern Europe with Jeremy. Introduced at a 16th birthday party, we attended different high schools but became best friends. After meeting me in Berlin, we set off for Prague, the Czech Republic, to complete our lost opportunity.

I had been there before and planned to get Mom to the center of the Charles Bridge, a sandstone span completed in 1402 across the Vltava River. The no-brainer idea vanished the moment beggars and street vendors bombarded me. For the first time, a preconceived location wasn't going to happen. I needed to improvise.

Off to the side stood a wall twice a person's height and the length of a few buses, attributed to John Lennon. The English singer, songwriter, and activist founded the *Quarrymen* in 1956, which evolved into the *Beatles* in 1960. Over the next decade, the Liverpool-based band became integral in the 1960s counterculture movement across much of the Western world.

The band broke up in 1970, and the members went their separate ways. Lennon wasted no time producing his debut solo album, *John Lennon/Plastic Ono Band*. A year later, he released his second album, *Imagine*, with the opening title track serving as an anthem for the anti-war movement. It asks people to imagine a world without heaven, countries, and possessions, where they lived in peace and shared the world. This idealized vision of a perfect society wasn't novel.

In 1848, the German philosophers Karl Marx and Friedrich Engels published the *Manifesto of the Communist Party*, aka *The Communist Manifesto*, one of the modern era's most influential documents. The introduction outlines their philosophy: "The history of all hitherto existing society is the history of class struggles." The remainder advocates a communist civilization—stateless, classless, and moneyless. When *Imagine* was released, Prague citizens lived in a version of this world, grimmer than Lennon envisioned.

In 1948, the Communist Party of Czechoslovakia took control of the country, which functioned as a Soviet satellite state. The regime forbade Western pop songs, especially those by Lennon, who praised something that didn't exist there—freedom.

Though he had never been to Prague, Czech youth idolized the former *Beatles* superstar. After Lennon's murder in 1980, activists painted his portrait, lyrics, and tributes on a wall beside the Charles Bridge. Over time, people expressed their own sentiments, which authorities suppressed. At the risk of imprisonment, citizens continued demonstrating with poems, paintings, and messages.

In November and December 1989, Czech dissidents took to the streets of Prague with nonviolent demonstrations that became the *Velvet Revolution*. Their peaceful efforts helped bring about the fall of communism in Czechoslovakia. It's been surmised that the John Lennon Wall helped inspire the bloodless transfer of power.

Live Your Dreams

A Catholic religious order now owns the Wall and welcomes daily messages of peace, love, and free speech. I left my mark of "Live Your Dreams." Inarticulate and unoriginal, it was the best I could muster. But I had been born and raised in a society that gave me every freedom to live mine. As my views of the world reshaped, I revisited the concept of freedom in various forms. This piece of graffiti-covered concrete beneath a bridge was the origin (M).

12 ♦ Budapest, Hungary

Standing in the hilly, wooded city of Buda, I saw its modern and flat counterpart, Pest, on the other side of the Danube River. The Széchenyi Chain Bridge linked the two. Come hell or high water, I would get Mom there, a task easier said than done when idiocy takes over.

Every Saturday during the summer, Budapest hosts one of Europe's best pool parties, which began in a balmy locker room that emerged to chest-thumping music and indiscernible conversations. Jeremy and I stopped at a pop-up bar and ordered the night's special, an unfortunate recurring math problem of two beers and three shots.

With beverages in hand, we stepped into the bath-temperature water. Supposedly containing minerals to help with joint diseases and arthritis, it didn't take long to add another ingredient—shame. In this modern-day Sodom and Gomorrah, half-naked silhouettes merged into full-naked behaviors. The water became so murky within a few hours that I couldn't see my feet. I didn't care. By night's end, I was unable to spell my name.

I awoke at 3 p.m., mouth parched, head throbbing, and stomach nauseated. Slated to leave early the next morning, getting to the bridge became my sole purpose for this wasted day. I slithered out of bed, threw on some clothes, and got Jeremy moving. After forty-five minutes of sweaty shuffling in the sweltering heat, we made it.

Before the bridge, floating wooden pontoons supported a flattish surface to cross the Danube. As the weather worsened and winter approached, the makeshift crossing was disassembled and rebuilt months later. Seeking a permanent solution, in the 1830s, the Hungarian statesman, writer, and politician Count István Széchenyi vowed to solve the problem.

The construction of the bridge bearing his name took place from 1840 to 1849. Destroyed by retreating Germans during the Siege of Budapest in World War II, it reopened on its hundredth anniversary. Most notably, it appeared in the opening scene of Katy Perry's music video *Firework*...OMG!!!

Two stubby grey stone towers with faded blue iron cables supported the roadway. A thick railing acted as a crutch for my weary legs. I had hoped to reach the center of the structure. But with each step meaning another back, one-third of the way sufficed (M). Mom would continue to Hungary, Croatia, Serbia, Romania, Bulgaria, Moldova, and Ukraine until she reached the Black Sea. My next stop was a late lunch and some acetaminophen.

The Széchenyi Chain Bridge

13 ♦ Oświęcim, Poland

An hour west of Kraków, Poland, is the town of Oświęcim. After the outbreak of World War II in 1939, the Nazis captured it and changed the name to its Germanic form—Auschwitz.

I was 14 when I saw the word plastered on a magazine cover commemorating the fiftieth anniversary of its liberation. I didn't understand what that meant due to my rudimentary education. I read the detailed article. An hour later, I was different, encountering terms like concentration camp, genocide, Holocaust, and the Final Solution to the Jewish Question.

I struggled to comprehend rounding people up, transporting them, and murdering as many as possible. How could such a thing happen? I threw myself into this question. I watched videos, read books, and asked Mom. I learned that the systematic destruction didn't happen overnight. It was a slow burn.

With the rise of Adolf Hitler, antisemitism and the severity of Jewish persecution grew. In 1933, the shunning of Jews, the boycotting of Jewish businesses, and the restriction of Jews from civil service began. In 1935, the Nuremberg Laws banned mixed marriages, racially defined a Jew, and declared that only those of German blood could be citizens. In 1938, civilians and Nazi paramilitary destroyed Jewish buildings, rounded up thousands of Jews, and killed at least ninety-one in a pogrom known as *Kristallnacht* (Night of Broken Glass).

Hundreds of thousands of Jews fled, but Germany acquired millions more by annexing Austria and Czechoslovakia in 1938 and invading Poland in 1939. The Nazis concentrated them in ghettos in major cities while simultaneously arresting members of the intelligentsia, artists, priests, and dissenters. The jails and camps became so overcrowded that they needed to resolve the problem.

In 1940, Auschwitz I, the first concentration camp in occupied Poland, was established in former army barracks. (Camps in Germany had been around since 1933.) New arrivals, who weren't immediately killed, were shaved, disinfected, tattooed with a serial number, and given a striped uniform with a color cloth triangle: red for political prisoners, green for criminals, purple for Jehovah's Witnesses, pink for gay men, black for asocial (Roma, vagrants, prostitutes), and a yellow Star of David for Jews. The hierarchy from top to bottom was German, non-Jew, Jew.

Camp life began early with prisoners filing out for roll call, often lasting hours before subjection to long days of labor with minimal rations. The more unfortunate endured medical experiments, including forced sterilization, virus injections, and anesthesia tests. The punished were strung up with hands behind their backs until their feet dangled, often losing consciousness as their tendons ripped or their shoulders dislocated. The "standing cells" forced prisoners to remain vertical. The "dark cells" had insufficient ventilation. Retributions often lasted days or weeks.

The first crematorium became active in the autumn of 1941. A munition bunker before the war, it functioned as a morgue until it was converted into a gas chamber, capable of killing several hundred at a time—a minuscule amount for what was to come.

Hitler invaded the Soviet Union in June 1941, capturing millions of prisoners of war (POWs). Needing somewhere to put them, in October, construction began on Auschwitz II-Birkenau, the largest and most notorious section of the complex.

Designed to house two hundred thousand prisoners, assuming all were accounted for in the evening, they filed into simple barracks and slept side-by-side on wooden or brick bunks covered in filth and excrement. Expectedly, vermin, disease, and death ran rampant.

In the spring of 1943, the purpose-built Crematorium II, equipped with a gas chamber, morgue, and ovens to dispose of the bodies activated. Within months, Crematoria III, IV, and V became operational. By that time, Auschwitz had shifted from detaining POWs to exterminating Jews and other undesirables.

Daily trainloads of prisoners arrived from Nazi-occupied Europe in cramped cattle cars for summary selection. Those capable of work went into the camp. Those incapable—primarily women, children, and the elderly—went to the gas chambers.

They disrobed under the guise of a shower and delousing. The Hygiene Institute, a special bureau of the Nazi paramilitary organization, the *Schutzstaffel* (SS), sealed the doors. Zyklon-B, a German cyanide-based pesticide invented in the 1920s, was dropped through roof vents. The thick concrete walls couldn't muffle the screams. But within minutes, there was silence.

The room was ventilated, the doors opened, and the corpses stripped. The cremated remains were buried, dumped in the river, or used as fertilizer. By the time the camp was liberated by the Soviet Red Army on January 27, 1945, the Nazis had murdered more than 1.1 million people there; 90 percent were Jews.

I arrived at Auschwitz I, sixty-eight years later. The black metal arch greeted me with the infamous words *ARBEIT MACHT FREI* (WORK SETS YOU FREE). Guard towers overlooked gravel corridors lined with barbed wire, bearing signs that translated to "CAUTION | High Voltage | Danger to Life." Rows of two-story red brick buildings lined the streets. These “blocks” held piles of the brutalities: hair, artificial limbs, shoes, spectacles, toothbrushes, suitcases, metal dental work, and children’s clothing.

Crematorium I—a drab, single-story, concrete structure embedded into a hill—housed reconstructed incinerators of metal tables connected to brick ovens. Corroding I-beams linked peeling camouflaged walls of brown, beige, grey, and black.

A few kilometers away, footprints of barracks with singular brick chimneys littered a sprawling field in Auschwitz II-Birkenau. Nothing obvious remained of the gas chambers. In October 1944, revolting prisoners destroyed Crematorium IV. Trying to hide their crimes, the SS destroyed the others just before the Soviets arrived.

Auschwitz I:
Barbed wire corridor (left) and reconstructed incinerators (right)

Auschwitz II-Birkenau:
Inside a barrack (left) and the remains of a crematorium (right)

Besides satisfying my curiosity from the magazine article I had read nearly two decades earlier, Auschwitz was personal. My family's genealogy was researched. From my perspective, it traced back eight generations to a Lithuanian-born Jewish man. He had four children, who then had more children, and so on.

Hitler's invasion of the Soviet Union included the newly created Lithuanian Soviet Socialist Republic.* The Nazis wiped out swaths of my relatives, some of whom I found in a database. Their lives were summarized on a sheet of paper. Mainly in Hebrew and Yiddish, I deciphered the CIRCUMSTANCE OF DEATH using translation software. A husband and wife—DEATH MARCH. Their son—SHOAH VICTIM. A mother—MAY 1945, STUTHOF, GERMANY. Her two children—MARCH 1944, GHETTO, KAUNAS, LITHUANIA, and KILLED BY NAZI GERMANS, MAY 1945, respectively.

It's unlikely any of my family met their demise in Auschwitz. Those victims came primarily from Hungary, Poland, France, the Netherlands, Greece, the Protectorate of Bohemia and Moravia, Slovakia, Belgium, Germany, Austria, Yugoslavia, and Italy. The pertinent question is, "How did I get here?"

In a fortuitous decision, my great-great-grandfather immigrated to America around 1907 and settled in Boston, Massachusetts. His son moved to Detroit, Michigan, where his daughter (my grandmother) met the man who became my grandfather. They had three children, with Mom being the youngest. In 1975, she married my father. Six years later, I was born.

With this discovery of our heritage, Mom always wanted to pay her respects to one of humanity's greatest atrocities. I passed through the main gate, a single-story brick building topped with a tower above an arched entrance. I followed the railroad tracks that had carried so many to their deaths until I was far away from the camp (M). The dead within had already consecrated the area.

---

* The Soviet Union invaded, occupied, and incorporated the sovereign Republic of Lithuania in the summer of 1940.

The main gate of Auschwitz II-Birkenau

14 ♦ Zermatt, Switzerland

I was nine when Mom went to Switzerland for ten days, and her parents from Florida came to watch me. Unable to comprehend how far she had gone, I didn't think planes could fly across an ocean. I cried the one time we talked on the phone. Back then, it cost a few dollars per minute to call from Europe. When she got home, I had never been so happy. Regaling me with stories, she hoped to return someday.

After a "see ya' later" to Jeremy, I flew to Basel, Switzerland, at the crossroads of Germany and France, where I was met by Matthew, a Swiss native and companion from my New Zealand trip. We drove to Zermatt (population 6,000), a charming town that became a mountaineering destination in the race to summit the Matterhorn, the sixth-tallest peak in the Alps.

Following numerous failed attempts by various Europeans in the mid-nineteenth century, in 1861, the Englishman Edward Whymper entered the fray. After eight tries from the southern slope, he approached from the east. Accompanied by six men, the group reached the top on July 14, 1865, but enjoyed a short-lived triumph. The party was tied together, and one man slipped on the descent.

Whymper and the two men above him held on, but the rope didn't. The falling man crashed onto the three below, who all plummeted to their deaths. The survivors searched for their companions but were stranded overnight and returned to Zermatt in the morning. Three bodies were recovered, so battered they were nearly unrecognizable. An inquiry found no evidence of wrongdoing.

We had no such aspirations or expertise for a similar undertaking, opting instead for an adjacent mountain and a mechanical ascent using three gondolas that whisked us to *Unterrothorn* at 3,104 meters (10,184 ft). A sign with arrows pointed in all directions, with corresponding ETAs—our goal read *1 h 05 min*.

We ambled down dirt and grass ski runs for three hours. Six hundred vertical meters (1,970 ft) below our starting point, we reached the elliptical lake of Stellisee, famed for its ability to reflect the distant Matterhorn's near-pyramidal peak so sharp that little snow clings—an image used for postcards. Despite the strong winds that had disrupted the mirrorlike qualities, I had returned Mom to Switzerland (M).

Stellisee and the Matterhorn

15 ♦ Cape Cod, Massachusetts

By the age of 31, I had buried my mother, father, and grandparents. My paternal uncle in California and my maternal aunt in Massachusetts were the only family I chose to keep. Both had differing opinions on the decision to quit my job. My free-spirited Uncle Curt, a freelance technology writer who had traveled extensively, supported me. He thought I should ride this gravy train until the biscuit wheels fell off. My strait-laced Aunt Karen, a former elementary school teacher, branded me insane. Although she had my best interests in mind, it disheartened me to seek her support, only to not receive it. It's tough when those close to you disagree with your chosen life.

Her dissent planted seeds of doubt. I questioned whether dedicating my peak career years to travel was worth it. Would losing those years haunt me? Was I sacrificing my long-term plans for short-term gains? I knew Mom wanted this, but I doubt she imagined the lengths I would go to.

As crazy as I drove my aunt, her door in Cape Cod, a ninety-minute drive south of Boston, was always open. The popular summer destination exemplifies the rural Atlantic Northeast, featuring beaches, lighthouses, and a small-town atmosphere. On the way back from Europe, a quick stopover seemed prudent.

I hadn't been there since Christmas. Eight months later, I became the topic of conversation. "Where's your favorite place?" "What's (insert activity) like?" "How's the food?" "Where next?" The last question was the easiest.

Accompanied by my aunt, uncle, and cousin, we arrived at a two-story building with a gray shingled exterior, white trim, and an expansive outdoor deck. Despite being a Tuesday, this seaside restaurant with a view Mom loved was packed.

Opting to eat outside, we got stuck with a cramped four-top, better suited for two, pressed against a window. Add some shirt-sticking humidity and relentless mosquitoes; it wasn't ideal. We ate the overpriced food, sipped the above-average cocktails, and shared stories about Mom, aiming to honor her at sunset.

As daylight faded, my aunt and I left early, walking through thigh-high grass toward rocky sand speckled with seaweed (M). She burst into tears, exclaiming, "I miss her so much!" Having been through this for almost a year, my role that evening was as a consoler. I hugged her and said, "So do I."

As the sun dipped below the horizon, my uncle and cousin arrived, carrying a jug of Mom's Mai Tais. I hadn't had one since the luau after her funeral. Enjoying her signature rum-laden drink, we toasted to her.

Joanne's Infamous Mai Tai
2 cups rum, light
1 cup rum, dark
1 cup rum, 151
1 cup orange liqueur
1 cup almond syrup
1 quart pineapple juice
1 quart orange juice

The beach on Cape Cod

STAYING CLOSE

16 ♦ Ontario, Canada

I returned home with a different disposition this time, having never formed a deep personal connection. I enjoyed not being depressed. Wanting to get a few more places in before year's end, a month after Cape Cod, I flew to Toronto, Canada, to meet up with Jason and Aarti. We had connected while traveling Europe in the summer of 2012, specifically trying to find Rome's cheapest bottle of wine.

Flashback to nine years earlier. I was home from university, waiting to start my final year. To Mom's dismay, I had failed to secure a summer job, the first time since I was 14 without one. Furious about the lost income, to make it up to her, I became her airport chauffeur, dropping her off every Monday and picking her up every Friday. On those drives home, I always asked about her week. She usually spent it working, but once, during a trip to Buffalo, New York, she made time to see Niagara Falls. With camera phones in their infancy, all I had was a description of what I envisioned as a mythical place. A ninety-minute drive from Toronto, I would never have a more accessible opportunity.

Garish casinos, extortionate chain restaurants, and cheap paraphernalia dominated Niagara Falls, Ontario. I had imagined something rustic and rural, but it was the Twelve Apostles on steroids. Though she had seen the falls from the U.S., I questioned using a place for her on the superior Canadian side.

Jason and Aarti coerced me into an open-air boat ride. As we puttered into the river, diesel fumes wafted in our faces. On the American side, the falls crashed over boulders, split by Luna Island, while the smaller Bridal Veil Falls barely made a ripple. But up ahead, the water of Horseshoe Falls, making up the main flow, cascaded from the height of a fourteen-story building.

The roar deafened, and the icy mist drenched us as we inched closer. My heart pounded with the same adrenaline I had felt bungy jumping and skydiving. Nature humbled me again as my discontentment of an hour earlier vanished.

On our way to the parking area, an outcropping with an unobstructed view called out (M). Niagara Falls lived up to the hype and gave me a brief connection with Mom, who once stood on the other side.

Niagara Falls

17 ♦ New York, New York, USA

Back at Aarti's apartment, Jason and I needed to figure out where to go. The limiting factor was our separate flights out of Washington, D.C., in two weeks. We settled on New York City. Like Berlin, *100 Places After in New York* wouldn't have been out of the question. Hard-pressed to narrow down my options, I settled on the Statue of Liberty.

We bought tickets for a typical morning, but when we arrived at the port, a ranger informed us that all national parks were closed. Our timing couldn't have been worse. It was the second day of the 2013 U.S. federal government shutdown, caused by the inability of my country's predominant political parties, the Republicans and the Democrats, to reach a compromise on the 2014 fiscal budget. I say *my country* because the democratically elected officials responsible for the citizens who elected them failed. I'm one of those citizens. The short version is that the two sides went back and forth in a partisan pissing contest, resulting in the federal government screeching to a halt from October 1 to October 17, 2013.

Instead of reaching the icon symbolizing the freedom my country prides itself on (a subject I will revisit later), we received a one-hour harbor cruise, passing ever so close. Unlike the Charles Bridge, I couldn't control this situation. For the first time (of many), I encountered failure. Looking for an alternative, I drew inspiration from the third most important day of my life.

I was a 20-year-old university student driving to campus with my roommate on a Tuesday morning. A radio broadcast announced that a small plane had hit one of the Twin Towers of the World Trade Center (WTC), assuming it was an accident. In 1945, a B-25 bomber inadvertently crashed into the Empire State Building, so a similar incident wasn't out of the question. Not thinking much of it, we parked and went to class. An hour later, the hallway buzzed. I told my roommate, "Remember where you are right now, as something big is happening." Back at our apartment, every TV channel broadcast the chaos.

A group of Islamic terrorists hijacked four commercial airliners. The "small" plane first incorrectly reported was a fully fueled wide-body Boeing 767, which they slammed into the North Tower. They flew another Boeing 767 into the South Tower. A Boeing 757 hit the Pentagon. Another Boeing 757 crashed in a Pennsylvania field.

We watched replay after replay of the planes vanishing into walls, balls of fire and smoke filling the New York skyline, panic spreading, and people leaping from the upper floors. By the end of the morning of September 11th, 2001, the towers had collapsed, the Pentagon lay in ruins, and nearly three thousand people were dead. It was the first attack on American soil since the attempt to bring down the towers in 1993.

I called Mom as we asked, "What the f*** is happening?!" It seemed surreal. I felt confused, sad, scared, and angry. Most of all, I felt helpless. Throughout my life, I had been preached to that we were the most powerful nation ever. That morning, nineteen men with box cutters sliced a gaping wound into the American psyche.

The events of September 11th were the deadliest terrorist attacks in world history—a tragedy in every sense of the word. Stepping back, realizing the next sentence may sound coldhearted, in no way is it meant to diminish the heartbreaking loss of life. The body count was insignificant.

In 2001, the U.S. death toll was 2,416,425, a daily average of 6,620 people. September 11th accounted for 0.12% of the annual total. Every day, more people died from just heart disease and cancer combined.* This sobering statistic led me to an obvious epiphany. The purpose of terrorism isn't to kill. The purpose of terrorism is to generate fear and disruption, which the terrorists achieved with unbelievable success.

In the days, months, and years to come, the effects were felt at home and abroad. The stock market plummeted. Hate crimes against Muslims and those perceived as Muslims increased. Conspiracy theories spread uncontrollably. Thousands fell ill due to the toxic dust from the towers' collapse. The Department of Homeland Security was created to protect the country from future terrorist attacks. The long-standing military campaign, the *War on Terror*, resulted in wars in Afghanistan and Iraq. The USA PATRIOT Act gave the government greater powers to monitor and detain suspected terrorists. And air travel changed forever.

---

* Deaths due to diseases of the heart were 700,142—a daily average of 1,918. Deaths due to malignant neoplasms were 553,768—a daily average of 1,517.

While I disagree with many aspects of my country, one thing I'm proud of is our resilience. It took nearly nine months to clear the WTC debris. The first step toward rebuilding was constructing the new One World Trade Center, the same name as the original North Tower. The colossal structure of concrete, steel, and reflective glass rose 1,776 feet, symbolizing the Declaration of Independence. The twenty-ton granite cornerstone of the Western Hemisphere's tallest building was inscribed with "the enduring spirit of freedom."

Disgruntled with the lackluster harbor cruise, we walked from Battery Park to the *National September 11 Memorial & Museum.* Arriving two years after its unveiling, a field of swamp white oak trees (M) surrounded two square reflecting pools set in the footprints of the fallen towers, bordered by bronze parapets engraved with the names of the dead.

A far cry from the savagery of Niagara Falls, the only sound was water trickling one story before disappearing into the earth. With the day's setback, I realized this search for 100 Places After wouldn't be the smoothest process. I would have to deal with disappointment and adapt. But I guess that's true for life in general.

The North Pool

18 ♦ Alexandria, Virginia, USA

Jason and I drove to Philadelphia, Pennsylvania, where the government shutdown had closed most of the city's landmarks, surrounded by armed guards and barricades. We continued south to Washington, D.C., where things went from bad to worse. Improvisation was again required.

Near Alexandria was Mount Vernon, the plantation home of George Washington, the "Father of his Country," aka *my country*. Born in 1732 in Popes Creek, Virginia, a British colony, he worked as a surveyor before beginning his military career in the Virginia militia, where he attained the rank of brigadier general, gaining combat experience during the French and Indian War (1754–1763).

After resigning his commission in 1758, the following year, at 26, he married Martha Dandridge Custis, a 27-year-old widow with two of four surviving children. Already a sizable property owner, the union made him one of Virginia's wealthiest men.

As George's stature rose, so did his dissension with the British Parliamentary influence over the Colonies without their representation. On behalf of Virginia, he attended the First Continental Congress in 1774, where delegates agreed to a boycott of British goods and a *Petition to the King* calling for a repeal of the Intolerable Acts—punitive acts stripping Massachusetts of the right of self-governance after the Boston Tea Party, a 1773 protest where colonists boarded ships and dumped tea into the harbor.

Tensions reached the boiling point on April 19, 1775, when members of the Massachusetts militia clashed with British Army regulars, marking the start of the American Revolutionary War. Unanimously chosen as Commander-in-Chief of the Continental Army, Washington had both military triumphs and setbacks. However, his leadership saw the colonists attain independence.

Two months after the war's end, he resigned his commission in November 1783 and returned home. Despite the estate's financial difficulties, he expanded the mansion and undertook landscaping projects. However, by 1787, Mount Vernon had failed to turn a profit for more than a decade.

That same year, he was unanimously chosen to preside over the Constitutional Convention in Philadelphia, where delegates aimed to create the framework of a new government. After four months of deliberation, he was the first to sign the Constitution of the United States, the supreme Law of the Land.

The government would consist of three branches: the legislative branch would make the laws; the judicial branch would interpret, defend, and apply them; and the executive branch would execute and enforce them. After much deliberation, a singular person would lead the executive branch. As expected, Washington became the first president in 1789, continuing his trend of being selected unanimously by the Electoral College, a system where each state is allocated a set number of electors based on the state's population.

Ideological disagreements emerged during his four-year term as factions transitioned into political parties. The Federalists and Democratic-Republicans clashed over the federal government's influence over the states and conflicts between Britain and France.

Hoping to retire to Mount Vernon, against Martha's wishes, he reluctantly ran for a second term to avoid further instability and was again elected unanimously. Despite his sacrifice, partisanship and infighting continued for the rest of his time in office. Setting the precedent of a two-term presidency, he stepped aside, fearing that his death in office might appear as a lifetime appointment.

On December 12, 1799, while tending to his farm, a wintry mix rolled in. Known for his punctuality, he stayed in his wet clothes for dinner. After more snow had fallen the following day, he completed additional outside chores.

After waking with throat pain and respiratory issues, he underwent bloodletting with no improvement. Over the next two days, he was bled thrice more, drank elixirs, received an enema, and induced vomiting. On the evening of December 14, George asked Martha to retrieve two wills from his study. He examined both and discarded one. Hours later, he passed away in his bed at age 67.

Mount Vernon passed through the generations to George's brother's great-grandson. Unable to maintain the estate, he sold it to the Ladies' Association of the Union in 1858, who still oversee it. Designated as a National Historic Landmark in 1960 and not run by the government, it's open daily. Hooray!!!

We drove a half-hour south from George's namesake capital city to his former residence. His beige, two-and-a-half-story Palladian-style house had black shutters and three entrances of different styles. He and Martha shared a room on the second floor with delicate dark wood furniture, a canopy bed, and a striped rug reminiscent of the 1970s.

The rest of the estate had gardens, greenhouses, a distillery, a blacksmith shop, a kitchen, a stable, a salt house, a coach house, a storehouse, and a smokehouse. The effort required to maintain it was enormous, but there was no shortage of (nearly) free labor.

Like many signers of the Constitution, Washington owned slaves. After the American Revolution, his views shifted from acceptance to a desire to eliminate it. During his presidency, he signed two pieces of slavery legislation. Neither moved the country closer to abolition. Slavery remained legally protected by the Constitution, but it became so divisive that it tore the nation apart.*

Martha's former husband died without a will. Like land inheritance, as slaves were property, Martha acquired one-third, with the remainder going to her children. In total, the Washingtons owned 123 of the 318 Mount Vernon slaves, with George unsuccessfully trying to buy and manumit some they didn't own. Following her death in 1802, the unemancipated slaves reverted to the Custis estate and were divided among her grandchildren. (Martha's daughter died in 1773, as did her son in 1781.)

Surrounded by dense woods in a remote corner of Mount Vernon, the slave memorial featuring three circular brick steps

---

* The Fugitive Slave Act of 1793 ensured the rights of owners to recover escaped slaves across state lines. The Slave Trade Act of 1794 forbade American ships from participating in the international slave trade.

displayed *Faith, Hope,* and *Love*. Signs of changing times, two plaques marked the burial grounds. One from 1983 memorialized the memory of the "Afro Americans" enchained there. The other from 1929 did the same for the "Colored Servants."

Up the hill was the final resting place of most of the Washington family, a brick mausoleum the size of a three-car garage (M). The American flag and a replica of Washington's Commander-in-Chief flag bordered an arched doorway with a black metal gate. George's elaborate marble sarcophagus was visible, while Martha's plain one was tucked away.

Still annoyed by the bipartisanship just a few miles away, in hindsight, Mount Vernon turned out to be the best outcome, as it taught me multiple lessons. First, political infighting will always be a part of my country. It was an issue Washington faced, as have every other president. Second, the importance of a will. Mom's was clear and concise, making the transfer of most assets straightforward. In the case of Martha's first husband, who had no will, the effects resonated for generations. Third, I had opened new possibilities for the future of 100 Places After. So many of the world's attractions are devoted to the dead. Compared to what was to come, the tomb of George Washington was modest.

The Washington family vault

SOMETHING DIFFERENT

19 ♦ Bangkok, Thailand

I endured my second Christmas without Mom. Sadness lingered but much less than the previous year. Time made a difference, and travel occupied me. I could have wandered around Europe for the remainder of the one hundred places, but that didn't embrace the spirit. Mom wanted me to do something different.

I had developed an inability to sleep on planes, an obvious problem for someone with lofty global aspirations. After three flights and twenty-eight hours of stewing in recirculated air, I couldn't bring myself to shower at the hotel in Bangkok. I slept hard, powered through the jet lag, and awoke before sunrise, adrenalized to be on a new continent. I knew little about the Thai capital, so I searched for "things to do." The Grand Palace ranked near the top. Within walking distance, it sounded like a superb first stop in Asia.

I waited until late morning to enter the bustling streets. Twenty minutes later, I followed a tall white wall to the main gate but couldn't enter due to my lack of full-length trousers. As a male, I had never struggled to get in anywhere with shorts as long as they covered my knees. (Women unfairly face stricter dress codes around the world.) Tired and sweating profusely, I decided to save the Grand Palace for the next day.

My focus shifted to religion. Roughly 95 percent Buddhist, Thailand was my first country not dominated by Christianity. I searched for a temple, aka a *wat.* Within minutes, I arrived at an open-air room with white walls, mirrors, fluorescent lights, dark metal chandeliers, and gilded Buddhas. Barefoot practitioners sat on the spotless black and grey tiled floor next to vases of fresh-cut flowers. I watched them pray. My knowledge of Christianity was nominal. I knew nothing about Buddhism. I questioned what they asked their god for. At that moment, I became curious about how others worshipped.

I arose early the next day to avoid the heat. A few blocks from the Grand Palace, I approached an intersection where a man on a weathered scooter was waiting. In a friendly manner, he told me it was closed until 2 p.m. and suggested I take a city tour for twenty baht ($0.62). I wasn't sure what that included. At least the price was right. The kicker was that I had to visit one or two shops. Having traveled to places where my biggest concern was a gypsy asking for signatures, I was naïve about how things worked here.

I walked to a kid no older than 14 sitting on a tuk-tuk, a three-wheeled auto rickshaw found in many developing countries. I hopped in, and he gunned the throttle. A plume of oily exhaust burst out, and polluted wind blasted my face. Like a homing pigeon delivering a message, he weaved through the sparse traffic, stopping at a gold stupa on top of a hill. (I later learned it was *Wat Saket*, the Golden Mount.) With broken English, he said, "Climb." I followed his instruction, ascending the staircase that wrapped the periphery for a bird's eye view of drab buildings and a filth-covered city.

I hurried down, surprising the driver with my quick return. He took me to *Wat something-something* (I can't remember the name) for the Lucky Buddha, where a man with a foot-long hair growing out of a pinky-nail-sized mole on his face greeted me. He claimed I was the first person of the day and that rubbing Buddha's hand would bring good fortune. With nothing to lose, I obliged. Next was *Wat Intharawihan* and its eight-story gilded Buddha. Not even noon, I'd had my fill of wats.

My driver got a stamp for gas at a suit shop. I humored the salesman for a few minutes and declined his offer of a jacket and three made-to-order shirts for 17,500 baht ($542). After more *wats*, it was onto a second suit store where I relented and purchased two shirts for two thousand baht ($62). The adolescent driver dropped me at my hotel after getting what he wanted from me.

I headed back to the Grand Palace as 2 p.m. approached. In theory, it should open soon. Wearing pants, I walked through the main gate to find a jam-packed complex. I had been bamboozled! Hoodwinked! Scammed! I felt ashamed of being fooled so easily, believing I was worldly and could sniff out bullshit. Since the deception led me to places I would never have gone and some custom souvenirs, I called it a wash.

The palace emerged with the establishment of the Chakri dynasty in 1782. It served as the official residence of the Kings of Siam until 1925 and functioned as the country's administrative and religious hub until the bloodless Siamese revolution of 1932, when a constitutional monarchy replaced the absolute monarchy along with a name change to Thailand.

Chapels, stupas, libraries, royal residences, administrative buildings, and lots of *wats* filled an area of forty football fields. Steep roofs and prangs topped gold-covered buildings. Strewn throughout were statues, guardians, and Buddhas, surrounded by flawless grass and flora. Exhausted from the morning tour, I wandered the grounds without purpose and found a pot with fuchsia flowers (M). After the last two days, I declared it a win.

Eager to remove my sweat-soaked clothes, I stepped out of the palace into a chaos of people, cars, trucks, and tuk-tuks. A 20-something driver saw me looking around and asked if I needed a ride. I hopped in and shouted the name of my hotel. He took off before I had a chance to get a fare.

I usually negotiate before entering any taxi, but I assumed it would be a fair rate of one hundred to two hundred baht ($3 to $6). Halfway there, competing with the whining high-revving engine, I yelled, "How much?!" I mistakenly heard "nine hundred baht" ($27). I asked him to repeat. Again, "nine hundred baht!" He said that if I went to five clothing stores, he would drop the price to five hundred baht ($15). I lied and said I didn't have that much, so he offered to take me to an ATM. After getting jerked around that morning, I argued, and he argued back before pulling over. I thought I was getting kicked out.

A Thai police officer on a motorcycle pulled up beside us after noticing the quarrel. He asked me what was going on, and I explained. He scolded the driver, who tried to argue back, but the officer wouldn't have any of it. Their conversation was in Thai, but I gleaned the situation from their facial expressions and hand gestures. The officer (in English) told me to get on his motorcycle.

We drove to the police station, where the two men (in Thai) argued further. After a few minutes of back-and-forth, the officer asked me to sit beside the driver and point my finger at him accusingly while he held up his license. The officer took our picture and apologized to me. He made the driver do the same. With our business concluded, I was close enough to get to the hotel on my own. I had gone in search of something different. I found it.

Inside the Grand Palace in Bangkok

20 ♦ Siem Reap, Cambodia

Four hours due east of Bangkok is Cambodian National Highway 5, a road that changed my definition of hardship. Within minutes, I encountered ramshackle dwellings made of rotted wood and rusted sheet metal on stilts. Ribs protruded from cows. Aluminum cans, garbage, and meter-diameter concrete piping littered the verge. Umbrellas sheltered open-air markets.

Scooters hauled three people. A woman peddled what I assumed was her grandson on a bicycle. Dust covered everything.

Staring at this perilous gravel motorway, shielded from the bone-permeating heat, I contemplated their lack of resources, poor education, and limited opportunities. While I used to dislike my job, complain about the weather, or fly coach, these First World problems weren't life or death. I never worried about my next meal, toiled to find clean water, had inadequate healthcare, or lacked electricity. I had finally confronted the Third World, which summated life's unfairness.

The road to Siem Reap

At the end of the road was Siem Reap, a popular tourist destination near Angkor Wat, the world's largest religious monument. Translating to "Temple City" in Khmer (Cambodia's official language), its design and construction began during the reign of King Suryavarman II in the early twelfth century, when he intended it as his mausoleum.

Initially a Hindu temple dedicated to the god Vishnu, the Khmer's old enemy, the Chams, pillaged it in 1177. When King Jayavarman VII restored the Khmer Empire, feeling slighted by the Hindu gods, he converted it into a Buddhist temple. Partially abandoned during the sixteenth century, it underwent restoration during the twentieth century, with work temporarily halted in the 1970s and 1980s due to civil war and political unrest. A symbol of Cambodia, it's featured on the country's flag.

At 4 a.m., I crossed a causeway bisecting a moat with natural reflecting pools. The larger left pool provided a superior view of the temple, assuming you reached the correct location. With over five hundred people jockeying for position, I peered at the smaller pool on the right, which had only two people. No signs indicated the area was off-limits, so I wandered over.

I exchanged pleasantries with the young *Québécois* as more people flocked to the left. Occasionally, some rebels migrated to the right. Those who did said hello or offered a nod of the head. But as the sun rose over the Cambodian countryside, we knew to shut up.

The sky shifted from purple to pink to orange as the temple's quincunx of four central jagged convex towers symmetrically placed around a taller fifth representing Mount Meru—a five-peaked mountain sacred in Hinduism, Jainism, and Buddhism—believed to be the center of the universe, reflected in the shallow, grassy, less busy pool (M). Only sporadic trees and the occasional wildlife ruined the perfect balance.

For a moment, I felt a near transcendence, where paradise and Earth merged. I appreciated life more than ever, wishing I could bottle this piece of time and periodically reopen it as a reminder of my good fortune. If Thailand had stimulated my religious curiosity, Cambodia did the same for my interest in poverty. I had gone in search of something different. I found it.

Angkor Wat

21 ♦ Phnom Penh, Cambodia

It is better to arrest ten people by mistake than to let one guilty person go free.

— Khmer Rouge slogan

With the Holocaust setting the genocidal benchmark for the twentieth century, three decades after the fall of the Nazis, the Communist Party of Kampuchea, aka the Khmer Rouge, implemented their utopia with the decimation of Cambodia. On April 17, 1975, after seven years, they emerged as the victors of the Cambodian Civil War, aiming to create an agrarian socialist society devoid of external influence. The transformation, termed *Year Zero*, meant destroying everything prior.

The regime abolished money, burned books, and seized property. They closed hospitals, schools, and factories. Foreigners weren't allowed in, and Cambodians couldn't leave. They forced the urban population of Phnom Penh and other cities, totaling nearly two million "new people," into the countryside to become "base people" through agricultural labor focused on rice production. Intellectuals, professionals, religious participants, and anyone suspected of being an enemy of the state were targeted for execution. Wearing glasses or speaking a different language could prove fatal. The Khmer Rouge's paranoia became so overwhelming that they arrested and imprisoned high-ranking officials.

In central Phnom Penh dwells Tuol Sleng, the Khmer Rouge's most notorious death facility. One of over 150 "security offices" across the country, it was designated Security Office 21 (S-21). Four months after coming to power, they converted the high school into a prison, interrogation, and execution center.

Inmates were photographed and forced to give an autobiography up to their arrest. Accused of being opponents of the revolution, often without evidence, they were tortured to extract confessions, while implicating themselves and others in fabricated conspiracies. With the confession obtained, prisoners were "discarded."

The Khmer Rouge wrought terror in the country for nearly four years, amidst sporadic border skirmishes with Vietnam. But on December 25, 1978, the Vietnamese launched an all-out offensive and, within two weeks, ended the Cambodian Genocide. A Vietnamese combat photographer discovered S-21 by following the smell. This is where I begin.

A high perimeter fence topped with razor wire surrounded three-story, open-air concrete structures resembling cheap motels, featuring burnt orange and cream-colored checkerboard floor tiles throughout. Most rooms had exterior bars and large windows with decorative metal shutters on the opposite side. Building A was used for jailing, interrogating, and punishing high officials. Buildings B, C, and D displayed mugshots of the dead, their belongings, and torture devices.

A prison cell (left) and the courtyard at S-21 (right)

Nobody left Tuol Sleng after mid-1976. Of the estimated fourteen thousand imprisoned, it's believed only twelve survived. Corpses were buried nearby during the first year, but the sheer volume drove prisoners to Choeung Ek, an orchard that became part of the Killing Fields.

Seven kilometers (4.3 mi) southwest resided some of the country's twenty-thousand mass graves where the Khmer Rouge beat victims with shovels, pickaxes, or sticks and smashed children against trees to save bullets before interring the dead in shallow pits. Wooden structures with grass-covered roofs and low wooden fences among sparse vegetation had signs detailing how many hundreds of bodies were haphazardly buried there. Without them, I wouldn't have known what I was looking at. It's common to see bones, teeth, or clothing protruding after a hard rain. A multi-story memorial stupa differing from the rest of the area—tall, modern, and made of pale stone—housed five thousand neatly stacked human skulls (M).

I had gone in search of something different. I didn't find it. Having studied the Holocaust, I had seen genocide. But I felt ashamed of my ignorance regarding the one in Cambodia. Ending two years before I was born, the estimated death toll was roughly one-quarter of the country's eight million people. Maybe it's not mentioned much because the body count wasn't as high. Or it was part of a regional conflict, not a global one? Or it was farther from the U.S.? Or they weren't white, and the West didn't give a damn? Whatever the reason, this most recent massacre of those deemed unworthy led to another epiphany.

Poverty arises from a range of causes: corruption, disease, environmental conditions, overpopulation, and under-education, to name a few. Days earlier, I had been perplexed by the conditions on the road to Siem Reap. I couldn't understand how things got so bad. It was now clear. These people endured a civil war and a genocidal government that purged the thinkers, innovators, difference-makers, and dreamers. Poverty was the only outcome.

Skulls at the Killing Fields

22 ♦ Hạ Long Bay, Vietnam

I occasionally turned to movies and TV for inspiration. One of my favorite shows, *Top Gear*, featured three presenters performing outrageous tests and skits with various vehicles. I've seen nearly every episode, some more than once. My favorite was when they bought used motorbikes and rode the length of the Vietnamese coastline from south to north.

I had postured buying a motorcycle in my adolescence to get a reaction from Mom, who shot that idea down, referring to them as "donor cycles" due to the likelihood of becoming an organ donor. My phobia of open-air vehicles ensured I would never own one. One mistake can have serious consequences. During my Southeast Asia stint, I saw innumerable road-rashed young men covered in bandages. With no desire to endure a comparable outcome, the 1,600-kilometer (1,000 mi) emulation wasn't for me.

Still eager to see the country similarly, I went from Ho Chi Minh City to Hoi An to Hue to Hanoi. Unable to find a place for Mom, I held high hopes for the last stop. A three-hour drive from the Vietnamese capital led me to Hạ Long Bay, where I boarded a small passenger cruise ship.

I envisioned my first glimpse of the bay to resemble the show with beams of light shooting through scattered clouds, illuminating the blue-green sea and limestone karsts in the Gulf of Tonkin. That's not how it happened. I could do nothing about the never-ending cloud sheet for the past ten days.

In the episode's final segment, the presenters convert their motorbikes into amphibious scooters. Desiring to do something on the water like them, I asked to go swimming, but couldn't due to the pollution. After some prodding, I arranged for kayaks. The kicker was that enough people had to consent to the 6 a.m. start time. I went from person to person, trying to persuade them. Some thought it foolhardy, while others waffled. Resorting to "sleep when you're dead," I convinced half of the sixteen-person group.

We set off at the crack of dawn through murky water with floating bits, paddling for paddling's sake. I find kayaking monotonous, but I do it as a means to an end. So far, sleep seemed the better option. Running short on time, someone noticed an opening in one of the islands. We raced towards a long, narrow tunnel with a ceiling just out of reach. On the other side, the world opened into a hidden cove of imposing limestone covered in dense foliage. The only sounds were the sloshing of our paddles and the echoes of our voices (M).

Returning to the boat at 8 a.m., those who had slept in lamented their decision, a sentiment that was common throughout my travels. I never heard anyone say they regretted doing something, only the opposite. Though my first attempt to recreate the fantasy world of television hadn't gone as planned, I had searched for something I knew about and had zero regrets that morning.

Zero regrets at Hạ Long Bay

TOWARD THE RISING SUN

23 ♦ Beijing, China

I sat in my aisle seat for the three-hour flight from Hanoi to Beijing, China. A white-haired white man in his 50s occupied the window. We gave the "it's nice to see a Westerner" nod I had acclimated to and commenced in generic conversation.

Rob was a widower from Canada who lost his wife to lung cancer two years prior. He considered selling everything and retiring in Vietnam. I briefly contemplated a similar move, but would have chosen somewhere else, maybe Berlin. He had spent six weeks visiting a younger Vietnamese woman, overemphasizing their platonic relationship.

He engaged the Chinese woman sitting between us, who spoke excellent English, though she didn't think so. Diane, the Western name she had chosen, was a salesperson heading home an hour outside Beijing. Cute but not stunning, she emitted a sweet modesty.

Rob inquired about her marital status. At the ripe old age of 32, the same age as me, she had missed her window. I sensed her lack of matrimony was an issue. (I later learned that an unmarried woman in China over the age of 28 is given the unfortunate title of "leftover.") I sympathized with Diane and empathized with Rob. When the plane landed three hours later, we wished each other safe travels.

I met a new group that evening. My guide, a Chinese native familiar with the communist regime, started with the "dos and don'ts." In particular, we weren't supposed to discuss the Three Ts—Tibet, Taiwan, and Tiananmen. Tibet, due to the heavy-handed Chinese rule and the Tibetan attempt to free its grasp. Taiwan (officially the Republic of China), the island outpost where the nationalist forces fled after their 1949 defeat by Mao Zedong's communists. And Tiananmen, referring to the 1989 Tiananmen Square protests and massacre. I was seven when the incident occurred, and I vaguely remembered it. As an adult, my curiosity about one of the defining moments of the twentieth century grew. It was an event forty years in the making.

On October 1, 1949, the Chinese Communist Party (CCP) founded the People's Republic of China (PRC) following its resounding victory over the Republic of China during the Chinese Civil War.* Tiananmen Square hosted the raising of the first National Flag of the People's Republic of China.

Over the next quarter-century, the CCP leader, Mao Zedong, implemented his Marxist–Leninist† ideology (I elaborate more on this later) by transforming China from a peasant-based society into one dominated by industry under a planned economy.

In 1958, his Great Leap Forward focused on grain and steel production. Farmers were stripped of their land and forced into state-run communes with grain quotas, where the harvest was taken by the state and used at its discretion. To produce steel, peasants diverted from agricultural labor melted scrap metal in backyard furnaces fueled by wood and household items. The poor quality yielded little economic value. Along with grain exports to save face, failed crop experiments, underreporting of output, and refusal of international aid, China suffered the deadliest famine in history. Additionally, political gatherings and propaganda replaced religious ceremonies. Objectors were publicly chastised, tortured, or killed. The Great Chinese Famine—and the murders, to a lesser extent—of the Great Leap Forward killed somewhere between fifteen and forty-six million people.

---

* During the Chinese Civil War, more than two million troops were killed, and five million civilians died due to combat, disease, and starvation.

† Marxist–Leninist is a communist ideology that became the state ideology of the Soviet Union and spread to China. It refers to the German philosopher Karl Marx and Soviet Union's first leader, Vladimir Lenin.

The failure diminished Mao's political power. Wanting to regain his status as the central figure, he launched the Socialist Education Movement in 1963 to purge high-ranking officials seen as disloyal. A year later, he published *Quotations from Chairman Mao Tse-tung*, aka the *Little Red Book*, due to its small size and bright cover. Containing snippets of his speeches and writings, nearly everyone in China owned at least one copy. Posters of people holding the book and portraits of Mao appeared everywhere. His soaring cult of personality set the stage for the Cultural Revolution.

Propaganda, rallies, and purges marred 1966. Inspired by the *Little Red Book*, the student-led paramilitary group, the Red Guards, massacred Beijing educators. The bloodshed ignited the Red Terror that spread across the country, leading to the destruction of the "Four Olds"—old ideas, old culture, old habits, and old customs. The process began with renaming streets and stores to sound more "revolutionary." It progressed to the Red Guards harassing individuals, namely intellectuals. It culminated in the destruction of buildings, books, artwork, and temples.

After suffering multiple heart attacks, Mao Zedong died on September 9, 1976, at age 82, and China experienced a reversal of the Cultural Revolution. Education and intellectuals reemerged, focusing on the Four Modernizations—agriculture, industry, technology, and defense. However, the country remained a one-party state under tight government control.

Following the death of reformist leader Hu Yaobang on April 15, 1989, posters sprang up, memorializing his policies, democracy, and free speech. A week later, his hasty funeral inside the Great Hall of the People on Tiananmen Square's western edge was broadcast to tens of thousands of students, who called for political reform and an end to government corruption.

The peaceful protest swelled over seven weeks, marked by hunger strikes, sit-ins, and the erection of the ten-meter-tall (33 ft) "Goddess of Democracy." After the government declared martial law, on June 3, outraged citizens—from the middle class to peasants, military members, and homemakers—set up roadblocks to stop the advancing army, which was ordered to clear the Square at the center of Beijing. Fighting broke out across the city as protesters did their best to block the soldiers and tanks with rocks, bottles, and Molotov cocktails. But just after midnight, the first armored vehicle breached the Square. The students tried to hold their ground amidst the threat of gunfire. However, by early morning, they abandoned their impossible position.

The next day, a convoy of tanks tried to leave the Square. The lead tank stopped a few meters from a lone man and attempted to go around him, but he remained in the way. The disgusted man climbed aboard and presumably conversed with the crew before jumping off. The tank lurched forward, and the man stood his ground again until plainclothes men led him away. Western journalists captured the moment, smuggled the images out of China, and displayed them on the front pages of newspapers worldwide. The man's identity remained unknown as he slipped into legendary obscurity, forever eternalized as Tank Man.

The official figures report 241 deaths (218 civilians, 10 People's Liberation Army soldiers, and 13 People's Armed Police) along with seven thousand wounded. Unofficial fatality estimates range from a few hundred to several thousand. The Chinese government maintains that no one died in the Square. There is no solid evidence to dispute this claim.

Like September 11th, the body count of the Tiananmen Square protests and massacre was minimal, but the consequences were vast. The government propagandized the event as an attempt to overthrow the socialist state and replace it with a Western capitalist system. Officials deemed responsible were removed, reassigned, or resigned. Thousands were arrested, often jailed or sent to labor camps without due process. Student leaders were imprisoned or fled the country to live in exile. The event was censored by banning contentious literature and movies, shutting down newspapers, restricting textbook information, and blocking internet resources.

I stepped into Tiananmen Square a few months before the twenty-fifth anniversary of the incident. Initially built in 1651, it had been expanded and modernized over time. Unlike other historically significant places, it lacked any mention of turmoil—no statues, plaques, or memorials.

On the perimeter, the Great Hall of the People, an imposing three-story building of light stone and vertical columns, served as the political center and home of the National People's Congress. In the middle stood the Monument to the People's Heroes, a ten-story obelisk honoring the martyrs of revolutionary struggles in the nineteenth and twentieth centuries (M). Despite wishing to be cremated, Mao Zedong was interred in a truncated version of the other structures. The Chairman Mao Memorial Hall put George Washington's final resting place to shame, a grand gesture for the man considered the greatest mass murderer in history, responsible for the deaths of forty to eighty million people.

Though Cambodia and Vietnam were communist, they didn't have the crushing feel of China. As military guards with batons and riot shields watched over the few thousand visitors wandering the pristine gray granite slabs, I was reminded of George Orwell's *1984*: "BIG BROTHER IS WATCHING YOU."

The Monument to the People's Heroes (foreground) and Great Hall of the People (background) in Tiananmen Square

24 ♦ Beijing, China

Chinese philosophy adheres to the concept of yin and yang, the theory that all things exist in contradictory opposites that attract, complement, and are interdependent—female and male, light and dark, old and young, poor and rich. If Tiananmen Square was the yin, across the street was the yang, a place equally important, diametrically opposite, yet interconnected.

I exited Tiananmen Square from the north and crossed the street, where Tank Man stood his ground. On the other side stood the Tiananmen, a city gate constructed in 1420. Destroyed numerous times, it carried an ironic translation, "Gate of Heavenly Peace."

Above the arched entrance hung a portrait of Mao Zedong—expressionless, with a receding hairline and a grey jacket. Replaced every October 1 on the country's national day, or when vandalized, it stared at his mausoleum. Maybe Big Brother was watching?

I funneled through the Tiananmen, crossing into the past, where in 1406, the third emperor of the Ming dynasty began building the Forbidden City, the world's largest imperial palace. Taking fourteen years to construct, it served as the political and ceremonial center for nearly five centuries and was home to twenty-four emperors from the Ming and Qing dynasties.

By the early twentieth century, the Chinese monarchy's power had declined. When the Qing fell in 1912, the last emperor, Puyi, was forced to abdicate but stayed in part of the palace until he was expelled in 1924. During World War II and the Chinese Civil War, many of the city's treasures were evacuated, with some eventually making their way to Taiwan.

Unlike the vast openness of Tiananmen Square, the Forbidden City was a bottleneck of thousands moving shoulder to shoulder through the Meridian Gate, the grand southern entrance once reserved solely for the emperor. I crossed a stone bridge over the Golden Water River and climbed toward the Hall of Supreme Harmony (M) with its yellow roof and towering pillars, once used for coronations and imperial birthdays.

The portait of Mao Zedong above the Tiananmen

The Palace of Heavenly Purity, a grand, rectangular hall set on a white marble terrace, served as the emperor's main residence. Further north was the Imperial Garden, a retreat of cypress trees, rock formations, and pavilions, before I finally exited through the Gate of Divine Prowess, the passage once used by guards and palace staff.

As much as I try to deny it, my slight claustrophobia was triggered by the press of the crowd. I was relieved to escape back into the open streets of Beijing.

While Tiananmen Square and the Forbidden City differed in appearance, their commonality was that neither mentioned violence. I again found it unsettling to have an "all is well, nothing to see here" façade when history told a different story. Like every empire, China's story is written in blood. To fully understand it, I would have to look further back in time.

The Hall of Supreme Harmony

25 ♦ Beijing, China

Sondre and Jan Ove were unofficial stepbrothers, although you wouldn't have guessed. Sondre was stereotypical Nordic—tall, blonde, and blue-eyed. Jan Ove was slightly shorter, with black hair, brown eyes, and a hint of Asian heritage. His mother moved to Norway as a child to escape the Vietnam War, met a Norwegian man, and had a child with him. They separated, and the Norwegian man later reconnected with Sondre's mom, his high school sweetheart from twenty years earlier. This unlikely reunion brought Sondre and Jan Ove together at age 12, and they grew up like brothers of blood. From the moment I met them, I liked them.

Halfway through a six-month journey, a few weeks earlier, they completed the *Top Gear* Vietnam scooter trip, each purchasing one and riding along the coast. Both were experienced riders who owned motorcycles. Hearing about their breakdowns, getting lost, and gastrointestinal distress, I had made the right decision.

I was seven years older than they were and remember feeling impervious at their age. But with each passing year, the more *risk vs. reward* influenced me. Was it worth doing *X* if the outcome was *Y*? Yes, I had done adventure sports in New Zealand. I considered that a phase rather than a lifestyle. Standing in the parking lot at Mutianyu, seventy kilometers (44 mi) northeast of central Beijing, the forces of adventurism and pragmatism collided. The question was: where to start walking the Great Wall of China?

As early as the seventh century BCE, Chinese states started building walls to defend against nomadic incursions. In 221 BCE, China unified under the Qin dynasty, with Qin Shi Huang emerging as the First Emperor. Tamped earth and gravel linked the previously separate fortifications.

Over the next one and a half millennia, dynasties rose and fell, each taking a different approach to wall construction. Some questioned their usefulness, while others built thousands of kilometers, often overburdening the populace and creating turmoil.

The rise of the Ming in 1368 and a continuous Mongol threat prompted the construction of thousands of kilometers of walls using brick and stone, offering better protection and durability. In the sixteenth century, new techniques allowed for the building of hollow towers, which provided space for food, water, weapon storage, living quarters, and defense against Mongol projectiles.

With the rise of the Qing in 1644, who controlled large parts of China beyond the Wall, preventing invasions from the north became unnecessary. As a cultural icon, it delineated the civilized (inside) and non-civilized society (outside). The Qing suppressed this idea and paid little attention to it until their fall in 1912. Erosion, neglect, and human activity damaged many sections, but China's economic reforms of the 1980s sparked a preservation campaign. It’s now the country's most popular tourist attraction.

We had two options to reach the walls built by the Northern Qi and reconstructed by the Ming—a gondola to Tower 14 or climbing to Tower 8. Joining us was Steve, a mid-50s American. I don’t know if it was machismo, peer pressure, or a desire to keep the group together, but when he sided with the Norwegians to take the challenging route, he made my decision for me.

We ascended a set of concrete stairs. Steve, dealing with a bad knee, was slow but steady. The Norwegians kept waiting for us. Half an hour later, we reached Tower 8, a fortified guard post made of bulky bricks with man-sized arched entrances leading into a protected room with tiny, curved windows. Stairs led up to an open-air parapet with battlements. Walkways, a few meters wide and hundreds of meters long, connected similar towers.

We set our sights on Tower 14, planning to take the gondola down to the parking lot. The Norwegians set off. Steve and I hurried to keep up. Our morning arrival beat most of the crowds, allowing swift movement. In a relentless hurry, we arrived at our objective within two hours. Enamored and eager for more, we pushed on to Tower 23, walking an unspecified number of uphill kilometers.

Everything had been in excellent condition, with smooth brick walkways and picturesque fortifications. But beyond Tower 23, the

Wall stopped being a wall, turning into a broken trail of ankle-twisting holes and shattered blocks. Even the Norwegians moved cautiously. A far cry from when ten people could stand shoulder to shoulder, the path often narrowed for one.

Vendors sold their usual trinkets—hats, flags, magnets, and other inexpensive items. They also offered necessities—water, chips, and beer. We each grabbed a (not so) cold one for our tertiary goal of Tower 26, where we sat atop the decaying structure, cracked open our brews, and gazed at the sprawling Yanshan Mountains with its serpentine backbone that had more or less protected this nation for over two millennia.

I hadn't told anyone about the 100 Places After in a long time. I couldn't keep it from these guys, who toasted to Mom (M). From that moment, we became friends for life.

♦♦♦

In the years to come, my bond with Sondre strengthened as we met in the world's corners. Two years after our day on the Great Wall, I received a message from him. Jan Ove had passed away in a motorcycle accident. He was 27 years old.

Me, Jan Ove, Steve, and Sondre at the Great Wall of China. Photo by fellow traveler.

26 ♦ Xi'an, China

In 246 BCE, at age 13, Ying Zheng ascended to the throne of the State of Qin. Thirteen years later, he began conquering the remaining independent Chinese kingdoms. By 221 BCE, he ruled a unified land and bestowed upon himself the invented title Qin Shi Huang, the First Emperor of China.

He divided the country into administrative units: commanderies, counties, and townships. Weights, measures, currencies, and lengths were standardized. A system of roads and canals enhanced trade and transportation. The walls from the previous four centuries were connected, paving the way for the Great Wall. The Qin script became the official text, forming a solitary language and communication system. To solidify his dominance, history books unrelated to the State of Qin were destroyed, and scholars were buried alive for possessing forbidden texts.

After unifying China, Qin Shi Huang turned his attention to his mortality, having survived multiple assassination attempts during his harsh rule. Hoping to avoid death, he searched for the legendary elixir of life. Mercury, a shiny, metallic element that is liquid at room temperature, was one potential candidate. Unable to achieve immortality, he died in 210 BC at age 49, possibly from mercury poisoning. Internal squabbling and weak leadership caused the fall of the Qin dynasty four years later.

In 1974, peasants digging a well near present-day Xi'an unearthed pottery fragments that revealed one of the world's greatest archaeological discoveries: Qin Shi Huang's mausoleum and the Terracotta Army.

Created to showcase the emperor's glory and immortalize the army that united China, he filled it with warriors, horses, and chariots made of terracotta (a type of clay-based ceramic) that would protect him in the afterlife. While a fear of booby traps has kept his tomb unexcavated, three nearby pits have been explored.

Having expended my enthusiasm quota at the Great Wall, I aimlessly strolled the immense complex, moving from pit to pit, arranged in an equilateral triangle. Pit 2, a story underground, contained cavalry and infantry laid out in narrow sections. Pit 3 served as the command center, housing high-ranking officers and a chariot. Pit 1 (M) held the bulk of the army.

A Terracotta Army soldier (left) and soldiers with cavalry (right)

Inside an aircraft hangar-sized building, rows of assembled warriors stood ready for battle. Each figure was life-size, with unique facial features, hairstyles, and uniforms indicating rank—infantry, cavalry, or charioteer. Some wore scale armor; others wore knee-length jackets with creases frozen in clay. The original paint had long since faded, leaving them in shades of grayish-brown, coated with fine dust. With an estimated strength of eight thousand soldiers, most of the army had yet to be revealed.

Pit 1 of the Terracotta Army

27 ♦ Shanghai, China

Walking one of Shanghai's main streets, surrounded by modern buildings and fast food, two Chinese girls approached me. They weren't attractive enough to be prostitutes, or at least expensive ones. Unbeknownst to me, they wanted to metaphorically f*** me.

They invited me to have some tea. I thought a simple cup would be harmless. Two minutes later, we entered a restaurant full of locals. But instead of sitting in the main dining area, they took me to a private room in the back. My neck hair bristled as the door closed, and I clutched my backpack, ready to run if needed. The girls sensed my anxiety and tried to put me at ease. I thought about leaving, but decided to let things play out.

A waitress entered and handed us menus in Chinese. Unsure of what was happening, I deferred. With the order placed, the waitress snatched the menus and left the room. A tray with a teapot, food, and several half-filled glasses of neat whiskey arrived. Something was up. Not wanting to cause trouble in a foreign land, I drank my drink, nibbled on the food, and made polite conversation. When I was ready to leave, I watched as another tray of drinks arrived. I grew agitated and insisted that the bill was the next thing the waitress brought. I sat there waiting, sipping the whiskey, though I despise it.

When the check arrived, I couldn't believe my eyes. We had been drinking some of the finest stuff in the bar. The girls insisted it was customary for the guest to pay. I offered to contribute my part. They gave me a sob story about how they couldn't afford their share. I angered them by insisting they empty their purses. I took their cash and would have preferred to leave if it weren't for the menacing man in the doorway. I paid the rest, which came to about one hundred dollars.

Back on the streets, I went through a mix of emotions. I felt joyous to be out of there, confused about what had happened, and ashamed of my foolishness. My instincts told me to leave, but I didn't trust them. There have been a handful of times my inquisitive nature overrode my intuition. The decision was always wrong. As the saying goes, "Curiosity killed the cat." In this case, curiosity cost me money. In the grand scheme, it wasn't much. But there's a difference between spending money and being cheated.

I was fooled in Bangkok a few weeks earlier, which led to a private tour and a couple of shirts. Then, a tuk-tuk driver tried ripping me off, followed by a trip to the police station and an amusing story. Shanghai was different. After a few drinks, I stopped trusting everyone I didn't know. I could have told my guide, but nothing would come of it. Even though the girls and the restaurant had deceived me, they hadn't done anything illegal. I had looked at the menu. Technically, I knew the prices.

Still reeling from the past half-hour, I put on a happy face for an evening cruise of the Shanghai Harbor, where I bought beers for Sondre, Jan Ove, and Steve. Although I had spent a lot on drinks for two treacherous girls, I enjoyed buying a round for friends as we savored them against one of the world's most impressive skylines (M). When the cruise ended an hour later, I felt better. In a way, a simple cup of tea became an investment in my real-world education. Never again would I be ripped off, robbed, or victimized.

Shanghai

28 ♦ Mount Kōya, Japan

The sub-cafeteria-quality food on the ferry across the East China Sea was so dismal that I resorted to "toilet noodles," prepackaged ramen cooked with hot water from the bathroom. At 3 a.m., I gripped my bunk in the cramped cabin as enormous swells nearly ejected me. I peered at the solitary porthole to black-grey-black-grey—sea to sky to sea to sky. I feared capsizing but could only hold on for dear life. Conditions calmed on the second day. Arriving in Osaka on the third, I had never been so glad to be on land.

I had planned an increase in living standards the further along I went. Though I coveted an initial challenge, I appreciated places with punctual trains, clean restrooms, and shops with visible price tags. Like Germany, as soon as I stepped onto Japanese soil, the country captured my heart. It was immaculate and functional, with people who exhibited a polite humility.

As diverse as Thailand, Cambodia, Vietnam, China, and Japan were in culture, economy, and climate, they all shared one thing—Buddhism. Each varied in practitioners and government support, but whether it was temples, monuments, monks, or souvenirs, its presence was unmistakable.

Raised a staunch Catholic, one of Mom's biggest regrets was the lack of religion in my upbringing. However, I attended a public school without a pious curriculum, my interests focused on math and science, and soccer often took up Sunday mornings. I lament not knowing more about Christianity, but only for educational reasons. I'm glad I never developed a blind belief that my solitary faith was the only true way and that anyone different was wrong.

Worldwide, about 84 percent of people believe in a higher power, including followers of Christianity, Islam, Hinduism, Buddhism, Judaism, and other faiths. I believe that as long as it doesn't harm others, what someone practices—or chooses not to practice—should be their fundamental right, devoid of external influence.

With my curiosity piqued in Thailand, I aimed to experience as many religions as I could. First was Buddhism, which traces its origins to the teachings of Gautama Buddha, a monk, philosopher, and teacher thought to have lived in India around the fifth century BCE. Like many new religions, the dogma spiderwebbed from the source. At some point during the first or second century, Buddhism reached China via the Silk Road, a network of ancient trade routes that extended from East Asia to Southern Europe and West Africa.

In 804, the Japanese-born Kūkai traveled to China, where he studied Buddhism under Master Huiguo and quickly received the full transmission of the teachings. After returning to Japan in 806, a decade later, he established a temple complex on Mount Kōya, cementing it as the headquarters of the Shingon (True Word) school of Buddhism. Near the end of his life, he retreated into meditation and passed away in 835 at age 62. Legend has it that he didn't die and instead resides in eternal meditation, awaiting the future Buddha.

I arrived at a Buddhist monastery on Mount Kōya and followed a monk to Okunoin, Japan's largest graveyard. After two kilometers (1.2 mi), the soft-spoken man with a shaved head and orange garb offered wisdom on the essentials of life: health and happiness. Regarding health, he emphasized that our bodies are our temples, and we must care for them. A clean body leads to a pure soul. Concerning happiness, he said people think money brings them joy—the more they have, the happier they'll be. But this false belief shatters when someone close to them dies, replaced by heartbreak.

I felt reaffirmed by my earlier realizations. I sometimes drank too much or overindulged in sugar. But I knew my body was my most valuable asset. And while I had inherited a significant sum of money, I would have traded it all for more time with Mom.

We had stopped just short of the Gobyō-bashi, the cemetery's third and most sacred bridge. As instructed, I washed my hands and mouth with the stream flowing beneath it before pouring water onto the statues as an offering for my departed family. Last, I bowed and crossed into the innermost grounds and the tomb of Kūkai, who is posthumously known as Kōbō-Daishi. In an anticlimactic letdown, it had closed for the evening.

A statue of Kōbō-Daishi

After an early breakfast, I had an hour before departure. I left the monastery, crossed the street, and speed-walked toward The Grand Master along an impeccable pink and grey brick path, slightly narrower than the Great Wall. On either side, two hundred thousand grey granite tombstones ranged from weathered to flawless. There were stacks of cubes, cuboids, spheres, and pyramids; figurines draped in pastel cloth; statues depicting people in prayer; and the occasional mausoleum.

The crisp air formed a layer of dew. The gleaming sun added the perfect warmth as it peeked through centuries-old pine trees. I had broken a sweat arriving at the Gobyō-bashi, where I repeated the cleansing ritual and crossed the arching concrete blocks with a low handrail. The path ended at stairs leading to a small building with black doors of delicate latticework. I couldn't see Kōbō-Daishi, a right reserved for only the highest-ranking monks who brought food as he meditated. Instead, I rang a bell on the porch and prayed for Mom (M).

As I silently wished to a different deity in a distant land, everything felt the same. I didn't understand what that meant. Had God, Buddha, or Kōbō-Daishi heard my plea? If they had, would it change anything? Would my hopes still be ignored? I looked for a sign. As usual, I didn't receive one. I only asked that bringing Mom to the most sacred cemetery in Shingon Buddhism might get her one step closer to salvation, if such a thing exists.

Okunoin Cemetery

29 ♦ Hiroshima, Japan

...and these atomic bombs which science burst upon the world that night were strange even to the men who used them.

— H.G. Wells, *The World Set Free* (1914)

As a testament to my nerdiness, for my 15th birthday, I asked for the DVD of *Trinity and Beyond: The Atomic Bomb Movie*. The documentary, narrated by the one and only William Shatner, chronicles the evolution of nuclear weapons. When the credits roll, my adolescent brain is filled with fearful anxiety about nuclear war, accompanied by a curiosity about these mysterious explosives, awed by their destructive power. Like the Holocaust, my interest in nuclear weapons intensified, and I developed into an atomic tourist. My first stop, Hiroshima, the site of the first nuclear attack in history.

On the morning of August 6, 1945, at 8:15 a.m. Japan Standard Time, the U.S. B-29 bomber Enola Gay dropped a 9,700-pound bomb, code-named "Little Boy," from an altitude of 31,000 feet (9,450 meters). Forty-four seconds later, at 2,000 feet (610 meters), one piece of uranium collided with another, initiating a nuclear chain reaction. The detonation unleashed an estimated explosive yield of fifteen kilotons (30 million pounds) of TNT, leveling the city with a supersonic shockwave while a 7,000°F (3,900°C) fireball ignited what remained.*

Those who survived, known as *Hibakusha* or "bomb-affected people," faced severe radiation exposure, which damages DNA and inhibits cellular division. In the days, weeks, and months that followed, acute disorders appeared: nausea, vomiting, hair loss, infections, and bleeding under the skin. Eighteen days after the bombing, actress Midori Naka became the first death certified as "atomic bomb disease."

After a multi-year latency period, radiation-induced cancers increased in the forms of leukemia and malignant tumors—breast, lung, and thyroid. One of the most well-known victims was Sadako Sasaki, who was two years old and one mile (1.6 km) from ground zero. Blown out of the window but showing no injuries, she and her mother encountered "black rain," nuclear fallout of rain darkened with soot and particulate.

Diagnosed with leukemia in 1955, her father told her about a Japanese tradition that anyone who created one thousand cranes would get one wish. Sasaki folded the requisite amount but wouldn't live to see her dream of world peace come true, dying at age 12 on October 25, 1955. That day, Mom celebrated her second birthday.

The Children's Peace Monument, dedicated to Sasaki and all the children who perished, was a one-story, three-legged marble arch topped with a bronze girl holding a crane. An inscription read: "This is our cry, this is our prayer: for building peace in the world."

Ground zero was the Shima Hospital. Everyone inside died, just like most of the city's medical personnel. A reinforced, earthquake-resistant building built in 1914 was the closest structure still

---

* For reference, iron melts at 2,800°F (1,500°C). The surface of the sun is 10,000°F (5,500°C).

standing. Only five hundred feet (150 m) from the hypocenter, no one survived. Initially scheduled for demolition, the Genbaku (A-Bomb) Dome became the centerpiece of the memorial park (M).

Almost seventy years after the bombing, only a few concrete and brick walls remained attached to the half-sphere of curved metal framework atop a five-story tubular central section surrounded by rubble. Lacking windows, doors, or anything flammable, it looked like a building ready to be demolished.

I had waited seventeen years to come here. Outside of the memorials and monuments, Hiroshima was a bustling, modern city, much like other parts of Japan that the U.S. had firebombed during World War II, often with more destructive results. The underlying difference with Hiroshima was how it was done. A single bomb blinked eighty thousand lives out of existence. By the end of 1945, an additional sixty thousand succumbed to radioactive fallout as the power of the atom unleashed a new, unimaginable kind of death.

The Genbaku (A-Bomb) Dome

IT HAS NOT GONE WELL

30 ♦ Rabat, Morocco

Travel is fatal to prejudice, bigotry and narrow-mindedness, and many of our people need it sorely on these accounts. Broad, wholesome, charitable views of men and things can not be acquired by vegetating in one little corner of the earth all one's lifetime.

— Mark Twain, *The Innocents Abroad* (1869)

As I crossed the East China Sea, a 73-year-old man motivated by antisemitism went on a shooting spree at a Jewish community center. Using illegally obtained firearms, he killed a physician and his grandson. He then drove to a Jewish retirement community and killed an occupational therapist visiting her mother. Ironically, the victims were Christians. The following year, the man was sentenced to death. I share this brief story because these events occurred ten minutes from my home.

Whenever I left for a trip, my friends and family reminded me to "be careful." Externally, I appreciated their concern. Internally, I rolled my eyes. Most who offered this obvious advice had never left the country.

While the prospect of being scammed was an unfortunate aspect of travel, I never considered myself to be in physical danger. I felt safer abroad than in my country, which has the highest gun ownership per capita of any nation and the only one with more guns than people. With mass shootings transitioning from breaking news to the back page, if the body count wasn't shocking enough, I had become numb to their regularity.

Though right-wing extremists carried out more acts, Islam became equated with terrorism in America. After September 11th, I harbored unfounded resentment toward Muslims because of my youthful frustration and ignorance. I knew nothing about their religion. It became my driving force to visit a 99 percent Muslim country.

One month after Japan, I arrived in Marrakech, Morocco. But in contrast to how I fell in love with some places, the hot, dirty, and inefficient airport annoyed me. I haggled with cab drivers for a fair rate to my riad and still didn't get one.

Hoping to shed my initial bias, I gave the place a second chance to make a better first impression. I entered the dusty streets, lined with faded yellow taxis and mule-drawn carriages, en route to the medina, the old part of the city, to experience the supposed true essence of Morocco.

I arrived at the walled courtyard and wandered toward thirty men gathered around an equal number of snakes. I was the only Westerner. A charmer approached me with a speckled serpent and asked if I wanted a picture. I recognized the ploy from my time in Asia and declined. Not liking my rejection, he put the snake around my neck. With thicker skin and a no-bullshit attitude, I scolded the man. As quickly as I had entered the medina, I left.

That evening, I joined a tour and met my roommate Brad, a postman from Australia, on a three-month journey across Africa and Europe. A decade older, his tall and muscular frame supported a perfectly shaved head. I enjoyed having someone similar to talk to. As much as I tried to embrace new cultures, it could be exhausting. Even unpleasant.

Casablanca was no better than Marrakech. Unlike the 1942 movie set in Vichy France, with its sharp-dressed, slick-talking characters gathering at a gambling den, the setting was old and run-down. Backdropped by the Atlantic Ocean, the Hassan II Mosque exemplified exquisite Islamic architecture with the finest wood, marble, granite, and metals. The breathtaking building, capable of holding over one hundred thousand worshippers, boasted the world's tallest minaret with a freaking laser beam aimed at Mecca, Islam's holiest city. In contrast to the majestic structures in China from a millennium or two ago, the mosque dates back to 1993.

Across the street, children played soccer on a dirt lot strewn with broken glass, surrounded by rundown buildings. With an estimated price tag in the hundreds of millions of dollars, I wondered why the money couldn't have been used for education or public services. But religion dominates in Morocco, as it does in many places.

We took a train up the coast to the capital city of Rabat. Brad and I sat in a compartment with a Moroccan man who bought us tea. We showed our gratitude with smiles. In a generous gesture, he began changing my opinion of his country.

Walking the streets, we met a local with jet-black hair that glistened from too much product, who offered to show us around. While he seemed friendly enough, if I had been alone, fearing a scam, I would have declined. My guide handled the details.

He led us to Shuhada Cemetery, a sun-bleached, walled graveyard that descended to the sea. More familiar to my Western eyes than the Okunion, thousands of uniform white, brown, and beige graves supported headstones in Arabic. A few had recesses with green plants, indicating watering in this desert environment. All pointed roughly northeast.

After an Islamic practitioner dies, their family members of the same gender typically bathe the body as soon as possible, wrap it in a simple cloth, and perform a funeral prayer. The body is then placed on its right side in a grave that is perpendicular to Mecca.

We exited via a dirt path to the Kasbah of the Udayas, a former citadel built in the twelfth century at the mouth of the Bou Regreg River. The ancient fort featured expensive homes inhabited chiefly by foreigners. The narrow, cobbled streets had coarse walls—white at the top and blue at the bottom—to keep mosquitoes away. We climbed to an expansive terrace overlooking the dark turquoise water, where the hot breeze sliced through me like a scimitar (M). I had finally found a place worthy of Mom.

The Kasbah of the Udayas

31 ♦ Moulay Idriss, Morocco

Morocco had been a mixed bag of mostly good people, with a few who weren't. But none of them were the scary monsters many in my country feared and hated. They were just individuals supporting their families, whose primary difference was how they worshipped.

Islamic tradition states that the Prophet Muhammad was born in 570 in Mecca, located on the Arabian Peninsula. Around the age of 40, he received divine revelations from Allah (God), delivered through the archangel Gabriel. His companions recorded these revelations and compiled them into the Quran, Islam's central religious text, believed to be God's literal words in Arabic.

Muhammad died in 632, and the Quran was finished, but a schism erupted. According to Sunnis, Muhammad never specified a succession plan. They supported Abu Bakr, Muhammad's father-in-law, whom they chose as the first caliph (leader). The Shia believed Muhammad delivered a sermon before his death, proclaiming that his cousin-in-law, Ali, would succeed him.

Islam fragmented and spread to the Middle East, North Africa, the Iberian Peninsula, and Central Asia. In 786, the Sunnis defeated a Shia uprising and forced Idris I, the great-great-grandson of Ali and Fatimah (Muhammad's daughter), to flee. In 789, he established Fez, which grew into the country's third-largest city and our next destination.

It had been a struggle finding alcohol over the past week, as Islam forbids its consumption. In a group of drinkers, this enchanted elixir became our top priority. We stopped at a supermarket, where the owner escorted us to his dingy basement without prices. I reached into a lukewarm refrigerator, pulled out a beer I had never heard of, and the man behind the counter shouted a number.

We smuggled our much-needed drinks into the medina for dinner. The waiter allowed them as long as we were discreet. Filling our glasses under the table made us feel like teenagers. We spent the evening laughing about the lengths we went to for a buzz.

With a few sore heads, we drove one hour west to Volubilis the next day. The city began around the third century BCE. Annexed by the Romans in the first century CE, it saw rapid growth driven by exports. During the third century, the Roman Empire nearly collapsed under the strain of plague, civil war, invasion, and economic depression. Volubilis fell due to its isolation, but remained inhabited by Christian and Jewish communities, eventually transforming into an Islamic one.

In 788, Idris I established his dynasty here, marking the founding of the first Moroccan state. He conquered large parts of northern Morocco but died three years later. Volubilis remained inhabited for a few more centuries before being abandoned, looted, and damaged by an earthquake.

The ruins of Volubilis

Stone dominated the footprints of temples, basilicas, houses, towers, and triumphal arches. Some were partially restored, others remained as they had for nearly two millennia. Dirt paths weaved among the crumbled remnants, surrounded by patches of green and brown fields under a bone-dry, dark sky.

A few kilometers away was the town of Moulay Idriss, nestled at the base of Mount Zerhoun. Founded in 789 by the one and only Idris I, his remains were housed in the center of this alcohol-free hamlet. Only Muslims could enter his mausoleum, so we walked uphill (M) for a birds-eye view of a simple green roof and white walls halfway up the packed hillside.

One of Islam's five pillars, regardless of sect, is the *Hajj*, a pilgrimage to Mecca that all Muslims should make at least once, assuming they are capable.* If unable, supposedly completing seven trips to Moulay Idriss is considered equivalent. With no intention of visiting Saudi Arabia, this felt like a suitable consolation prize. Watching the last light slip behind the low mountains, it's possible Allah was present. God, all I wanted was a beer.

The town of Moulay Idriss

* The five pillars of Islam are *shahadah* (profession of faith), *salah* (prayer), *zakat* (charity), *sawm* (fasting), and *Hajj* (the pilgrimage to Mecca).

32 ♦ Toledo, Spain

We had spent the last week heading north toward Tangier, a port city with a looser, more Mediterranean vibe. Eager for a taste of Europe, we found a dim and sticky pub. As the only customers, we received a complimentary platter of fried foods as gratitude for the hefty tab.

A few plates in, a sharp stomach pain emerged. Back at the hotel, I tossed and turned for hours as the discomfort grew. I induced vomiting to no effect and spent the next six hours curled up in the fetal position, only moving to take care of business at the other end.

I thought of Mom during the agony, partly wishing she could care for her sick child. More importantly, it gave me insight. Nights like this were typical for her. Every morning, I asked how she felt, hoping she was better than the day before. She often wore a look of exhaustion. For a few moments in a Moroccan hotel room, I caught a glimpse of her world.

It seemed nature had run its course by early morning. Having avoided the toilet for a few hours, I got a wink of sleep before boarding the ferry to Spain, where high winds churned the Strait of Gibraltar, the gateway between the Mediterranean Sea and the Atlantic Ocean. As the boat swayed, crew members handed out vomit bags. Somehow, I didn't need mine, so I gave it to a little girl who needed a second one. As bad as I felt, she looked worse.

We arrived at Tarifa an hour later. Assuming the worst was behind me, I forced down a sandwich while awaiting the bus to Seville. Four hours later in the hotel lobby, my stomach rumbled. Confident it was just gas, I gave a gentle push. It wasn't just gas. A streak of warm badness filled my underwear. I had been skydiving, hiked a glacier, and survived one of the highest bungy jumps. None compared to the fear of feces running down my leg in public.

I snatched my room key and waddled like a penguin up two flights of stairs. I inserted the credit card-like key into the electronic lock. The red light flashed. I tried again. The red light flashed. The third time's a charm. The red light flashed. Struggling to hide my horror, I shuffled down to have the key reprogrammed. When I returned to my room, the light turned green. Victory!!!

I finished what I had started and cleaned myself up. I told Brad about my situation. He sniffed the air, wrinkled his nose, and said, "Whew, there is some meat on that taco!" I knew he wouldn't judge, having shit his pants a few days earlier in Rabat. Our lack of bowel control became an ongoing joke just between us. I cracked open my ciprofloxacin, a potent antibiotic. I had traveled with it everywhere, but never needed it. Leaving Seville the following day, I had found the road to recovery.

After a few days of not venturing far from a bathroom, Brad and I popped over to Toledo, an hour's train ride southwest of Madrid. When we arrived at *Mirador del Valle* (M), the Tagus River formed a natural boundary around the "City of the Three Cultures," named so due to the coexistence of Muslims, Christians, and Jews.

Having traveled through places dominated by a single faith, I had yet to find a spot where multiple beliefs intersected. Toledo checked that box. I got the warm fuzzies, partly due to the peaceful coexistence, but mainly because I felt healthy. Remembering what the monk in Okunoin said, our bodies are our temples. With mine restored, I was able to enjoy life fully.

Toledo, Spain as seen from Mirador del Valle

Dead Men's Legacies

33 ♦ Barcelona, Spain

Barring a changing of the stars, my story will wither into oblivion after a generation or two, whittled to dates on a calendar and bullet points. But for some, their lives shaped the world long after they left it.

I begin with Antoni Gaudí, a tale of professional success and personal struggles. Born in 1852 in Catalonia, Spain, the son of a coppersmith had an affinity towards geometry and nature. After earning his diploma in architecture, he was tasked with creating a Benedictine monastery and a church in 1882. That same year, the foundation stone was laid for the Roman Catholic Church, *Basílica i Temple Expiatori de la Sagrada Família*, aka *Sagrada Familia.* When the original architect resigned a year later, Gaudí took over, radically revising the blueprints, excluding parts of the already completed apse and crypt.

He never married, showing interest in only one woman, who didn't reciprocate. After losing many of his close family and friends, he felt he had nothing. Once a young man who dressed well, enjoyed the theater and fine food, he aged into someone who wore tattered clothes and ate cheaply. Often mistaken for a beggar, by 1914, he had dedicated his entire life to the church, eventually moving into the *Sagrada Familia* workshop.

On June 7, 1926, while walking to church for his daily prayer and confession, a tram knocked him unconscious. His poor appearance and lack of identification caused delayed medical attention. After transport to the hospital and some basic care, it wasn't until the next day that the *Sagrada Familia* chaplain recognized him. By then, the injuries were too severe, and he died two days later.

I exited the metro, and Gaudí's crane-covered opus greeted me. At the time of his death, only 25 percent of the work had been completed. Progress slowed due to a reliance on private donations and the raiding of Gaudí's workshop during the Spanish Civil War (1936–1939). Construction reached the midway point in 2010.

Brad and I walked the perimeter of the Gothic/Art Nouveau hybrid, with a monochrome stone canvas depicting ornate biblical scenes. I admired their beauty but failed to comprehend the references, wishing once more that I knew more about Christianity. The Catholic-raised Brad patiently explained their meaning.

The Nativity Façade commemorated Jesus's birth and faced northeast toward the rising sun. The Passion Façade, dedicated to Jesus's suffering during the crucifixion, faced west to catch the day's last rays. The still-to-be-completed Glory Façade, representing Jesus and man within the general order of creation, faced south to obtain as much sunlight as possible. Eight bell towers signified two-thirds of the Twelve Apostles. Four more were in the works, as were those for the Virgin Mary and the four Evangelists. Last, the tallest would represent Jesus. The estimated completion date was 2026, one century after Gaudí's death.

I had seen more churches than most, but this one felt like art. The Latin cross design had bone-colored pillars reaching for the heavens. An octagonal chandelier with a crucified Christ hung in the center. Thousands of stained-glass windows cast kaleidoscopes.

I found a secluded prayer area and said one for Mom. I reemerged and noticed windows overlooking a small church below ground level. Older than the ornate encapsulating icon, with only a few pews, it felt out of place. Unable to find the entrance, a volunteer directed me to the street and around the corner. I grabbed Brad, and we entered as the eight o'clock mass began. Strolling the periphery, we stopped at a marble tablet raised a few centimeters above the floor. The inscription read:

Original Text	English Translation
Antonius Gaudí Cornet. Reusensis. Annos natus LXXIV, vitae exemplaris vir, eximiusque artifex, mirabilis operis hujus, templi auctor, pie obiit Barcinone die X Junii MCMXXVI, hinc cineres tanti hominis, resurrectionem mortuorum expectant. R.I.P.	Antoni Gaudí Cornet. From Reus. At the age of 74, a man of exemplary life, and an extraordinary craftsman, the author of this marvelous work, the church, died piously in Barcelona on the tenth day of June 1926; henceforward the ashes of so great a man await the resurrection of the dead. May he rest in peace.

We had stumbled into the crypt where Gaudí was buried days after his death (M). Over the following decades, his projects experienced neglect and disapproval. However, his reputation recovered in the 1950s, as he gained international recognition, becoming the centerpiece of documentaries, books, musicals, and film awards.

My question is: "Was it worth it?" Would Gaudí have traded his posthumous greatness if he had found love? Or new friendships? We will never know. Instead, he took solace in the one thing he couldn't lose—his work. But his lifelong sacrifice paid off. As his religious faith grew more evident in his projects, he earned the nickname "God's Architect."

Sagrada Familia exterior (left), the interior (center), and Antoni Gaudi's grave (right)

34 ♦ Oslo, Norway

I have never felt war. Never endured another man trying to end my life, nor me trying to end his. Never carried scars on my mind, body, or soul from a bomb, bullet, or blade. Never known the life-altering fear that comes with it. The closest it came to touching me was four hijacked airplanes, the nearest one crashing in a Pennsylvania field over eight hundred miles (1,300 km) away.

Following September 11th, the idea of joining the military crossed my mind, but it quickly faded away. Born under different circumstances, whether by choice or chance, my story could have been different. U.S. military conscription had been around since my country's founding, but in 1973, active service became voluntary. If my hypothetical number had been called, I believe I would have done my duty. Hopefully, I will never have to find out.

I had seen the repercussions of war throughout my travels. There was never a lack of tributes to battles, military leaders, or massacres. I had yet to find a place dedicated to the antithesis of war. I discovered such a place in Oslo, Norway, attributable to a man responsible for countless wartime deaths.

Born in 1833 in Stockholm, Sweden, Alfred Nobel moved with his mother and brothers to St. Petersburg, Russia, where his father owned an armaments factory that supplied weapons for the Tsar's army. The family's newfound success allowed private tutoring for the young Alfred, who mastered five languages and demonstrated an aptitude for the natural sciences, particularly chemistry and physics.

The end of the Crimean War in 1856 bankrupted his father's factory. Alfred and his brothers tried to restart it by experimenting with nitroglycerine, aiming to improve the safety of the finicky explosive liquid. But an 1864 blast in his Stockholm factory killed five people, including his brother, Emil. The tragedy strengthened Alfred's resolve, leading to his 1867 invention of the easier-to-handle dynamite. Not intended for the battlefield, both sides used it during the Franco-Prussian War a few years later.

Nobel invented the smokeless propellant ballistite in 1887. With increased military applications, he offered it to the French (he was living in Paris at the time), but they declined due to their development of a similar product. The consummate businessman, he presented it to the Italians, who adopted it for their new rifle.

The perturbed French launched a smear campaign, accusing Nobel of high treason and banning further experiments in France. When his brother Ludvig died in 1888, a French newspaper mistakenly published an obituary for Alfred, chastising his invention of dynamite with quotes like "The merchant of death is dead." This mistake made him question his legacy.

Although he had produced munitions, Nobel was an idealist and pacifist who strived for disarmament and peaceful solutions to military conflicts. After several revisions, he signed his will less than a year before suffering a stroke and passing away on December 10, 1896, at his home in San Remo, Italy, at age 63.

As one of the world's wealthiest men, having never married and with no direct heirs, in a surprise to his extended family, his will included a clause to invest his remaining assets into secure investments to establish a fund, where the interest earned would be awarded annually to those who, in the previous year, have done the most to benefit humanity.

This laid the groundwork for the Nobel Prizes in Physics, Chemistry, Medicine, Literature, and Peace.* For reasons unknown, Nobel specified that the first four awards be given in Stockholm while the Peace Prize would be bestowed in Oslo. I was six months away from the award banquet at City Hall. However, the next best option was just a few blocks away, the Nobel Peace Center.

A soft yellow covered the three-story former railway station. Inscribed above the wheelchair-accessible entrance were BROADMINDEDNESS, HOPE, and COMMITMENT in

---

* In 1968, the Nobel Memorial Prize in Economic Sciences was established for outstanding contributions to the field of economics. While it's not technically a Nobel Prize, it's awarded in conjunction with them.

Norwegian and English. A replica of the Peace Prize medallion—a right-facing image of Nobel, circled by ALFR • NOBEL • NAT • MDCCCXXXIII • OB • MDCCCXCVI—hung above them.

Two posters advertised the temporary exhibit, BE DEMOCRACY. One displayed a solemn young man with a shaved head holding an automatic rifle, wearing a blood-splattered white tank top, a cheap silver chain, and #outfitoftheday superimposed on top of him. The other showed a cute girl making duck lips with aviator sunglasses, a swimsuit, pierced ears, and #revolution.

Inside was an exhibit dedicated to the 2013 Nobel Peace Prize laureate, the *Organization for the Prohibition of Chemical Weapons* (OPCW). Founded in 1997, the OPCW had, by the time of my visit, grown to 190 Member States and overseen the destruction of more than 80 percent of the world's chemical weapons in sixteen years.

My eye gravitated to an Andy Warhol-stylized poster of the 2009 laureate, Barack Obama. Nearby, some Norwegian schoolchildren watched a video of the "I Have a Dream" speech by Dr. Martin Luther King, Jr., the 1964 laureate. I had seen it on American television a year earlier. Observing it in Norway, emotion overwhelmed me. I don't know if it was the surroundings or if his words rang truer after all I had seen.

BE DEMOCRACY focused on social media's impact on the basic right of freedom of expression. Besides posting the occasional travel photo, I didn't use social media. But in countries where the government controls the information, social media has exposed war crimes, combated racism, and fought for women's rights.

A children's craft area sat adjacent, inviting people to express what democracy meant. Thousands of colored pipe cleaner messages and symbols adorned a wall—"*amor*," "1913," hearts, hashtags, and Stars of David. I pulled up a chair wide enough for one butt cheek, grabbed a wire (M), and formed "hope"—the sentiment that fleeted every time I visited a war memorial or mass grave. Nearly illegible, it appeared to be the work of a child. I have never been good at art. It was my proudest moment in the pursuit of 100 Places After.

The Nobel Peace Center

35 ♦ Stockholm, Sweden

I reflected on the elation from the Nobel Peace Center and wanted more. My best chance to find it again resided in Stockholm, where on December 10, 1901, a group of 113 male guests gathered at the Grand Hôtel for the Nobel Dinner. As the event's popularity grew, in 1930, the rebranded Nobel Banquet relocated to the City Hall. Formerly known as Eldkvarn, the site was an old gristmill that burned down in 1878 in the "fire of the century." Today, the nearly eight million red bricks feature a tower in the southeast corner, anchoring it to the city's skyline.

I stepped into the Blue Room, which, ironically, lacks any blue. The architect liked the look of the exposed brick so much that he scrapped his plan to paint the walls blue. Now, it serves as the dining room for 1,300 guests, located beneath its high windows and grand staircase, surrounded by the arches of the recessed hallway.

During the dinner, each laureate (apart from the Peace Prize laureate) delivers a speech before two ceremonial cheers—one honoring the Swedish monarch and the other to Alfred Nobel himself. In 2013, laureates received 8,000,000 SEK ($1,225,000), a diploma, and a gold medal bearing Nobel's image.

The Stockholm City Hall

I walked to the other side of the building and entered the Golden Hall (M), where the post-dinner dancing takes place in one of the world's blingiest rooms amidst its eighteen million gold-tiled mosaic dedicated to the Queen of Mälaren.

She sat atop a clamshell, Stockholm resting on her lap, symbolizing it as the center of the world. Holding a scepter in one hand and a crown in the other, she was flanked by symbols of East and West—a mosque, an elephant, and the Ottoman flag to her left; the Eiffel Tower, a modern ship, and the New York skyline to her right.

Despite the grandeur, my time at the Stockholm City Hall didn't elicit the joys of Oslo. Had I attended the banquet, it might have been different. What mattered was the posthumous atonement of a brilliantly flawed man and the path it set me on as I searched for those who have done the most to benefit humanity.

36 ♦ St. Petersburg, Russia

I took European History in my sophomore year of high school. The course covered the Renaissance, the Reformation, the Enlightenment, the Industrial Revolution, and World War I. To my chagrin, the teacher excluded World War II due to his obsession with the Romanov dynasty, the last imperial house of Russia.

The death of the heirless Feodor I in 1598 marked the end of the Rurik dynasty, propelling Russia into the *Time of Troubles*, a period of chaos, famine, and succession crises. In 1613, parliament elected Michael I of the House of Romanov as tsar. The father of ten, his bloodline produced some of history's greatest rulers.

His grandson, Peter I, aka Peter the Great, was the first significant player. An avid traveler, he emulated the policies of

Western Europe with sweeping reforms that modernized Russia. In 1703, he founded St. Petersburg (named after the apostle Saint Peter). Nine years later, construction of the Russian Orthodox Church, Peter and Paul Cathedral, began on the north bank of the Neva River. Completed in 1733, it's the city's oldest landmark.

The slender, pastel-yellow Baroque-style building featured a multi-tiered bell tower with a gold spire and an angel holding a cross. Its permanent residents included nearly every ruler of the Romanov dynasty since Peter the Great. Their idealized portraits adorned the main room's gilded walls, and waist-high fencing protected their gleaming white marble sarcophagi with golden Orthodox crosses. The first in line got the best spots near the iconostasis—Peter the Great, Catherine the Great, and Alexander I. Further back sat some of the lesser-known actors. Conspicuously absent were Nicholas II and his family. Of all the tsars, his story is the most notable—a tale of tragic incompetence.

He was born in 1868 in St. Petersburg to Alexander III and Maria Feodorovna, a Danish princess. In 1881, Alexander III assumed the throne at the age of 36, and did little to teach the young Tsarevich, dying thirteen years later. The 26-year-old, ill-prepared Nicholas inherited the third-largest empire in history.*

A few weeks later, he married the love of his life, Princess Alix of Hesse and by Rhine, a beautiful German girl. Confirmed by the Russian Orthodox Church, she took the name Alexandra.

The couple was crowned Emperor and Empress of Russia in May 1896. Days later, a formal celebration at Khodynka Field in Moscow attracted half a million people, fueled by rumors of free bread, sausage, and commemorative cups. Reports swirled that there wouldn't be enough for everyone. The ensuing stampede killed about 1,400 people and injured thousands more. The distraught newlyweds visited the wounded in hospitals but unwisely attended a lavish ball that evening. The Khodynka Tragedy foreshadowed the Tsar's reign.

---

* The British Empire was the largest, followed by the Mongol Empire.

On Nicholas's recommendation, the First Hague Conference convened in 1899, resulting in one of the first statements of the laws of war. His efforts earned a nomination for the first Nobel Peace Prize, but these pacifistic ideals couldn't avoid armed conflict.

The Japanese attacked Russia in February 1904, as both countries sought territorial expansion. After multiple defeats, despite military advice, Nicholas kept Russia in the fight. The Japanese triumphed in September 1905, marking the first time in the modern era that an Asian power defeated a European one.

On January 22, 1905, thousands of unarmed demonstrators upset with the war and tsarist autocracy marched on the Winter Palace (the Tsar's official residence) to present a petition. Unaware that the imperial family had left St. Petersburg the night before, as the unwitting and nonviolent crowd approached, troops opened fire. Casualty estimates ranged from a few hundred to several thousand. The incident became known as *Bloody Sunday*.

Nicholas's ineptitude set the stage for revolution. Strikes spread across the empire, cities lacked electricity, and the railroads ground to a halt. To reduce discontent, the newly drafted October Manifesto granted basic civil rights, made progress toward universal suffrage, and created an elected parliament, the Duma. Nicholas hesitated to sign the document but ultimately relented, hoping to avoid further massacres and lacking military options. The manifesto's release eased the strikes, but its flaws allowed the Tsar to retain too much power.

The Romanovs celebrated the monarchy's tercentenary in 1913. A year later, World War I erupted, drawing Russia into the conflict after Germany and Austria-Hungary declared war. Besides manpower, Germany exceeded the unprepared country in nearly every aspect, including transportation, heavy industry, and equipment. Russia suffered severe defeats in the war of attrition, with Nicholas taking symbolic command of the army in 1915. Little changed, and the losses mounted.

With the Tsar away from Petrograd (formerly St. Petersburg, renamed in 1914 to sound less Germanic), domestic decisions shifted to his wife. The granddaughter of Queen Victoria of the United Kingdom, Alexandra was a carrier of hemophilia, a disease that impairs blood clotting, common among European royalty in the nineteenth and twentieth centuries. The mother of five passed it to her youngest child and only son, Alexei, the heir to the throne.

By 1917, revolution was in the air again as Russia stood on the precipice of ruin. The railway nearly collapsed, stifling shipments of food and fuel. Inflation skyrocketed. Looting broke out across Petrograd. Members of the Duma and the Soviets formed a Provisional Government, demanding that Nicholas abdicate. With no option, he acquiesced. As the Tsarevich's hemophilia made his ascendancy undesirable, Nicholas's brother, Michael, was named successor, but he unceremoniously declined. After three centuries, the Romanov dynasty came to an undignified end.

Initially placed under house arrest in a former imperial residence south of Petrograd, the family was moved to western Siberia in August 1917 as civil unrest swept the nation. The fear for their safety was justified.

The Bolsheviks—a far-left, revolutionary group founded and led by Vladimir Lenin—seized power in October. Six months later, they transferred the family to the remote town of Ekaterinburg, 1,800 kilometers (1,100 mi) east of Petrograd, and imprisoned them in the Ipatiev House, aka "The House of Special Purpose."

Fearing the family's liberation, in the early hours of July 17, guards awoke Nicholas, his wife, their children, the physician, valet, maid, and cook. Under the guise of relocation, they led them to a room in the basement to await the supposed transport.

A group of men entered, the execution order was read, and a barrage of bullets tore through the unsuspecting targets who tried to flee. The gun smoke became so thick that it obscured the solitary light. The executioners couldn't see what they were shooting at and opened the door for ventilation. Only Nicholas, Alexandra, and two servants were dead. The grand duchesses had jewels sewn into their clothes that acted like bulletproof vests. Bayonets, rifle butts, and bullets to the head finished off the survivors.

The men carried the bodies outside, stripped, dismembered, burned, covered in sulfuric acid, and tossed them down a shallow abandoned mineshaft. Hand grenades were thrown in to cover them with debris. To the men's dismay, limbs remained visible, so they removed the dead, hoping to find a deeper mine. By then, the drunk and inexperienced makeshift undertakers had lost all motivation. The effort of loading, unloading, and slogging through thick mud with underpowered trucks and horse-drawn carts had taken its toll.

They dug a shallow grave in a clearing and tossed in Alexei and one of his sisters, whom they burned and buried. By then, the mass grave for the others was ready, whose faces they smashed and doused the bodies with more acid. Earth was shoveled on, and railroad ties were placed atop. The process took two days.

The missing bodies fueled decades of speculation, rumors, and impostor claims. In 1979, amateur investigators discovered the first remains. Fearing government reprisal, they kept their secret for a decade before revealing the find. The government exhumed the mass grave in 1991, which contained nine skeletons believed to be Nicholas, Alexandra, three of their daughters, and the servants.

Initial forensic analysis suggested the remains were those of the Romanovs. To obtain definitive proof, a science in its infancy in 1993 emerged—DNA testing. The government enlisted both Russian and Western experts. After confirming their identities, the family was laid to rest on the eightieth anniversary of their murders, July 17, 1998, in St. Catherine's Chapel at Peter and Paul Cathedral.

The interment happened a year after I finished European History. I was ignorant of the event and the discovery of the bodies. For my final assignment, I created a timeline of every significant dynastic event, ending at 1918. As a prolific procrastinator, I completed it the morning it was due. Before I could print it, I had to catch the bus. These were the days when the dot matrix printer dictated your schedule. Realizing I was in a pinch, Mom finished it and dropped it off at school before work. If memory serves, I earned an A-.

Seventeen years later, life came full circle as I stood at the edge of the roped-off chapel (M). A chandelier hung from a lavish ceiling above vases of flowers. Sunlight shone on the family's off-center, white marble sarcophagus through a lone window. Eight white gravestones with gold inlay covered the wall. Those for Nicholas and Alexandra were in the middle, bordered by their children. Those for Alexei and his sister, Maria, lacked burial dates. Their remains, discovered in 2007, seventy meters (230 ft) from the mass grave, were being held in the state archives at the church's insistence, pending further DNA testing.* The final marker contained abbreviated information about the servants.

I don't know much about the Bible, but Deuteronomy 24:16 says, "The fathers shall not be put to death for the children, neither shall the children be put to death for the fathers: every man shall be put to death for his own sin." A falsehood for the devout Romanovs, who were sacrificed for the patriarch. But as tragic as their deaths were, their suffering was acknowledged. After much controversy, in 2000, the Russian Orthodox Church bestowed the honor of passion bearers, someone not killed for their faith but died in a Christ-like manner.

Peter and Paul Cathedral

Unlike Gaudí, who left us his life's work or Nobel's gift of hope, Nicholas II's limitations paved the way for a new world as his upended empire emerged as something radically different. But as often happens, to quote the nineteenth-century French novelist Jean-Baptiste Alphonse Karr, "*Plus ça change, plus c'est la même chose*." The more things change, the more they stay the same.

* DNA testing in 2018 confirmed the authenticity of all the bodies.

37 ♦ Moscow, Russia

Capitalism: An economic system where private individuals or businesses own and control the means of production (factories, land, machinery, etc.) and operate them for profit.

Proletariat: The working class who don't own the means of production and sells their labor to survive.

Bourgeoisie: The capitalist class that owns the means of production and derives its wealth from exploiting the proletariat.

Socialism: A socioeconomic system where the means of production are controlled by the community rather than private individuals or businesses. The goal is to create a more equal distribution of wealth and resources.

Communism: A stateless, classless, moneyless society where resources are owned collectively, and everyone contributes and receives according to their abilities and needs.

Marxism: A nineteenth-century socioeconomic and political theory developed by Karl Marx and Friedrich Engels. It focuses on class struggle and the eventual transition from capitalism to socialism to communism.

Leninism: The political theory and practice of Vladimir Lenin, which adapted Marxist ideas to the conditions of Russia and emphasized the need for a revolutionary vanguard party to lead the proletariat.

Marxism-Leninism: A combination of Marxist and Leninist principles developed by Joseph Stalin, which served as the official ideology of the Soviet Union and other communist states. It further emphasizes the necessity of a revolutionary party to guide the proletariat towards socialism and communism.

Of all the classes that stand face to face with the bourgeoisie today, the proletariat alone is a really revolutionary class.
— Karl Marx and Friedrich Engels,
Manifesto of the Communist Party (1848)

I entered Moscow on the seventy-third anniversary of Operation Barbarossa.* The ill-fated Nazi invasion of the Soviet Union during World War II created the Eastern Front, humanity's largest military conflict that claimed the lives of thirty to forty million people. A monument marked how far the Germans pushed into Russia, as they fought toward Red Square. Like veins of an empire, all streets emanate from Moscow's central marketplace, six percent the size of Tiananmen Square.

I walked through the gate on the northwest end. To my right stood Russia's largest historical museum. Behind were Kazan Cathedral and the GUM shopping center. At the opposite end was Saint Basil's Cathedral with its ice-creamlike domes. In front was the Kremlin, the former home of tsars, Soviet leaders, and the official residence of the President of the Russian Federation. Jutting out was a multi-tiered red brick pyramid with **ЛЕНИН** printed on it. Inside resided the yin to Nicholas II's yang.

Born Vladimir Ilyich Ulyanov in 1870 in Simbursk, Russia, his early life was forged by the death of his father and the execution of his older brother for plotting to assassinate Alexander III (Nicholas II's father). Following his expulsion from university, where he studied law, Vladimir embraced the works of the nineteenth-century German philosophers Karl Marx and Friedrich Engels, who developed the socioeconomic and political theory of Marxism.

A simplified version of Marxism posits that in capitalist societies, class conflict arises from material desires between the oppressed majority wage laborers—the proletariat—who produce goods for the minority ruling class—the bourgeoisie—who own the means of production and earn the profit. The proletariat would rise

* Operation Barbarossa began June 22, 1941.

in revolution, resulting in socialism, characterized by social ownership, compensation reflective of a person's contribution, and production based on use instead of profit. After some time, the transition to communism would create a stateless, classless, moneyless society based on common ownership and the fundamental Marxian principle, "From each according to his ability, to each according to his needs."

In 1889, Vladimir's family moved to Samara in southeastern European Russia, where he produced a Russian translation of *The Communist Manifesto*. In 1902, he published an influential pamphlet under the pseudonym *Lenin*. The following year, he founded the Bolsheviks (majority), a faction of the Russian Social Democratic Labour Party that had split from the Mensheviks (minority) over ideological disagreements. Lenin believed the party should consist of dedicated full-time revolutionaries, while his Menshevik opponents felt membership should be open to anyone who supported the party.

In the wake of the failed 1905 Revolution, Lenin returned to St. Petersburg. To finance Bolshevik activities, he advocated a series of heists, most notably the 1907 Tiflis bank robbery. In the heart of the Georgian capital, a group of men robbed two mail coaches of roughly a quarter-million rubles (equivalent to U.S. $3.4 million in 2008), killing about forty guards and civilians in a flurry of bombs and gunfire. All the robbers escaped, but most of the funds were unusable. The 500-ruble bills had serial numbers on file, and anyone who exchanged them was arrested. None of the organizers faced justice, including Ioseb Jughashvili, who became one of history's greatest mass murderers.

Fearing tsarist government suppression, Lenin fled the country, bouncing around Europe and developing his ideology, *Leninism*, while writing about class struggle and revolutionary strategy. With the abdication of Nicholas II, he returned to Russia as the leader of the Bolsheviks, who, in an armed insurrection in October 1917, overthrew the unpopular Provisional Government that had kept Russia in World War I. Lenin could now build his utopia.

He nationalized banks, railroads, utilities, and large industries; redistributed aristocratic and church lands; limited workdays to eight hours; provided free education; fought illiteracy; promoted gender equality; suppressed the freedoms of the press and religion; and made Russia the first country to legalize abortion.

In March 1918, the party's name changed from the Russian Social Democratic Labour Party to the Russian Communist Party. Moscow resumed its role as the capital, with Red Square serving as the official governmental address.

The country simultaneously withdrew from World War I at great expense, with the Treaty of Brest-Litovsk ceding substantial western portions of the land acquired in the mid-seventeenth century to Germany. But with the German defeat to the Allies (Russia, France, the UK, the U.S., Italy, and Japan) in November, the Bolsheviks declared the treaty void. They attempted to regain some territory and spark other European revolutions by warring with the newly independent Poland, but lacked the resources to achieve victory. They had bigger problems within their borders.

The monarchy's downfall plunged the country into civil war between the Red Army (Bolsheviks) and the White Army (anti-communists). The overwhelming Red manpower proved insurmountable, as the White Army had been severely weakened by 1920 and collapsed three years later.

The drought in the spring of 1921 worsened the crisis. By the end of 1922, famine had claimed five million lives. Various epidemics added another two to three million. Throw in combat fatalities and massacres during the civil war, the revolution cost the lives of nine to ten million people.

To stabilize the economy, Lenin enacted his New Economic Policy (NEP), a temporary measure creating "a free market and capitalism, both subject to state control." The program allowed private ownership of small and medium enterprises, while the state maintained control of large industries, banks, and foreign trade.

At this point, he was seriously ill, having suffered a stroke in May 1922 and another in December. That month, Russia, along with the Transcaucasian Socialist Federative Soviet Republic (Armenia, Azerbaijan, and Georgia), the Ukrainian Soviet Socialist Republic, and the Byelorussian Soviet Socialist Republic, coalesced into the Union of Soviet Socialist Republics (USSR), commonly known as the Soviet Union. Notwithstanding his poor health, Lenin was elected leader. Nearly incapacitated, he made few appearances. A third stroke in March 1923 sidelined him further. On January 21, 1924, he slipped into a coma and died at age 53.

Thousands attended his Red Square funeral in freezing conditions. His brain was removed, and the embalmed body went into a wooden vault on the northeast side of the Kremlin. (A brain dissection revealed extreme sclerosis, an abnormal hardening of body tissue.) Six years later, his mausoleum of concrete and granite was finished. Besides relocation during World War II, his body has been on public display.

Open five days a week for three hours a day, I got in line early. Rain and sleet plagued the summer morning. A group of Russian dignitaries bypassed everyone, prolonging the misery. An hour later, beyond the airport-like security, the girl beside me put her hands in her pockets. A menacing guard in the dark corridor chastised her. Hands by my hips, I inched into the black room, shuffling along the one-way path around three sides. Guards at each corner stared. Things not allowed: stopping, talking, smoking, hats, and pictures. I felt guilty of thoughtcrime. Beware of Big Brother.

A transparent bulletproof sarcophagus in the center of the room, with a simple brushed metallic roof and an ornate base, housed one of the most influential men of the twentieth century. Lenin had closed eyes, his arms neatly resting on his thighs, dressed in a black suit, white shirt, and black tie. He had a goatee, a bald head with hair at the sides, and skin that looked like a poorly made wax sculpture. Dead for ninety years, I couldn't be too critical.

The Kremlin Wall Necropolis waited outside. The tall red brick wall housed a *who's who* of communism: mass graves of October Revolutionaries, victims of a communist school bombing, and those killed in the derailment of an experimental railcar fitted with an aircraft engine. Cremated burials into the wall began in 1925, including high-altitude balloonists, cosmonauts, the crew of a crashed fighter jet that took the life of Yuri Gagarin (the first man in space), military leaders, politicians, and scientists.

The *crème de la crème*, like former leaders Leonid Brezhnev, Yuri Andropov, and Konstantin Chernenko, had slabs of polished granite, the height of my shins, with granite blocks reaching upwards, cresting with lifelike busts. A medium-sized spruce tree stood behind each. Unable to read the names, I glossed over most. One bust, however, was unmistakable—Ioseb Jughashvili.

Born in 1878 in Gori, Georgia, in what was part of the Russian Empire, he was raised in a poor family with a violent alcoholic father. To escape the beatings, he and his mother moved around Europe for a decade before settling with a friend. The young Ioseb attended seminary school but abandoned his religious studies, declared himself an atheist, and devoted himself to Marxism.

Introduced to Lenin in 1905, the following year, he married a Georgian seamstress, who bore him a son. The high-profile 1907 Tiflis bank robbery forced the three to flee to Baku, Azerbaijan, where the stress of a foreign land and hot climate affected her health. Upon returning to Tiflis, she drank contaminated water and likely contracted typhus. Her death in November devastated Jughashvili, who abandoned his young child to be raised by her family.

In January 1913, he wrote an article for the Bolshevik journal *Prosveshcheniye* (Enlightenment) under the pseudonym *Stalin*—derived from *stal*, the Russian word for steel. His new surname would become synonymous with fear and death.

With the Provisional Government's suppression of the Bolsheviks, Stalin smuggled Lenin out of Petrograd and assumed acting leadership of the party. Upon Lenin's return and the October Revolution, the two collaborated to establish the new government. Stalin co-signed Lenin's decrees, shared his support for violence, and chaired the committee to draft a new constitution.

Seeking an ally, Lenin appointed Stalin to the newly created position of General Secretary of the Communist Party in 1922, an administrative role responsible for membership oversight. As Lenin's health declined, Stalin became the main point of contact.

Despite being at the top of the Soviet food chain, the men weren't friends. They disagreed on trade, the incorporation of Georgia, and the country's name.* Notably, Lenin disliked how his wife, Nadya, was treated by Stalin. Following Lenin's death, against Nadya's wishes, the party had the body embalmed and interred in Red Square.

Nadya turned over *Lenin's Testament* to the Communist Party. The following clause echoed his sentiments:

> Stalin is too rude, and this fault, entirely supportable in relations among us communists, becomes unsupportable in the office of General Secretary. Therefore, I propose to the comrades to find a way to remove Stalin from that position and appoint to it another man who in all respects differs from Stalin only in superiority – namely, more patient, more loyal, more polite and more attentive to comrades, less capricious, etc.
>
> January 4, 1923 Lenin

Due to its sensitive nature, only high-ranking officials were permitted to see the document. (A revised version became the official one. Referencing the original was met with punishment.) The embarrassed Stalin offered to resign, but his modesty allowed him to remain as General Secretary, a role that previously wielded little power. But with Lenin out of the way, Stalin gained control of the government and attempted to create his utopian society.

He consolidated power by installing loyalists, ended the NEP, and reintroduced collectivized agriculture. A class of wealthy peasants, *kulaks*, were eradicated by exile or concentration camps. The resulting famine of 1932-33 killed five to seven million people.

---

* Lenin originally wanted the *Union of Soviet Republics of Europe and Asia.*

Created cities underwent large-scale industrial projects using forced labor. Science (in line with Marxism) was encouraged, literacy was promoted, and religion was further suppressed. With the Wall Street crash of 1929, the USSR's policies were seen as establishing socialism, while capitalism was in its last throes.

Beginning in 1936, a series of show trials saw members of the Politburo, the highest policy-making authority, found guilty of crimes such as treason or attempting to assassinate Stalin, who, with the reduction in members, further consolidated power.

During this Great Terror (1936–1938), members of different political parties, religious figures, minorities, foreigners, peasants, White Army soldiers, Red Army soldiers, and former criminals fell victim. Upwards of seven hundred thousand were killed, and one and a half million went to forced labor camps, the Gulags.

With the rise of the Nazis, a military buildup replenished the purged Red Army. Stalin bought the country time by signing a non-aggression treaty (the Molotov–Ribbentrop Pact) with Germany, including a secret protocol outlining how the two countries would dismember Eastern Europe. A week later, on September 1, 1939, World War II ignited with Germany's invasion of Poland from the west. Sixteen days later, the USSR invaded from the east. The juggernauts conquered Poland in twenty days.

Germany violated the non-aggression pact in June 1941. Stalin wrongly believed Hitler would honor his promise despite intelligence reports and the buildup of German troops near the Soviet border. The Germans decimated the unprepared Soviet Air Force. Belorussia, Ukraine, and the Baltic states fell. By October, Germany had pushed deep into Russia for the assault on Moscow.

To boost morale, on November 7, the 24th anniversary of the Bolshevik Revolution (October 25, Old Style), Stalin ordered a military parade through Red Square. Troops marched past the Kremlin directly to the front. By December 2, German reconnaissance had advanced within nineteen kilometers (12 mi) of central Moscow but made it no further.

Expecting a swift victory, the Germans lacked cold-weather gear. The European winter was the coldest of the twentieth century. The average Moscow temperature in January 1942 was –36°C (–32°F). Machine guns seized, vehicles ran constantly, soldiers looted corpses, and frostbite filled the hospitals.

Having weathered the storm, the Red Army launched a counter-offensive. In April 1942, despite military advice, Stalin unsuccessfully attempted to regain eastern Ukraine. In June, the Germans tried to capture Stalingrad in the war's bloodiest battle, but the Soviet victory in February 1943 marked a turning point on the Eastern Front. By the end of the year, the Soviets reclaimed half of the territory ceded to the Germans and gained control of most of Eastern Europe in 1944.

With the Allies closing in on Germany from the west, Stalin prioritized reaching Berlin first. The Red Army captured the city in May 1945, leading to Germany's surrender. Aiming to exert influence in Asia, the focus shifted to the Pacific War. With the Soviet invasion of Manchuria on August 8, bookended by the atomic bombings of Hiroshima and Nagasaki, Japan had little choice but to surrender. World War II was over.

The USSR suffered the highest death toll of any nation—26.6 million. Fourteen percent of the population perished due to military deaths, crimes against humanity, famine, and disease. In June 1945, the triumphant Stalin stood atop Lenin's Mausoleum to watch a victory parade.

As Britain's global influence waned, the U.S. and the USSR rose as superpowers. In 1949, the Soviets tested their first atomic bomb in the Kazakh desert. Similar in design to the first U.S. nuclear bomb and the one dropped over Nagasaki, Soviet spies had stolen the plans. The West codenamed the bomb *Joe-1*, referencing Joseph (Ioseb) Stalin. Rising hostilities between the former allies triggered the Cold War, a decades-long rivalry fueled by political tension, proxy wars, and nuclear threats.

Found unconscious on March 1, 1953, Stalin had suffered a stroke, urinated on himself, and vomited blood. Moved to a couch, he lay there for three days as high-ranking members scrambled in fear. After his death on March 5 at age 74, crowds flocked to see his body lying in state, with thousands trampled and hundreds killed. Despite not leaving instructions, his embalmed body was placed next to Lenin's.

To eliminate the cult of personality left in Stalin's wake, his successor, Nikita Khrushchev, launched a de-Stalinization campaign by renaming places, destroying monuments, and removing lyrics from the national anthem. References to Lenin remained. His body was removed from Lenin's Mausoleum in 1961 and placed in the Kremlin Wall Necropolis.

His granite bust had a full head of perfect, slicked-back hair, bushy eyebrows, an intense nose, a slight turkey neck, and a fierce, disapproving gaze. The *pièce de résistance*—a striking, gargantuan, borderline hypnotic, moustache. Of the twelve graves, his had the most red flowers. Unlike Lenin, there were no guards, but I still feared Big Brother. I followed the ropes back into Red Square (M), having completed my tour of the implementation of Marxism and what remained of the men most responsible for its (r)evolution.

Red Square:
GUM shopping center (left), Saint Basil's Cathedral (center), and Lenin's Mausoleum in front of the Kremlin (right)

38 ♦ Berlin, Germany

In this period my eyes were opened to two menaces of which I had previously scarcely known the names, and whose terrible importance for the existence of the German people I certainly did not understand: Marxism and Jewry.

— Adolf Hitler, *Mein Kampf* (1925)

I left my Berlin apartment near Hackescher Markt and walked to Bebelplatz, a square adjacent to Humboldt University. Set into the cobbles was a quote by the German poet Heinrich Heine. From his 1821 play, *Almansor*:

Original Text	English Translation
Das war ein Vorspiel nur, dort wo man Bücher verbrennt, verbrennt man auch am Ende Menschen.	That was but a prelude; where they burn books, they will ultimately burn people as well.

On May 10, 1933, as many as twenty thousand books were burned there, one of many university sites across Nazi Germany where flames cleansed "un-German" literature.

I passed through the Brandenburg Gate, a feat I accomplished a year and two days earlier. Once again, a chill ran down my spine. I turned left towards the *Memorial to the Murdered Jews of Europe*, a square block of undulating concrete slabs dedicated to the Jews who perished in the Holocaust. I emerged on the other side and crossed the street, stopping at the place where, eight meters below my feet, one of history's greatest orators stopped talking.

Born in 1889 in Braunau am Inn, Austria-Hungary, a stone's throw from the German border, Adolf Hitler was the fourth of six children to Alois Hitler and his third wife, Klara Pölzl. Like Stalin, the young Adolf endured an abusive father.

In 1907, he moved to Vienna and unsuccessfully tried to get into art school. After running out of money two years later, he stayed in men's dormitories, trying to make a living by selling his paintings.

Bebelplatz (left) and
The Memorial to the Murdered Jews of Europe (right)

Four years later, he went to Munich, Germany, to avoid military service but was arrested for evasion and conscripted into the Austro-Hungarian Army. The years as a vagrant deemed him medically unfit. But with the outbreak of World War I in 1914, he enlisted in the Bavarian Army (a German state army), which shouldn't have been allowed due to his Austrian citizenship. It was most likely an error on the part of the government. Serving as a dispatch runner in France and Belgium, he received the Iron Cross, Second Class; Iron Cross, First Class; and Black Wound Badge.

In October 1918, he learned that Germany had lost the war. The fanatical corporal couldn't fathom the possibility of military defeat. Along with the right-wing, he adopted the stab-in-the-back myth, a conspiracy theory claiming that the failure came from within, perpetrated by Jews and Marxists.

With limited career options, he returned to Munich, stayed in the military, and was assigned as an intelligence agent to infiltrate the recently formed German Workers' Party (DAP). He attended his first meeting in September 1919 and interrupted one of the speakers with such a furor that the man left in a huff. The party's chairman, enamored by Hitler's oratory skills, gave him a nationalist leaflet with views against Jews, Marxists, and capitalists. Hitler joined the party within a week. To increase interest, the trivial nationalist group rebranded itself as the National Socialist German Workers' Party (NSDAP), colloquially known as the Nazi Party.

Discharged from the army in March 1920, he went to work full-time for the party, usurped the leadership, and designed the banner—a red background with a white circle and a black swastika at its center. A charismatic speaker, his demagogic rhetoric of populism—combined with the scapegoating of Jews, Marxists, and politicians—attracted audiences of hundreds, then thousands. NSDAP membership followed suit.

On the night of November 8-9, 1923, the NSDAP attempted to overthrow the government. Accompanied by the paramilitary group, the *Sturmabteilung* (SA), they interrupted a meeting at a Munich beer hall, declared the formation of a new government, and demanded support. The ill-planned coup failed, resulting in the deaths of sixteen NSDAP members and four police officers. Hitler suffered a dislocated shoulder when he was dragged to the ground by the man beside him, who had been shot and killed instantly.

The Beer Hall Putsch propelled Hitler into the national spotlight. Arrested two days later, he was tried, convicted of high treason, and sentenced to five years at Landsberg Prison. During his incarceration, he dictated the first volume (of two) of his autobiographical manifesto, *Mein Kampf* (My Struggle). Full of grievances and conspiracy theories, he outlined his plan to transform German society into one based on race.

Paroled in December 1924, he served nine months of his light sentence. The Bavarian government attempted to deport him to Austria, but the Austrians argued that his service in the German Army voided his Austrian citizenship (which he renounced in 1925).

Learning from the failed coup, Hitler sought to achieve power democratically, an arduous task as the NSDAP withered to obscurity during his absence. He briefly returned to public speaking, but a fiery speech in February 1925 resulted in a two-year ban from the platform. Following the ban's removal, he wasted no time ratcheting up the vitriol against Jews and Marxists while adding the concept of *Lebensraum* (living space), the belief that Germany's survival depended on expanding and removing non-Aryan indigenous populations, either by deportation, enslavement, or death.

This fearsome tale of a doomed Germany fell on deaf ears. Aided by American loans, the country had rebuilt its economy reasonably well after World War I. Germans were unwilling to disrupt the status quo for a man like Hitler. He needed a catastrophe. He got it.

The collapse of the U.S. stock market in October 1929 sent shockwaves across Europe. Hitler capitalized on the opportunity created by the Great Depression, targeting veterans, farmers, the middle class, and the youth. He portrayed a vision of a renewed and prosperous nation. But only he and the Nazis could make Germany great again. Amid extreme unemployment, the party's support skyrocketed.

In the 1928 *Reichstag* (German parliament) elections, the NSDAP garnered 3 percent of the vote and secured 12 seats. Two years later, they increased their share to 18 percent and 107 seats, becoming the country's second-largest party.

In the wake of the NSDAP's electoral success in 1932, Hitler was appointed as a low-ranking government official, giving him German citizenship. Finally able to run for public office, he set his sights on the presidency by ramping up his speaking engagements. That year, he finished second in the presidential race, losing to the incumbent, Paul von Hindenburg.[*]

On January 30, 1933, Hindenburg grudgingly appointed Hitler as chancellor. The Nazis held an impromptu torchlit march of thousands of uniformed men through the heart of Berlin. A month later, the *Reichstag* burned. The culprit was a lone Dutch communist protester. Nazi leadership spun it as a grand communist plot to overthrow the government. At Hitler's request, Hindenburg issued the Reichstag Fire Decree,[†] suspending sections of the Constitution protecting individual and civil liberties. It declared:

---

* 1932 German presidential election results: Paul von Hindenburg (53 percent), Adolf Hitler (37 percent), Ernst Thälmann (10 percent).

† The full title is the *Decree of the Reich President for the Protection of the People and the State.*

Article 1

Sections 114, 115, 117, 118, 123, 124, and 153 of the Constitution of the German Reich are suspended until further notice. Therefore, restrictions on personal liberty, on the right of free expression of opinion, including freedom of the press, on the right of assembly and the right of association, and violations of the privacy of postal, telegraphic, and telephonic communications, warrants for house searches, orders for confiscations, as well as restrictions on property, are also permissible beyond the legal limits otherwise prescribed.

The decree further granted the federal government control over the states, with the authority to arrest, detain, and sentence individuals (including the death penalty) without due process. Four thousand members of the German Communist Party (KPD), along with Social Democrats and liberals, were arrested, sent to barracks, and tortured. Their party newspapers were suppressed, and meetings were banned. Only the Nazis and their allies could operate freely.

Following a new round of parliamentary elections on March 6, 1933, the NSDAP secured the most seats in the government but fell short of a majority (44 percent). Their response was the Enabling Act,* granting the passage of laws without the *Reichstag's* consent for four years, often bypassing the Constitution.

The Reichstag Fire Decree authorized the arrest of all eighty-one KPD members and prevented many Social Democrats from participating in the next government vote. With a tally of 441 to 84 (84 percent), the Enabling Act secured more than the necessary two-thirds majority. On March 23, 1933, German parliamentary democracy voted for its destruction, and Hitler became *de facto* dictator.

---

* The full title is the *Law to Remedy the Distress of People and Reich.*

On August 1, 1934, Hindenburg was in the final stages of lung cancer. The hastily passed *Law on the Head of State of the German Reich* declared that upon his death, the position of president would be eliminated and merged with the chancellorship. Hindenburg died the next day, and Hitler emerged as *Führer* (Leader). Already the head of government, adding the title of head of state made him the supreme commander of the armed forces. The *Reichswehr* (soldier's loyalty oath) was changed to swear loyalty not to Germany but to him.

> I swear by God this holy oath, that I will render to Adolf Hitler, Führer of the German Reich and People, Supreme Commander of the Armed Forces, unconditional obedience, and that I am ready, as a brave soldier, to risk my life at any time for this oath.

Hitler prepared for war. German forces reoccupied the Rhineland (a region in western Germany) in March 1936, marking the first time since World War I that they had troops in the region. Two years later, Germany annexed Hitler's birth nation. Applauding Austrians and chants of "*Heil*!" welcomed the *Führer* as he shed tears of joy.

In September 1938, he negotiated the annexation of the Sudetenland, an area of Czechoslovakia mainly inhabited by ethnic Germans. Facing the threat of invasion, the rest of the country was surrendered in March 1939, providing Germany with vital raw materials, weapons, aircraft, monetary reserves, and industrial facilities. The Czechs showed less enthusiasm than the Austrians.

So far, the acquisitions had been nonviolent, but Hitler still wanted his war, at least a small one to start. Germany invaded Poland on September 1, 1939. Britain, a Polish ally, issued Germany an ultimatum to withdraw its troops or face the consequences. The Germans did nothing. On September 3, Britain called Hitler's bluff and declared war (followed by France, Australia, India, and New Zealand). He supposedly looked to his adviser and said, "What now?"

With Germany unprepared for a large-scale conflict, the Phoney War began, a six-month period of limited fighting during military expansion and strategic positioning. But in April 1940, the now overwhelming German war machine invaded Denmark, which capitulated in hours. Norway succumbed within two months. Belgium, Luxembourg, and the Netherlands fell in May. Hitler entered Paris a month later, avenging the humiliating defeat of World War I. He stood at the pinnacle of his power.

Following Britain's rejection of Hitler's half-hearted peace offers, Germany set its sights on the island empire, aiming to achieve air, then sea superiority, before a land incursion. None of those happened. The Royal Air Force bent but didn't break. The flustered Germans resorted to strategic night bombing of London and other cities, which only strengthened British resolve.

Suffering his first significant defeat, Hitler concentrated on the Soviet Union, hoping to gain resources, remove them as a military adversary, eliminate "Jewish-Bolshevism," and create *Lebensraum*. Germany swept Yugoslavia and Greece aside over a few weeks in April 1941, setting the stage for the largest invasion in the history of warfare.

After conquering significant areas, despite the advice of the Army High Command, Hitler ordered the assault on Moscow to be redirected toward Leningrad and Kyiv. The blunder allowed the Red Army to resupply its forces with what appeared to be endless men. When the attack on Moscow resumed in mid-October, the weather had changed. Heavy rains slowed progress to a crawl as roads turned into impassable mud. Within weeks, snow arrived. The Germans, so unprepared, asked their citizens to send winter clothing to the troops.

On December 7, 1941, the Japanese attacked the American naval base at Pearl Harbor. Four days later, Germany declared war on the U.S., which responded in kind. For two and a half years, the U.S. and its allies prepared for what would be the largest sea invasion in history.

On the morning of June 6, 1944 (D-Day), they landed in Normandy, France. Hitler's subordinates were instructed not to wake him for any reason. When he got up around noon, he doubted the legitimacy of the invasion. By August, over two million Allied soldiers had arrived in France, gaining control of the Western Front.

Things were worse in the east. On June 22, 1944, exactly three years after the start of Barbarossa, Stalin launched Operation Bagration and inflicted the German force, half the size of the Soviet army, with their most significant military defeat. Hitler deserved much blame and took none.

As his military miscalculations mounted, so did his physical decline. He aged noticeably, developing gray hair, bloodshot eyes, insomnia, a heart condition, and stomach issues. In 1942, symptoms likely of Parkinson's disease worsened—quivering left arm, twitching left leg, and lumbering walk.

He gave fewer speeches—nine in 1940, seven in 1941, five in 1942, two in 1943, and none in 1944. He avoided Berlin, the people, and any places where bombs had fallen, spending time at his mountain retreat, the Berghof, or at field headquarters in East Prussia, the Wolf's Lair.

His paranoia about the Army High Command was bolstered on July 20, 1944, when disgruntled officers detonated a bomb as part of a coup during a meeting at the Wolf's Lair. Four men died, and twenty were injured. By pure luck, not "Providence," as he claimed, Hitler survived with minor injuries, the worst being ruptured eardrums. It was one of at least forty-two failed assassination attempts and "confirmed" that past military losses were due to a conspiracy, not poor tactics. Hitler still believed Germany could win the war.*

---

* In the aftermath of the July 20 plot, more than 7,000 people were arrested, and 4,980 were executed.

On September 25, all able-bodied males aged 16 to 60 were conscripted. The six million militiamen swore a loyalty oath to Hitler and supplied their gear: clothing, cooking utensils, and blankets. The futile effort only increased the death toll.

By October, the Americans had reached German soil from the west, just as the Soviets had from the east. Hitler dismissed officers who suggested retreat, retreated, or ignored his flawed orders. It made no difference.

With the Third Reich wobbling, Hitler had no choice but to withdraw to an air raid shelter in the center of Berlin on January 16, 1945. The *Vorbunker* (forward shelter) was a temporary measure constructed in 1936. As the situation worsened, the *Führerbunker*—a self-contained concrete labyrinth with heat, lights, and water pumps powered by a diesel generator—was built in 1944 beneath the garden of the Reich Chancellery.

On his birthday, April 20, 1945, the gaunt man made his final trip to the surface to award Iron Crosses to a group of Hitler Youth, a sign of what the defense of Berlin had come to. Later that day, just before the Red Army began its bombardment of the city, he met with the remaining leaders of the Third Reich as they swore their undying loyalty. Two days later, he suffered a nervous breakdown after an attack didn't happen and scolded his generals for their incompetence and betrayal. He had finally realized all was lost.

Hitler refused to leave the crumbling capital despite numerous pleas. However, he capitulated on one point—Eva Braun. She had met him in 1929 at age 17 as an assistant to the official Nazi Party photographer. They became lovers, but their relationship remained secret from all except the inner circle. Hitler wanted to maintain the bachelor persona of a man devoted to Germany. Just after midnight on the night of April 28-29, he married his longtime companion in a solemn ceremony.

Hours later, he dictated his will, leaving his art collection to his hometown of Linz, Austria, and a few objects to relatives. Everything else went to the Nazi Party. Next came his political testament, a regurgitation of his fury. Hitler's final written sentence:

> Above all I charge the leaders of the nation and those under them to scrupulous observance of the laws of race and to merciless opposition to the universal poisoner of all peoples, international Jewry.
>
> Given in Berlin, this 29th day of April 1945. 4:00 A.M.
>
> ADOLF HITLER

That day, his ally, former Italian dictator Benito Mussolini, and his mistress were executed in Italy. Civilians kicked, spat upon, stoned, and hung the bodies upside down by meat hooks. Hearing of his friend's demise, Hitler wouldn't suffer the same fate.

On the afternoon of April 30, 1945, a cyanide capsule was successfully tested on his dog, a German Shepherd named Blondi. After saying their goodbyes, he and Eva retired to the study. An hour later, a gunshot rang out. The door was opened, and the lifeless bodies were discovered. She had ingested cyanide, and Hitler shot himself in the head. She was 33, and he was 56. Per his instructions, they were taken outside, covered in petrol, and set on fire. With Soviet artillery falling like rain, nobody stuck around. The former *Führer* and his new bride burned alone in an open pit.

The Soviets arrived at the bunker days later and found the charred bodies. They confirmed the dental remains, which—at Stalin's request, who didn't want relics—were sent to Moscow. A bullet-holed skull fragment found in 1946 also went to the Russian capital. The other remains were buried in an unmarked grave outside Berlin, moved to a forest near Magdeburg in 1946, then exhumed, cremated, and scattered in 1970 when the Soviets returned the land to East Germany.

The Soviets attempted to destroy major Nazi landmarks. The *Führerbunker's* three-and-a-half-meter (11.5 ft) thick reinforced concrete walls and ceilings made it a formidable task. When the Berlin Wall went up in 1961, the proximity left the area neglected. Just before the Wall fell, the bunker's ceiling was removed, allowing gravel, sand, and rubble to fill the cavity.

Now, the site is a gravel parking lot with mundane trees and half-dead grass, surrounded by upscale condos. A simple gate and shin-high wooden barriers prevent unauthorized vehicles from entering. Unlike the rest of Berlin, which has memorials for everything, the only marker was a sign installed in 2006.

It was late afternoon. Nobody was around the most inconspicuous place (M), a fitting tribute to an unremarkable man. Hitler wasn't educated; he didn't understand foreign policy, economics, or military tactics; he didn't listen to advice; he didn't drink, smoke, or eat meat; he was awkward with women and sickly. What set him apart was words.

Hitler's right-wing populist scapegoating and fearmongering struck a chord in those so disillusioned and desperate that they were willing to sacrifice their moral currency, regardless of the costs. His fiery rhetoric blamed Germany's issues on Jews, Marxists, and anyone the Nazis despised. He practiced, rehearsed, and refined his speeches, propelling him from local beer halls to municipal concert halls to regional sporting arenas to national radio. But he didn't create the hatred; he was a manifestation of it.

It's horrifying what humans can do when given permission. It was those who greenlit his demagogic rhetoric that made Nazism possible. They rationalized the dirty work: beating, shooting, and gassing. They were the puppets of the puppet master. And when it all went to hell, the man pulling the strings revealed his true colors.

Hitler held the title of *Führer*, but he was an abysmal leader. When the Third Reich's situation—which he created—became untenable, he hid, committed suicide, and left his shambolic country to clean up the mess. But that's what demagogues do. Their rabble-rousing promises, lacking substance, leave a wake of destruction.

World War II broke records in every aspect. The most significant was the death toll—seventy million people, three percent of the world's population. In human history, there's arguably never been a darker period than those six years. It was because of words.

Above the Führerbunker

39 ♦ Berlin, Germany

The practical measures proposed in them – such as the abolition of the distinction between town and country, of the family, of the carrying on of industries for the account of private individuals, and of the wage system, the proclamation of social harmony, the conversion of the function of the state into a mere superintendence of production – all these proposals point solely to the disappearance of class antagonisms which were, at that time, only just cropping up, and which, in these publications, are recognised in their earliest indistinct and undefined forms only. These proposals, therefore, are of a purely Utopian character.

— Karl Marx and Friedrich Engels,
Manifesto of the Communist Party (1848)

Following World War II, the victorious Allies claimed their spoils by splitting Germany into four occupation zones. The U.S., Britain, and France combined their zones to form West Germany, which developed into a capitalist democracy. The Soviets controlled East Germany, implementing communist policies that nationalized property and industry, enforced Marxist-Leninist education, and kept the population under strict surveillance. Despite these efforts,\ East Germany lagged economically, and the higher Western standard of living led to mass emigration: 198,000 in 1950, 166,000 in 1951, 182,000 in 1952, and 331,000 in 1953.

By the mid-1950s, East Germany had fortified its border with West Germany, effectively closing it. Berlin, however, situated deep inside the Soviet zone and similarly divided, remained a loophole. With easy subway access to West Berlin and no barriers, by 1961, nearly 20 percent of East Germany's population, about three and a half million people, had fled. This "brain drain" undermined the credibility of the East German government.

To halt the exodus, at midnight on August 13, 1961, East German troops unrolled barbed wire, ripped up streets, and shut down transit across the city, sealing West Berlin behind 155 kilometers (96 miles) of barricades. Overnight, Berlin went from the easiest escape route to the hardest. The day became known as *Barbed Wire Sunday.*

Within days, East German authorities expanded the barrier, adding concrete blocks, fences, minefields, and other obstacles, all placed entirely within East Berlin to avoid crossing the border. Armed paramilitary guards shot at anyone attempting to flee.

Over the following decades, the Berlin Wall evolved into a massive system of reinforced concrete walls up to twelve feet (3.6 meters) high, lined with guard towers and searchlights. Between the inner and outer walls lay the infamous "death strip"—a barren, floodlit expanse raked smooth so footprints were visible, lined with barbed wire, tripwires, guard dogs, and armed patrols.

As the Cold War thawed in the 1980s, reform movements in Eastern Europe gained momentum. On May 2, 1989, Hungarian guards dismantled border sections with Austria, allowing East Germans to escape. Czechoslovakia followed suit in the fall. The outflow grew so large that on November 9, authorities relented and approved travel from East to West Germany.

That evening, a confusing announcement by an East German official saying that travel abroad was now permissible led thousands of citizens to flock to the city's six checkpoints. Bewildered guards called their superiors. None of the East German authorities would take responsibility for authorizing deadly force. Just before midnight, the border guard commander ordered the gates to be opened, allowing jubilant East Germans to flood into the West. The city, known for partying, hosted one of the twentieth century's most epic celebrations.

During the twenty-eight years of the "Anti-Fascist Protection Rampart," one hundred thousand people risked their lives trying to defect, with five thousand succeeding. At least 140 people were killed, more than ninety of them shot by border guards. No matter how close a wounded person was, Western intervention was prohibited. East Germany dissolved and reunified under the West German Basic Law in October 1990. By December, most of the Wall had been destroyed. Today, in Berlin, three main sections remain.

I left the *Führerbunker* and walked one kilometer (0.6 mi) south to a cracked and weathered eighty-meter (260 ft) portion twice my height running along *Niederkirchnerstraße*. Large chunks had been removed, and a rough texture had replaced the smooth surface of the pipe covering the apex.

I took a fifteen-minute metro ride north to *Berlin Nordbahnhof* station and followed a two-wide row of bricks embedded in the ground, found all over the city, tracing where the Wall once stood. I marveled at how easy it was to cross from one side to the other until I reached the Berlin Wall Memorial, a 1.3-kilometer (0.8 mi) stretch covered in graffiti next to *Bernauer Straße*. A preserved watchtower loomed above the death strip.

A half-hour metro ride southeast took me to the *Warschauer Straße* station near the East Side Gallery. Founded in 1990, the 1.3-kilometer (0.8 mi) section along the Spree River displayed more than one hundred murals. Most of the messages confused me. A few I comprehended:

A hybrid of the German and Israeli flags
Leonid Brezhnev and Erich Honecker kissing, the leaders of the Soviet Union and East Germany, respectively, during most of the Wall's existence.
The Brandenburg Gate, the German flag, and the American flag (M).

The most powerful force in the world is an idea. It can propagate borders, infiltrate without warning, mutate, and infect. The Berlin Wall was a result of Marxism, the nineteenth-century philosophy created by Karl Marx and Friedrich Engels.

In *The Communist Manifesto*, derivations of *utopia* appear nine times in the twelve-thousand-word document. Sir Thomas More coined the term in his 1516 book *Utopia*, depicting a fictional island paradise. It's a world where everything is by the numbers—elected officials, hours of work, leisure hours, population, occupation, dinner etiquette, and travel. Wealth is despised, and modesty is coveted. Men can't marry until they are 22, and women until they are 18. Premarital sex is discouraged, and divorce isn't allowed unless in cases of adultery or perverseness. Lawyers don't exist; people plead their cases. Multiple religions exist, but one dominates. People worship as they wish and can persuade others to join through reason, not violence. Derived from the Greek words *ou* (not) and *topos* (place), *utopia* ironically means "nowhere."

Though the concept of communism had existed for a long time, like a religion, the variation of Marxism spread and splintered, taking on whatever form those in power contorted it into: Leninism, Stalinism, Maoism, Marxism–Leninism, Marxism–Leninism–Maoism.

When Mao Zedong took control of China, combined with Soviet satellite states, Marxist-derived nations controlled one-third of the world's population. They stretched to Asia, Europe, the Middle East, Africa, and Cuba. But after the Berlin Wall fell, so did Marxist governments. The Soviet Union collapsed in 1991, leaving only a handful of states. The results of a failed social experiment.

As much as I covet a world John Lennon imagined, with free education, ample employment, no homelessness, no religion, equality of the sexes, and free healthcare, humanity hasn't evolved to the point where the greater good is more important than individual needs. I doubt we will.

The flaw in this so-called "perfect" design is that it relies on imperfect participants. Humanity is far from uniform. We are as unique as our fingerprints, motivated by selfishness, pettiness, and desires that often exceed our needs. Societies divide into haves and have-nots, comprised of those who can and those who can't. We form tribes shaped by geography, held together by faith. Power is hoarded by those who possess it and desired by those who don't. It's this division that defines us, and it's the struggle that makes us human.

The Berlin Wall

40 ♦ Pamplona, Spain

The streets were solid with people dancing. Music was pounding and throbbing. Fireworks were being set off from the big public square. All the carnivals I had ever seen paled down in comparison.

— Ernest Hemingway, *Toronto Star Weekly* (1923)

I flew to Pamplona, Spain, for one of the year's most splendid celebrations, its popularity attributable to Ernest Hemingway. Born in 1899 in Oak Park, Illinois, he briefly reported out of high school for the Kansas City Star (my hometown newspaper). Turned away by the U.S. Army due to poor eyesight in 1917, he served as an ambulance driver in Italy during World War I. Wounded in a mortar attack, he recuperated for six months before living in Toronto, Chicago, and Paris.

He visited Pamplona in the summer of 1923 for the festival of San Fermin. Three years later, his timeless classic, *The Sun Also Rises,* told the story of American and British expatriates living in Paris who did the same. The book unveiled the event to the world and put this quiet city in northern Spain on the metaphorical map.

The festival's origins combine the fairs that date back to 1324, the bullfights introduced in 1385, and the arrival of the second relic of Saint Fermin, the co-patron saint of Navarre, in 1386. (The first relic arrived in 1186.) On October 10, 1386, the initial event centered on prayer, the Procession of Saint Fermin, and a feast for the city's poorest residents. The date was moved to July in 1591 for better weather.

The present-day festivity is a far cry from the original. Every year, from July 6 to 14, Pamplona's population surges from two hundred thousand to over one million. I followed the crowd on the first morning to Plaza Consistorial, a square near City Hall. Swelled to its twelve-thousand-person capacity, I found a spot around the corner with the thirty thousand others wearing red and white.

The *Chupinazo* rocket fired at midday. The MC shouted into the microphone, "Pamplonesas, Pamplonesas…Viva San Fermin!" The crowd roared, "Viva!" The microphone bellowed, "Gora San Fermin!" A thunderous reply of "Gora!" ("Long live Saint Fermin," in Spanish and Basque, respectively.) The balconies above and the crowd below unleashed beer, wine, and sangria. Clothes became a speckled pastel pink or a comprehensive dull crimson for those who dumped buckets on their heads. I had never seen anything like it. Hemingway might have been onto something.

While some came for food, friends, and nightlife, the main attraction is one of Earth's most idiotic yet thrilling spectacles, the Running of the Bulls. I vowed to be one of those idiots. I planned to stay out all night and drink away any misgivings to overcome my fear. I entered the city at midnight, becoming so enthralled with the atmosphere that the adult beverages plunged down my throat. I stumbled back to the apartment around 4 a.m. and stayed in bed until noon, having missed my first opportunity.

The run happens every morning during the festival. Unlike Budapest, I had another chance. To avoid failing, I exercised unusual self-control. Up at 6 a.m., I reached Plaza Consistorial an hour later. Along with the other brave buffoons, we were locked in the pen next to City Hall at 7:30 a.m. An estimated 3,500 people run on weekends and 1,800 during the week. It was a Tuesday.

Rules of the run: no hiding, no touching the bulls, no photographs, no loose objects, no improper footwear, nobody under 18, and no running in the opposite direction. The biggest one—no running drunk. Many had disregarded their sobriety, and police plucked out the blatant violators. For once, I appreciated restraint.

The gates opened a few minutes before 8 a.m., and everyone dispersed. The advice I received from Day 1 runners was to find a spot halfway along the 875-meter (957-yard) course. If I started at the beginning, I wouldn't reach *Plaza de Toros* before the gates closed. If I began near the end, I would beat the bulls to the bullring, jeered by the crowd for my cowardice.

I jogged what I thought was a few hundred meters along the cobblestoned street, wide enough for two cars, bordered by buildings and tall walls. At 8 a.m., the first rocket fired, the corral opened, and exhilaration radiated through the city. The second rocket signaled that the bulls were in the streets, and the runners grew restless. Some scampered, but I waited for the pack to start moving. It didn't take long. Terror spread through the sheep as we dashed in the same direction. Pursuing us were fifteen bulls, six wild and nine steers (castrated males), familiar with the course.

I had watched videos of previous runs and observed that the bulls usually stayed in the middle, so I hugged the walls. In the chaos, entangled runners tumbled and coalesced. I leaped over the human dominos, covering two hundred meters (660 ft) without incident. In a flash, one ton of horned muscle raced past. My heart skipped a beat, my eyes widened, and my backside clenched. Another burst by. Then another. I couldn't keep track.

With a few more twists and turns, the glorious *Plaza de Toros* appeared. I sprinted into the tunnel, and darkness descended. I couldn't discern ground, ceiling, or walls—only human silhouettes gliding toward a light, creating an eerie heaven-on-earth sensation. I chased the shifting shadows as the brightness increased, entered the twenty-thousand-seat arena, and hooked a sharp left (M).

My hands shook, my legs ached, my lungs burned, and adrenaline coursed. But I had survived nearly unscathed. Someone had stepped on my heel and removed a chunk. It was nothing a bandage and a cocktail couldn't fix. At some point, the third rocket fired, signaling the bulls were in the ring. The fourth marked the end. I didn't hear either. The *encierro* lasted four minutes.

To complete my San Fermin experience, I attended the bullfights held every night during the festival. The bull was released into the ring and encircled by three *matadors* who tormented him as he tried to impale their pink capes. Minutes later, two *picadors* on padded horses stabbed the bull atop the neck with pikes, creating soda-can-sized holes. Next, three *banderilleros* pierced barbed spears into the bull's neck, and the crowd cheered if both stuck. With blood streaming from his wounds, the bull began to weaken.

A man carrying a red cape and a sword entered. He enticed the bull to charge. With each successful pass, the crowd shouted, "*Ole!*". When the bull barely stood, it was time for the man to earn his official title, *matador de toros*—killer of bulls. He thrust his sword into the docile animal's neck, aiming for the heart or aorta in hopes of a quick death. This man hit his mark, but the bull clung to life briefly before succumbing to its injuries. A team of horses removed the carcass. This scene was replayed five more times until the wild bulls from the morning run were dead.

I sat in the cheap seats near the top, where the emphasis was on chanting and spraying alcohol. The boisterous upper deck paid little attention to the fight. I initially concentrated on the partiers and was numb to the slaughter. By the end, the carnage turned my stomach. As much as I disagreed with the practice, it was a Spanish tradition. Those bulls probably led better lives than the beef in the supermarket. The difference was that I never saw my steak being butchered.

I flew home the following day, having squeezed every drop I could from the festival Hemingway* made famous. He loved it so much that he returned eight more times. I hoped to get there at least once more. Of all the Dead Men's Legacies, his was the most fun.

Inside Plaza de Toros after running with the bulls

* After *The Sun Also Rises*, Hemingway married four times and had three sons. In 1954, he won the Nobel Prize in Literature for *The Old Man and the Sea*. He developed headaches, high blood pressure, and obesity that led to diabetes due to years of heavy drinking. On July 2, 1961, he committed suicide, suffering the same fate as his father, sister, and brother.

CHALLENGES

41 ♦ Quito, Ecuador

Two weeks after running with the bulls, I embraced a challenge—getting Mom to the Equator via public transportation. Seventy-nine percent of this imaginary line at zero degrees latitude crosses water, with only eleven countries owning real estate.* Quito, the capital of the *República del Ecuador* (Republic of the Equator), a mere twenty-six kilometers (16 mi) south, provided my best opportunity to get there.

I asked the man at the front desk of my hostel for instructions. He provided them in Spanish, a language I had taken throughout high school but never tried. Fifteen years later, my minimal skills had withered. I had brushed up on them in Spain and could order food, a beer, and find *el baño*. I was useless beyond that.

Another skill I lack is a sense of direction. I can get lost in a shopping mall. To compensate, I had honed my map-reading abilities. With smartphones becoming more brilliant by the second, navigation apps were my greatest asset. The problem I faced was the haphazard nature of Quito's public transit system. I put my hopes in a paper map and luck.

My first leg was a one-kilometer (0.6 mi) walk where I boarded a long bus with a pliable accordion connecting two sections and bought a ticket for a quarter. I appreciated that the national currency was the U.S. dollar. The hostel man told me, or at least I think he did, to catch another bus at an airport. I counted the stops until I

* The Equator passes through São Tomé and Príncipe, Gabon, the Republic of the Congo, the Democratic Republic of the Congo, Uganda, Kenya, Somalia, Indonesia, Columbia, Brazil, and Ecuador.

reached the place circled on my map. I knew it was a mistake as soon as I got off at the disused airfield.

I tried asking a security guard where the other buses were. Again, my broken Spanish was rubbish. He spoke so fast that I only shrugged. He pointed to a taxi, a mode of transportation I try to avoid using alone due to its costliness and larger carbon footprint. Sometimes, they are a necessary evil. I got a preset rate of fifteen dollars. Had I taken one from the start, it would have been forty. My frugality felt better. Thirty minutes later, I arrived at *Mitad del Mundo*—the Middle of the World.

An eighteenth-century debate arose over whether the Earth's circumference was longer at the poles or at the Equator. The French dispatched two expeditions to conduct scientific measurements to settle the dispute. In 1736, one team reached Lapland, a northern region in present-day Finland near the North Pole, while the other arrived in Quito. The North Pole expedition first demonstrated that our planet is flatter at the poles (imagine sitting on a ball and it becomes a little wider than it is tall). Despite finishing second, a monument was erected to commemorate the Equator expedition.

Mitad del Mundo resembled a tiny town down on its luck. Most of the buildings for scientific displays were neglected. A thick, yellow line ran through the middle of the park, marked with a large "N" and "S" on opposite sides. I had researched this place and learned that the team had come close, but their calculations weren't exact. The Equator was supposedly a few hundred meters north.

I walked along an industrial road to the smaller *Intiñan Solar Museum,* which required a tour showing the validity of their red line (M). Water poured down drains on either side demonstrated clockwise vs. anti-clockwise rotation, eggs balanced on nails, and people walked the line with closed eyes to show muscle weakness. To solidify their line, they emphasized that GPS had confirmed the accuracy. The whole thing was silly, but it was marketed well.

It was nearly 4 p.m. At that latitude, the sun rises around 6 a.m. and sets around 6 p.m. daily. I didn't want to be in a supposedly sketchy city after dark. Determined not to take a taxi, I left the museum and asked a random man, "Quito?" He pointed to the bus stop. I boarded the first one that came by. The ride to the outskirts took an hour, but we weren't heading to the city center. I exited three kilometers (1.9 mi) from my hostel and hurried back, arriving minutes before sunset, content with the day's festivities.

The Equator

42 ♦ Cotopaxi, Latacunga, Ecuador

The idiom, "It's like riding a bike," implies that a skill, once learned, is never forgotten. Just because you have learned something doesn't mean you're good at it. For me, that's riding a bike.

I taught myself to ride when I was eight. I then biked the half mile (0.8 km) to elementary school before taking the bus to middle school. Now, I only hop on a bike for the occasional city tour. I rarely travel in a straight line, but I get from Point A to B without incident. Knowing my skills were marginal, I came up with the idea to bike down one of the world's tallest active stratovolcanoes.

I met at a coffee shop in central Quito with two couples, and we all piled into a van for the fifty-kilometer (31 mi) drive south along twisting paved roads to Cotopaxi National Park. We joined forces with a large group of guys from Amsterdam, a city where bikes outnumber residents and outnumber cars four to one.

After transferring to off-road trucks, the pristine road held for five kilometers (3.1 mi) before changing to gravel. I wasn't too concerned until that morphed into a corrugated washboard. We ascended the rattling mountain pass for twenty minutes, reaching a parking lot at 4,560 meters (14,960 ft), a new altitude record for me. The doors opened to a frigid blast. The summit, 1,351 meters (4,432 ft) higher, was cloaked in fog that touched us.* I tried a test ride, made hopeless by a wind that heaved me toward the cliff's edge with certain death below. Realizing my futile efforts, I walked to the parking lot entrance for the descent.

I started near the front, but almost everyone passed me. The road jarred my bones, and the wind froze them. My throbbing hands spent over an hour clamping the handbrake, wishing it all would end. But the lower we went, the more bearable it became. When the sun appeared, I regained feeling, and the road smoothed.

We stopped for the obligatory lunch amidst a landscape of wispy grasslands and dark mountains. Not wanting to get back on the bike, I had no choice but to do so. Cruising along, the path ahead looked precarious. A few meters next to me seemed a less imposing route. I spotted a rock-free area appearing as a good transition point. I rode straight into grey volcanic ash, my front tire stopped, and I flew off the bike. Dazed and sore, I hadn't broken or torn anything. But the abrasive ash ripped through my gloves and pants. I couldn't see the extent of the damage, only that there was blood.

The few people behind me offered help. I declined, not wanting to bruise my ego further. Ahead was another hour of rocks, gravel, and sand. It wasn't until my tires hit asphalt that I breathed a sigh of relief, raced to the national park entrance (M), and jumped into the truck. If I had to choose between running with the bulls or biking Cotopaxi again, that's a no-brainer. Bring on the bulls.

---

* Cotopaxi is Ecuador's second-highest peak at 5,911 meters (19,388 ft).

Cotopaxi

43 ♦ Galápagos Islands, Ecuador

Despite my battered knee, I threw on my backpack and walked a few kilometers to my new hotel. I could have grabbed a taxi for two dollars, but I reeled from the one to the Equator. In my room was Collin, a good-looking guy in his early 50s, with salt-and-pepper hair, a matching beard, and kind blue eyes. I had no trouble discerning he was Irish. He ascertained I was American. I apologized for my sweaty appearance, and he said two things to me. The first: "Most Americans don't walk." The second: "You're skinnier than most Americans."

He confided that a group of my countrymen inspired him to travel. I mistakenly perked up at the backhanded compliment. A few months earlier, a friend of a friend asked Collin to serve as a tour guide for some elderly and overweight Americans. Watching them struggle with simple tasks, like climbing a flight of stairs, he vowed to see the world while he still had the strength, courage, and desire. He sorted out his affairs and set out on a six-month journey. While I was disappointed to hear about these semi-stereotypical compatriots, the silver lining was that they motivated Collin to change his life.

We joined a group and flew to San Cristóbal, the easternmost island of the Galápagos archipelago, located a thousand kilometers (620 mi) off the west coast of Ecuador. Named after Saint Christopher, the patron saint of travelers, San Cristóbal is where a young scientist made a discovery that changed the world.

In August 1831, the 26-year-old British naval captain, Robert FitzRoy, sent a letter to the 22-year-old geologist and naturalist Charles Darwin, asking the recent college graduate if he wanted to embark on a two-year journey around the world on the second voyage of the *HMS Beagle,* which intended to generate nautical charts of the southern part of South America for naval and maritime commerce, as previous expeditions had left discrepancies in the data. Darwin accepted the invitation.

The *Beagle* departed in December 1831 from Plymouth Sound in the southwest of England and sailed to the Canary Islands and Cape Verde Islands before crossing the Atlantic to Brazil, Uruguay, Argentina, Chile, and Peru. Darwin collected species and kept meticulous notes.

Reaching Chatham Island (later renamed San Cristóbal) in September 1835, Darwin observed wildlife unlike anything he had seen: marine iguanas, birds, and giant Galápagos tortoises. He went from island to island, collecting flora and fauna. His key takeaway was the variance of mockingbirds on each island, a tiny twist of fate that became the foundation for his groundbreaking theory.

The *Beagle* continued to Tahiti, then to New Zealand, Australia, the Keeling Islands, Mauritius, South Africa, St. Helena, Ascension Island, and back to Brazil, the Azores, before returning to England in October 1836, nearly five years after embarking.

Darwin published works about the voyage, geology, fossils, and crustaceans. In 1859, he published his pioneering book *On the Origin of Species*, laying out his hypothesis that populations evolve over generations through natural selection, which became the cornerstone of the theory of evolution.

Overlooking the ocean on San Cristóbal's western edge stood a statue of Darwin. Towering above me, slicked-backed hair clutched his balding head, and a scowled face wrinkled his brow. He donned an overcoat, trousers, and a fancy tie while holding a book titled *Galápagos*. A tortoise and a sea lion lounged at his feet (M).

That night, I boarded a modest vessel with a capacity for sixteen passengers and a crew of six. Not luxurious, it was a far cry from the ferry from China to Japan, featuring a swimming deck, a stocked bar, and edible food. With our first dinner in the books and the anchor raised, we motored toward the next island. Within minutes, the faces of every passenger greened, and some prayed to the porcelain Poseidon. Seasickness has rarely been an issue for me. I was no match for a top-heavy vessel at the mercy of Pacific swells.

I awoke to the calm of Santa Fe Island, located in the center of the archipelago, home to a diverse array of wildlife, including sea lions, iguanas, turtles, lizards, crabs, and birds. With no infrastructure, we took a skiff to a skinny beach surrounded by volcanic rock. A narrow, uphill path led to a barren landscape of trees, shrubs, and cacti. Hours later, we returned to the ship to snorkel along the shoreline, home to equally sundry wildlife: fish, turtles, stingrays, and sharks.

The Charles Darwin Statue on San Cristóbal Island

The next four days were rinse-and-repeat—explore, swim, and move on. South Plaza was a tiny spot on the map covered in red flowers. Genovesa was a horseshoe formed from a collapsed caldera, home to over two hundred thousand birds. Santiago was filled with rippling black lava flows stretching as far as the eye could see. Rabida had beaches the color of coagulated blood. For a naturalist like Darwin, this was paradise. I yearned for something new, happy not to spend five years on a boat.

44 ♦ Cusco Region, Peru

I awoke in Ollantaytambo, Peru, to a magnificent blue sky with frothy clouds on an August morning, one of the driest months of the year. I despised the thought of hiking to Machu Picchu in the rain.

Leading me was Jhon, an Incan descendant from Cusco (the historic capital of the Inca Empire), fluent in Spanish, English, and Quechua. His cultural passion surpassed that of any guide I had encountered. A stocky man with short black hair and dark skin, I mistakenly questioned his fitness. He had walked the trail more than five hundred times but couldn't recall the exact number. The yin to Jhon's yang was his apprentice, Jose, a jokester who had done it nearly one hundred times, with a personal record of six hours.

Along with fifteen other trekkers of all ages and nationalities, we set off from kilometer (KM) 82 on a flat dirt path at an altitude of 2,700 meters (8,860 ft). We gasped to keep up with Jhon as a team of porters, equal in number to the hikers, blew past carrying packs weighing up to twenty-five kilograms (55 lbs). Items included tents, sleeping bags, air mattresses, clothes, food, water, and anything we didn't want to lug in our day packs.

The porters would break down camp in the morning, pass us, set up lunch, break that down, pass us again, and then set up camp for the night. I had the utmost respect for their marvelous abilities. I also felt guilty about doing this for fun, while they did it four to five times a month to make a living. Again, life comes down to privilege, opportunity, and luck. On the other hand, if I created employment, then some good came from it.

We reached Wayllambama at 2,950 meters (9,680 ft) around 3:30 p.m., having covered eleven kilometers (6.8 mi) in excellent time. Dinner was at dusk, illuminated by the glow of electric lanterns and headlamps. Roughly 1,500 kilometers (900 mi) south of the Equator, the sun set around 6:30 p.m., so bedtime came early.

Day 2 began with a wake-up from Jose and a cup of coca tea. Relatively flavorless, it curbed the effects of altitude. I welcomed the hot drink. After breakfast, our blood pumped by 7 a.m. Stairs dominated the morning. Up and up and up. By midday, we reached the trail's apex, Dead Woman's Pass, at 4,215 meters (13,830 ft), perched above the cloud forest surrounded by Andean Peaks.

Our respite was brief as the winds picked up and the cold set in again. It was a never-ending struggle to stay warm. The descent was quicker, but not a picnic. I ran down the variable-height steps for three hours, reaching camp at 1:30 p.m. at Pacamayo, at an elevation of 3,600 meters (11,810 ft). We had missed Jhon's group record of the twelve kilometers (7.5 mi) by forty-five minutes.

Day 3 was the coldest yet, with overnight temperatures dropping to –5°C (23°F). Up again at 5:30 a.m., another downhill stretch of thousands of steps took us to 2,650 meters (8,700 ft) as we reached Wiñaywayna around 4:30 p.m. Another sixteen kilometers (10 mi) down.

Jose woke me for the final time at 3:30 a.m. We left camp an hour later for the short walk to queue for the national park. I sat silently as a gentle rain fell. The gates opened an hour later, and the pitch-black night gave way to a dark grey dawn. Our blistering pace covered four kilometers (2.5 mi) to the Sun Gate, offering our first glimpse of Machu Picchu. *Inti*, the sun god, is the most worshipped deity in Inca culture. I prayed he would bless us with his benevolence. As usual, my prayer went unanswered as we arrived just after 6 a.m. to thick fog conquering the valley.

We hiked to the Machu Picchu fringes and waited as the chunky clouds transitioned to thin haze. Contours of stone buildings set into sloping hills appeared. Long parallel walls, bisected by short ones, outlined roofless houses and rooms. A grassy area separated the upper and lower sections. We entered the abandoned citadel as the sun's rays burned the fog. The lush, green, looming mountains and the iconic, rounded peak at the city's center emerged. I understood why the Inca chose this place.

Built during the empire's zenith around 1450, Machu Picchu translates to "old mountain" in Quechua. Most archaeologists believe it served as an estate for the emperor, Pachacuti Inca

Yupanqui. With a capacity of three hundred to one thousand people, the Inca abandoned it during the Spanish conquest. The inhabitants possibly died from smallpox, a disease introduced by Europeans around 1520.

The city lay undisturbed for nearly four centuries. With the help of an 11-year-old boy, it was discovered in 1911 by Hiram Bingham III, a Yale University lecturer searching for Peruvian ruins. Restored over the years, it's now Peru's top tourist destination.

We exited to have our passports re-examined and stopped at the snack bar. At 8 a.m., with messy hair, filthy skin, dusty clothes, wobbly legs, and colossal smiles, many grabbed a beer and toasted a triumphant journey.

Back inside (M), Machu Picchu had swelled with bus-takers, clogging the place up. After four days, forty-five kilometers (28 mi), early mornings, thousands of steps, heat, cold, rain, sun, and bugs, I had never felt more accomplished. I had earned my prize, whereas they had taken the easy way. Seeing many of them struggle reminded me of Collin's story. It took a moment to get off my high horse and commend every one of them. Getting there isn't simple, no matter how you do it. Sometimes, taking the challenging route isn't possible. The day approached when I would take the easy way.

Machu Picchu

THE MISSING DINNER TABLE

45 ♦ Kansas, USA

I was six months old when my parents bought a modest three-bedroom, two-bathroom, two-car garage house in a quiet Kansas City suburb. One of only six houses on the street, I fed apples to horses in the pasture at the end of the cul-de-sac. They threw backyard birthday parties for me with cake, ice cream, and games. I played soccer with friends when the weather allowed.

One day after school, Mom unexpectedly picked me up and took me home. She sat in the front room chair where my father watched TV, put me on her lap, and told me he had died that morning. I cried in her arms until I ran out of tears.

With him gone, Mom dedicated her life to me. She drove me to soccer practices and games, helped me with homework, took me on trips, and bought me a car. When I graduated from high school, she invited my aunt, uncle, and grandma from my father's side to stay with us and watch me walk across the stage.

Three months later, I attended a nearby college on a soccer and academic scholarship. I liked being only forty-five minutes away, allowing me to come home for Sunday dinners, our longstanding tradition. They were the best meals I had all week and provided leftovers.

I transferred a year later to the University of Kansas, also about forty-five minutes away, where I graduated with a Bachelor of Science in Aerospace Engineering. Mom had attended Michigan State University for two years but stopped due to a lack of funds. She wished she had graduated and considered finishing school. After my father died, those hopes faded.

Like many wayward graduates, I had no idea what to do, so I moved back home and took an entry-level job in the financial services sector while pursuing my Master of Business Administration (MBA) at nearby Rockhurst University. Mom never charged rent, allowing me to pay off my student and car loans. After earning my MBA, I was debt-free and had saved enough for a down payment on a house. I strode an admirable path.

On my last day at home, right after Sunday dinner, I packed the final load of my belongings. Her silhouette waved from my bedroom window as I left the driveway. I couldn't see the tears, but I knew they were there. Living only ten minutes away, I stopped by my old house to mow the lawn, fix something, and have Sunday dinners. But once she was gone, the house became silent.

Mom was as savvy as they came regarding paperwork. As a widower with no other children, she appointed me as her power of attorney, healthcare proxy, and executor of her will. Having dealt with contracts for years, I handled most items without trouble. But her house remained a hurdle. She had drawn up documents to put it in my name, but never signed them. To obtain ownership, I enlisted a lawyer who recommended that I sell it. I was offended. How dare she tell me to get rid of my childhood home! The idea was unfathomable. Instead, I would rent it to earn a little money while keeping what I loved.

It took nearly a year to transfer the house into my name. During that time, whenever I wasn't traveling, I would go there, sorting through the belongings I wanted, donating what I didn't, and throwing away the rest. Some days, I made great progress; on others, I felt aimless, overwhelmed by the task. Mom wasn't a hoarder, but she had accumulated a lot over thirty years. After combing through every room, only large items were left. I hired an estate sale company to sell them. When I returned, my footsteps echoed, and the wood creaked in unfamiliar ways. I hardly recognized the place. Still, my plans remained the same. I couldn't let go.

I contacted several contractors to fix a few things. All were either too expensive or full of broken promises. The headaches mounted as my long-term travel plans developed, and the idea of selling emerged. Before heading to South America, I told myself I would decide what to do after finishing the Inca Trail.

Four days of trudging the muddy paths and climbing stairs gave me time to think about why I wanted to keep it. It was the story of my life—the place where I experienced every significant event. But with nobody there, all that remained were memories. I could have moved back and made new ones, but it wouldn't have been the same. I decided to sell it.

In the hospital, before losing her ability to speak, Mom said she wanted to go home. On the second anniversary of her passing, I entered the empty house for the last time, walked around the unfinished basement, peeked into the barren bedrooms, and listened to the echoes. I passed the spot where my father's chair used to be, stepped into the kitchen, and stood where our table had once been for Sunday dinners (M).

In the months that followed, I randomly drove by. Sometimes, my eyes welled up. I didn't know anything about the family that lived there. I hoped their memories would be as happy as mine.

The missing dinner table

Around the World

46 ♦ Bohol, Philippines

I had removed the burden of Mom's house, my roommate could look after mine, and our digital world allowed me to take care of anything from anywhere. With my life streamlined, I planned the most ambitious journey yet. It took some guts to pull the trigger a few times, but after sorting the details, anxiety set in.

I had recently fulfilled my duties as best man for the fourth time. Watching my friends marry, some divorce, and others become parents, I examined my life. Was traveling holding me back? Was I missing out on what truly mattered (hopefully not the divorce)? Was Middle America changing my view of how life should be? Was I wasting my time and money traveling? Should I give all of this up and get a job like the one I had? I debated changing the book to *50 Places After*. Eventually, I removed my head from my ass and realized how rare this opportunity was. My apprehension turned into enthusiasm when I boarded a plane to the Philippines.

It took thirty-three hours to get from my door to Manila. Still struggling with my inability to sleep on planes, I passed out when my head hit the hotel pillow. I awoke to a knock on the door from Sondre, my Great Wall buddy. He had invited me to join him for three weeks, along with two girls from his neighborhood.

The young Norwegians weren't picky about planning. The only thing we had booked was a flight to the island of Coron. As is common in Southeast Asia, things rarely run on schedule. The supposed 3:15 p.m. departure turned into 4:00, then 4:15. When the boarding call rang out at 4:30, we rushed aboard the eighty-seat propeller plane. With the engines humming, the captain came over the intercom to inform us that the flight had been canceled due to the lack of landing lights in Coron. Welcome to the Philippines.

We received a complimentary hotel room in the red-light district and a flight the next day that boarded an hour late at 12:30 p.m., sat on the tarmac for an hour, and landed at a bumpy airstrip an hour later. It made sense why nighttime landings were prohibited. With no public transportation, private vans sold cheap tickets for the hour-long ride to civilization.

There wasn't much to do in the modest beach town geared towards scuba divers, so travelers suggested we visit El Nido. Not wanting to fly again, we bought tickets for a ferry that would take six to ten hours.

The open-air wooden vessel had benches and little else. It didn't sell water, so I rationed my half-empty 500 ml bottle, a task in the scorching heat. At least there was a breeze for part of the eight-hour trip. We stayed four nights in the backpacker-friendly town, snuggled among limestone cliffs, turquoise waters, and white sandy beaches. Despite my efforts, I never found a suitable place.

We feared for our lives as the driver whipped the fourteen-passenger van through mountainous roads en route to Puerta Princessa. I mistakenly sat in the back next to the luggage. Anticipating the van rolling over or falling into the water, I would break the rear window with my elbow wrapped in a shirt. Feeling nauseous from a hangover and the air conditioning not reaching me, I dreaded vomiting on Sondre's head in front of me.

I went to bed early after dinner, hoping to sleep off how awful I felt. Lying in the humid room, I developed chills and chest pains as my heart raced. I shifted to every position, trying to slow it down, but any movement only quickened my pulse. Nothing helped as I drifted in and out of a sweaty fog, fearing a heart attack or that I might never wake up. I thought about calling the girls, who were nurses. They couldn't do much, so I remained motionless. Ten hours later, my body normalized, and I fell asleep. I awoke feeling like someone had sat on my sternum all night, but I knew I was out of danger.

We flew to Cebu and caught a respectable ferry to the island of Bohol. After three days of calm, we took a two-hour drive into the island's interior to the Chocolate Hills, named for their transformation from green to brown at the end of the dry season. A climb of two hundred not steep steps took me to a viewing platform of these unique conical mounts, thirty to fifty meters (100 to 160 ft) tall, stretching into the distance. Surrounded by lush green trees, most had become the color of drumroll…chocolate. Having been to so many other places without luck, I called this one good (M). I was damned if I would spend two weeks of hard travel in vain. Little did I know things would only get worse.

On the morning we were leaving Bohol, I woke up with minor stomach discomfort. I didn't think much of it, took care of it, and went back to bed. When I had to go again twenty minutes later, I knew my old adversary, food poisoning, had found me. Not as bad as Morocco, having avoided shitting my pants, it was no picnic. One of the girls caught the same bug as I did, which I think came from a yogurt parfait. We alternated noxious trips to the bathroom for the next five hours. It became so repetitive that we jokingly called ourselves "poo buddies." The levity made the situation bearable.

We caught the ferry back to Cebu that afternoon. I hadn't eaten in a day. Not learning from Morocco, I assumed the worst had passed and forced down convenience store ramen and snacks. I awoke late at night and headed to the bathroom. After doing my business, something shifted in my stomach. Vertigo replaced the nausea, and my world dimmed. I slid to the tile floor as darkness engulfed me, and I lost consciousness for an unknown amount of time. When I came to, there was only black. My brain functioned, and I knew I was on the floor. But I couldn't open my eyes.

A few minutes passed, and the blackness receded. Lying in a pool of cold sweat, I pulled myself up and dried off before shuffling back to bed to pass out. When I woke up, I took some ciprofloxacin and felt well enough to catch the ferry to Boracay. As one of the world's most acclaimed islands for its beaches and nightlife, notwithstanding all the prostitutes that come out after the sun goes down, I did my best to enjoy what time I had left with the Norwegians. But I had grown tired of the Philippines.

The Chocolate Hills

47 ♦ New Delhi, India

We resist British Imperialism no less than Nazism. If there is a difference, it is in degree. One-fifth of the human race has been brought under the British heel by means that will not bear scrutiny. Our resistance to it does not mean harm to the British people. We seek to convert them, not to defeat them on the battle-field.

— Mahatma Gandhi, *Letter to Adolf Hitler* (1940)

The most nerve-racking part of travel is arriving somewhere unfamiliar at night. I'm generally cautious when choosing transportation. Not wanting to figure out the metro and assuming it was closed for the evening, I foolishly took the first taxi offered to me at the airport in the Indian capital of New Delhi.

I followed the man to his tuk-tuk. He looked confused from the get-go and stopped at a tourist office. I quietly followed him inside, where he spoke to another man. Distrustful of everyone after Shanghai, I clutched my small backpack with valuables. I could manage with that for a while if I needed to run. The man at the office sensed my edginess and reassured me that everything was fine. He directed my driver, who dropped me off at the hotel just after midnight. Still annoyed about only finding one place in the Philippines, I knew India would be better. Without a doubt, the first would be dedicated to another "Father of the Nation."

British rule in India began in the mid-eighteenth century, solidifying its grip after the defeat of local rulers and establishing the British East India Company as the dominant power in the region. But by 1857, widespread resentment against colonial rule culminated in the Indian Rebellion, a mutiny of Indian soldiers commanded by the British East India Company that spread across northern and central India. The British government suppressed the uprising, leading to the direct rule of India by the Crown in 1858.

Born eleven years later to a Hindu family in Porbandar, Mohandas Gandhi was the youngest of four children. After finishing high school, he moved to London to train as a lawyer before practicing in the Colony of Natal, a British territory in southeastern Africa. Despite his education and proper attire, he encountered prejudice and racism. When challenging the authorities, violence often met his disobedience.

In 1906, a regulation requiring the registration of Indians and Chinese prompted Gandhi to develop his non-violent resistance methodology, *satyagraha* (truth force). Thousands of defiant Indians refused to carry their registration cards. Despite being beaten, jailed, or shot, they didn't forcefully resist. Gandhi's pacifist approach sparked a public outcry that led to a compromise with the local government, earning him the honorific title of *Mahatma* in 1914, Sanskrit for "Great Soul." A year later, he returned to his homeland, applying lessons learned in the struggle for Indian independence.

In March 1919, the British legislature in India passed a law allowing authorities to arrest without a warrant and detain without trial for up to two years. After the apprehension of two national leaders on April 13, thousands of unarmed, peaceful protesters gathered at Jallianwala Bagh, an area bordered by high walls on three sides. Fifty British Indian Army troops cut off the exit, didn't order the crowd to disperse, and opened fire for ten minutes until their ammunition was depleted. British casualty figures were 379 dead and 1,100 wounded. Unofficial estimates were higher.

The unwavering Gandhi upheld his non-violent principle by initiating the *non-cooperation movement*, a large-scale boycott of British goods, government services, elections, and taxes. In March 1930, in defiance of the British salt tax, he led seventy-eight others on a 385-kilometer (239 mi), twenty-four-day march to the sea, speaking to thousands along the way. Reaching the Arabian seaside town of Dandi, he illegally produced salt and was detained. Salt-making protests erupted across the country, and the march continued without him.

Upset by the disruptive campaign, the British beat hundreds of pacifists, killed two, and imprisoned thousands. Gandhi was freed in January 1931 and negotiated the release of political prisoners, but his push for independence remained ignored.

He delivered his Quit India speech on August 8, 1942, amidst the shadow of World War II, insisting on the end of British rule. He, his wife Kasturba, and most of the Indian National Congress, a political party he led, were arrested within hours.

After a series of heart attacks, Kasturba died in prison in her husband's arms in February 1944 at age 74. Authorities feared the backlash of a similar fate for Gandhi, who was suffering from malaria and dysentery. Believing his health would limit his political threat, he was released three months later.

As the war drained British resources, the demand for independence became unavoidable. On August 15, 1947, the Indian Independence Act came into effect. After more than thirty years, Gandhi achieved victory, but it didn't take the harmonious form he had hoped. During his imprisonment, the growing rift between Muslims and Hindus widened, leading to the call for a separate Muslim state. The result was the independent country of Pakistan alongside a free India.

The new lines drawn on the map triggered one of the largest migrations in history. About fifteen million refugees traveled to new homelands—half were Muslims to Pakistan, half Hindus and Sikhs to India. Riots, rapes, and violence broke out, causing the deaths of anywhere from a few hundred thousand to two million people. An atmosphere of mistrust and resentment developed.

On January 30, 1948, Gandhi went to the garden for his evening prayer at his current residence, Birla House, a grand home in the New Delhi suburbs. Nathuram Godse—a right-wing Hindu nationalist who believed Gandhi favored Muslims and Pakistan and blamed him for the violence during the partition—pushed through the crowd and fired three shots into the 78-year-old's midsection. The father of four was carried inside and died shortly after.

The next day, millions watched as his body was taken in a procession from Birla House to Raj Ghat, where he was cremated in Hindu tradition. His ashes were placed in urns and scattered across India.

I took the metro from the city center to an affluent neighborhood. I entered the former Birla House, a white, colonial-style mansion with a columned entrance, which the government had purchased, converted into a museum in 1973, and renamed *Gandhi Smriti* (Gandhi Remembrance).

Details of his life, quotes, and looping videos adorned the walls. A diorama of his Salt March featured a figurine with fringe around a bald head, round glasses, a white robe, a walking stick, sandals, and a red, dripping bindi on his forehead. A more elaborate diorama of his cremation depicted mourners gathered around an unlit pyre covered in flowers, with various national flags at half-mast.

I followed a winding hallway to his sparse meeting room. A low railing cordoned off a mattress on the floor, a pillow, and some tables. A shadowbox on the wall held his WORLDLY REMAINS. A hardcore minimalist before there was such a thing, it had a walking stick, two forks, two spoons, a butter knife, a large curved knife, a pocket watch, spectacles with a case, and a coin purse.

Down the hall, his bedroom had a windowed alcove with a shin-high table covered by a worn cloth, where he meditated. A single-person bed with a large pillow sat nearby. Everything was white, brown, or dingy beige. A young security guard followed me. I asked if there was anything else to see. She told me to go outside.

In the back, low hedge rows blocked a path with raised footprints. I followed an adjacent trail to a manicured garden with electric lanterns, a fountain, and golf-course-quality grass. It had been sixty-seven years since he had taken that walk. Every step I took felt mirrored by a ghost. Goosebumps covered my arms despite the searing heat. After fifty meters (160 ft), I reached a pillared gazebo with lattice fencing, removed my shoes, and approached the one-meter-tall column marking the site of the man's murder (M).

Gandhi was the yin to Hitler's yang. Both lived through the same conflicts, yet emerged as opposites. Tolerance, non-violence, and kindness clashed with hatred, genocide, and cruelty. Ironically, the tyrant chose when to shoot himself, while the pacifist was chosen. But Gandhi had the last posthumous laugh.

In 1948, he was nominated for the Nobel Peace Prize for the fifth time, having never won. Assassinated before nominations were closed, the committee didn't award the prize, as there was no appropriate living candidate. His theories on non-violence inspired future Nobel Peace Prize laureates, including the 14th Dalai Lama, Nelson Mandela, and Dr. Martin Luther King Jr.

The location of Mahatma Gandhi's assassination

48 ♦ Pushkar, India

When we think of the Hindu religion, we find it difficult, if not impossible, to define Hindu religion or even adequately describe it. Unlike other religions in the world, the Hindu religion does not claim any one Prophet, it does not worship any one God, it does not believe in any one philosophic concept, it does not follow any one set of religious rites or performances; in fact, it does not satisfy the traditional features of a religion or creed. It is a way of life and nothing more.

—Supreme Court Of India (1966)

A person could spend a lifetime exploring India. It wouldn't be enough. A three-week tour, primarily in the largest state, Rajasthan, had to suffice. I went to Jaisalmer, Jodhpur, Udaipur, and onto Pushkar, one the most sacred cities in Hinduism, a religion that, unlike Buddhism, Islam, and Christianity, doesn't have a founder and is a blending of faiths.

The religion evolved over millennia through a fusion of traditions and influences from migrating Indo-Aryans, with its earliest roots traced back to the Indus Valley near present-day Pakistan. The Vedas, Hinduism's oldest sacred texts, appeared around the fifteenth century BCE, with the concept of deity worship emerging a millennium later.

Islam reached northern India in the seventh century, as Hinduism spread in the south and Southeast Asia. The Muslim takeover of the Indian subcontinent commenced in the tenth century, marked by periods of both religious tolerance and conflict. The Islamic reign peaked in the late seventeenth century but spiraled downward as the Hindus reconquered much of India. The British colonial era led to a modernization of Hindu practices. After India's independence, Hinduism influenced the nation's laws, traditions, and identity.

Having checked off the second (Islam) and fourth (Buddhism) most popular religions, I set my sights on the third, of which India has more than 94 percent of its worshippers. Within Hinduism lies the central theme of the *Trimūrti* (Hindu Trinity), consisting of three gods: Brahma, the creator; Vishnu, the protector; and Shiva, the destroyer. Brahma, the least worshipped, has few temples dedicated to him. The most prominent one, however, resides in Pushkar.

Legend has it that a demon tried to kill Brahma's children, so Brahma slew him with a lotus flower that dropped three petals, each creating a lake. He came to Earth and named one of them where the flower (pushpa) fell from his hand (kar). Brahma was to perform a ritual there, but his wife, Saraswati, wasn't present. The timing was so crucial that he took another wife, Gayatri. The angry Saraswati cursed Brahma, declaring he would only be worshipped in Pushkar, where it's believed immersing oneself in the lake brings salvation.

Shops, trash, and animals encircled the sacred lake. The free-range hippies added to the chaos. Hordes of Westerners with tragic haircuts, smoking weed and hash, lingered for months to "find themselves." Next to a hippy jam session, our dinner came with a free concert of random half-songs and whiffs of whacky tobacky.

We gathered in the early dawn to climb Ratnagiri Hill on the city's outskirts. A grand white arch led to stairs that transitioned to haphazard rocks halfway to the summit. Monkeys, the size of large cats to large dogs, pestered us for food. After half an hour, we reached the small-house-sized Saraswati Temple (M), dedicated to Brahma's scorned wife. The antithesis of most shrines, it was ragged and windowless. As daylight broke over the mountains, I struggled to discern Pushkar's details through the smog.

Back in town, visitors swarmed the much nicer Brahma Temple. With elements dating back to the fourteenth century, marble steps lead to a vibrant, pillared hall and an inner sanctum featuring a small, dark marble statue of him, resting cross-legged, wearing a red robe and necklace of yellow flowers. His four heads and four arms pointed in different directions. Behind sat statues of Gayatri and Saraswati on either side. It's ridiculous that a guy cheats on his wife and gets a high-end shrine in the middle of town while she, who was running a little late, gets a shack in the suburbs.

Pushkar, as seen from the Saraswati Temple

49 ♦ Agra, India

I had never had better food during my travels, unable to get enough vegetarian curry, garlic naan, chai masala tea, and mango lassi. The problem with dining in India is the likelihood of Delhi Belly. Of the ten people in my group, only I avoided food poisoning. Even my guide, an Indian man who had lived there his entire life, was incapacitated for days.

Maybe my stomach developed a steel lining in the Philippines. Or maybe it was the temporary vegetarianism. Or the unanticipated sobriety. Whatever it was, I had never felt better. I couldn't say the same for the 22-year-old British girl, Haley, whom I met strong, spirited, and vibrant. Already thin, she had withered to a skeleton with skin in less than a week. So weak I carried her luggage from city to city. I offered her some ciprofloxacin, but she refused, ever stoic. The road to Tordi Sagar changed her mind.

Buses, jeeps, and motorcycles swerved to avoid each other and animals along the trash-filled one-lane corridor, each honking at every move. The terrible suspension forced Haley to grip the seat each time we hit a bump. As one of the toughest travelers I had met—much tougher than me—she never complained. Arriving three hours later, she accepted my offer of antibiotics and needed four days' worth. For comparison, I have only ever needed two.

We were slated to visit an elementary school the next morning, but it was closed for Good Friday, a Christian holiday commemorating the crucifixion of Jesus Christ. I found this strange as India's religious breakdown is roughly 80 percent Hindu and 14 percent Muslim, with Christians, Sikhs, Buddhists, Jains, and others making up the rest. But the size of the religion didn't matter. Regardless of faith, most major holidays were observed, a far cry from the West's Christian obsession.

A few days later, everyone had recovered from their stomach issues in Agra as we entered the queue at 5:30 a.m. to see the Taj Mahal. When the gates opened half an hour later, we sprinted one hundred meters (330 ft) to the inner gateway, turned the corner, and the ivory-white marble icon greeted its first visitors of the day.

A finial sat atop an onion dome, flanked by smaller domes. The vaulted arch below created a pleasing negative space. A long reflecting pool—lined with trees, manicured grass, and walkways—stretched to where I stood. Elegant Islamic geometry of flowers, vines, fruits, lattices, and Arabic calligraphy set light into dark and dark into light. I had never seen a more beautiful structure.

The inspiration for this grandiose display dates back to the 1607 engagement of Mughal Prince Khurrum to Arjumand Banu, the daughter of a Persian noble. Both were about 15 years old and married five years later, making her the second of his three wives. (The other two marriages were for political reasons.) Possessing such deep affection, Khurrum bestowed the title of *Mumtaz Mahal*, "The Exalted One of the Palace."

Khurrum became the fifth Mughal emperor in 1627, taking the name Shah Jahan I. Four years later, Mumtaz died from blood loss while giving birth to the couple's fourteenth child at age 38. (Seven of her children survived to adulthood.) To honor his favorite wife, he commissioned a mausoleum. Completed in 1643, it employed more than twenty thousand artisans and laborers.

Shah Jahan fell ill in 1657, triggering a war of succession among his sons. Despite recovering, he went under house arrest until dying nine years later, thirty-five years after Mumtaz.

Two sarcophagi resided in the Taj Mahal's main chamber—a centered one representing Mumtaz and a more prominent, out-of-place one for Shah Jahan, creating the only unbalanced aspect (M). (For security purposes, their actual sarcophagi are in the basement, with their faces turned right toward Mecca.)

I have always been obsessed with symmetry, and this off-center "flaw" disheartened me. But it served as a metaphor. While everything on the outside may look perfect, the imperfections make a relationship unique. I had been to places commemorating the dead for several purposes. This was the first for love, perhaps the ultimate reason to remember someone. At the time, it was a subject I knew nothing about. It would be two years before I met the woman I would fall in love with.

The Taj Mahal

50 ♦ Varanasi, India

We arrived in Varanasi just after sunrise, where bodies burned along the banks of the River Ganges. When I chose to cremate Mom, I picked a coffin and a vessel for her remains. The funeral home did the rest. Days later, I received an engraved urn with her ashes.

An example of cremation grounds in Nepal. (Photos in Varanasi are prohibited)

In India, the body is washed, and the last rites are preferably performed within a day of death. Men are wrapped in white cloth, while women are wrapped in red. The big toes are tied together, and a red mark is placed on the forehead. The family carries the body to the cremation grounds and places it on a pyre with the feet facing south towards Yama, the ruler of the dead. The eldest son (or a priest) bathes, performs a ceremony, sets the pyre alight, and makes offerings of ghee. The cremator and relatives walk around the burning body and consecrate the cold ashes at the nearest river or sea.

Within Hinduism lies the central belief of *saṃsāra*, the recurring cycle of birth, life, and death—commonly referred to as reincarnation. This concept is intertwined with *karma*, the idea that our actions influence our future—good deeds lead to good *karma* and rebirth, while evil deeds lead to the opposite. Those who die in Varanasi and are cremated along the riverbank receive instant salvation, ending the cycle and bringing them closer to *moksha*—freedom or liberation. If a person dies somewhere else, salvation is still possible if a relative deposits the ashes in the most sacred river in the holiest city.

As I sputtered along the Ganges in a shabby wooden boat, buildings with faded paint lined the riverfront. Ghats led down to concrete walkways where Hindus bathed to respect their lost loved ones and be cleansed of their sins. At least, that's the theory.

Some four hundred million people live along the river, turning it into a dumping ground for sewage, industrial waste, and garbage. Confounding the problem are improperly (or not at all) cremated bodies. Those who use it are at risk of cholera, dysentery, hepatitis, and typhoid. I questioned subjecting Mom to such a filthy place, but an elegant solution presented itself. After half an hour, the oil-burning engine stopped, and I received five candles in flower-shaped vessels (M) that represented:

1) Peace, harmony, and prosperity in the universe.
2) Peace, harmony, and prosperity in my country.
3) My community.
4) Family, friends, and relatives.
5) Me.

I lit the candles, set them in the river, watched them drift away, and prayed for Mom, again hoping to bring her salvation, if such a thing exists.

The River Ganges in Varanasi

51 ♦ Lhasa, Tibet Autonomous Region, China

The Tibetan nationality is one of the nationalities with a long history within the boundaries of China and, like many other nationalities, it has done its glorious duty in the course of the creation and development of the great motherland. But over the last hundred years and more, imperialist forces penetrated into China, and in consequence, also penetrated into the Tibetan region and carried out all kinds of deceptions and provocations.
— Seventeen-Point Agreement (1951)

With my backside clenched, I peered at the gray outside the window as the turbulence intensified on the approach to Kathmandu, Nepal. I blinked, and we broke through the clouds over the runway. The pilot shoved the stick forward and slammed the landing gear. We bounced. Another forceful push stuck the wheels to the ground as he crushed the brakes. I exited with frayed nerves.

I caught a cab to my hotel just in time to meet my new group. Still shaken, the next morning, we boarded a flight that would go one of two ways—smooth with beverage service and spectacular views of the world's highest mountain range, or the opposite. Upon reaching the Himalayas, the wide-body Airbus A330 pitched in sinusoidal arcs, and I discovered a new fear-induced reaction. The adrenaline surge caused debilitating lower back pain.

After a hair-raising landing, I asked my guide how this ranked on his scariest-flight scale. He gave it a seven out of ten. If the plane had been smaller, it would have been his worst. Even with my education and understanding of turbulence, these back-to-back gut-wrenching flights instilled a fear of flying. At least I wouldn't have to get on a plane for another ten days, with the first four spent in Lhasa, the capital of the Tibet Autonomous Region and the former home to many of the Dalai Lamas.

The spiritual leader of Tibetan Buddhism traces its origins back to Avalokiteshvara, the bodhisattva of compassion, whom the Dalai Lamas are believed to be reincarnations of. The 1st Dalai Lama, Gendun Drubpa, emerged in the fifteenth century, becoming the head of the Gelugpa school of Tibetan Buddhism. His successor, Gendun Gyatso Palzangpo, strengthened the institution's influence as a respected educator who traveled, wrote, and taught in Central Asia.

In the late sixteenth century, the 3rd Dalai Lama, Sonam Gyatso, accepted an invitation from the Mongol ruler, Altan Khan, who adopted the teachings and called his friend *Dalai*, the Mongolian word for Gyatso, meaning "ocean" or "big." Combined with the Tibetan word *Lama*, meaning "master" or "guru," the title *Dalai Lama* officially emerged. (The titles of 1st and 2nd were bestowed posthumously on Sonam Gyatso's predecessors.)

It wasn't until the Great Fifth, Lobsang Gyatso, consolidated political power in the early seventeenth century with the support of Mongol forces that the Dalai Lamas became the leaders of Tibet. In 1645, he began building the future seat of government, the Potala Palace, which took over forty-five years to finish.

In the early eighteenth century, the Qing dynasty emerged as a protectorate of Tibet, as successive Dalai Lamas either died young or defied their role. The 13th Dalai Lama, Thubten Gyatso, restored the position in the early twentieth century and modernized the country by opening it up to foreigners, implementing a national tax system, overhauling the penal system, abolishing the death penalty, and electrifying Lhasa. After the fall of the Qing in 1912 and the rise of the Republic of China (later Taiwan), he declared Tibetan independence.

The 14th Dalai Lama, Tenzin Gyatso, was thrown into political chaos when Mao Zedong's communists seized control of China in 1949. They wasted little time declaring their intentions for Tibet, which had been a *de facto* independent state, and hoped to stay that way.

A year later, the "Chinese invasion of Tibet," as Tibet calls it, or the "Peaceful liberation of Tibet," as China refers to it, began. After unsuccessful negotiations to assert Chinese control, forty thousand People's Liberation Army (PLA) soldiers entered Tibet in October 1950 and subdued their eight and a half thousand less prepared counterparts. A month later, the Dalai Lama was ordained at age 15.

Tibetan delegates went to Beijing in 1951 to discuss terms, hoping to avoid further conflict. The result was the *Seventeen-Point Agreement*,* a document affirming China's sovereignty. Supposedly, Tibetan delegates couldn't suggest alterations, communicate with Lhasa, and weren't authorized to sign, but did so under duress using seals not sponsored by the Tibetan government.

The Tibetan regions under Chinese control, Kham and Amdo, were subjected to socialist land reform and redistribution. In 1956, a guerrilla resistance erupted there, aided by Tibetan monasteries and villages, which fell victim to Chinese reprisals. Having initially complied with the *Seventeen-Point Agreement* and allowed *de facto* independence, Lhasa joined the uprising.

On March 10, 1959, fearing that the Chinese would abduct the Dalai Lama, thousands of Tibetans surrounded Potala Palace. A week later, Chinese artillery landed nearby. Disguised as a soldier, he fled under the cover of night, escaped to India, and established the *Central Tibetan Administration* in Dharamsala. Eighty thousand Tibetan refugees followed him. In 1965, the Chinese renamed the area formerly controlled by the Dalai Lama's government to the Tibet Autonomous Region.

Stepping off the plane in Lhasa felt like China—sterile and modern. The city had noticeable Chinese-style buildings on the outskirts and Tibetan architecture near the center. Located at *35 Beijing Middle Rd* was the Potala Palace, named after Mount Potalaka, the legendary home of Avalokiteshvara.

---

* The full title is the *Agreement of the Central People's Government and the Local Government of Tibet on Measures for the Peaceful Liberation of Tibet.*

The towering structure contained a thousand rooms, ten thousand shrines, and two hundred thousand statues that we couldn't photograph. More importantly, due to all the guards, as part of the Three Ts, we weren't supposed to ask questions. The safest place to talk was a restaurant. Beware of Big Brother.

I stopped at the former bedroom of the 14th Dalai Lama, who hadn't been there in fifty-six years, but everything looked in order (M). With amenities similar to Gandhi's but with more flair, a geometric rug displayed pastel flowers in pink, blue, maroon, and white. A seating area was in one corner, and his bed was in another. Painted religious figures covered the walls.

In the wake of his exile, Tenzin Gyatso became a Buddhist educator who advocated for religious freedom, nonviolence, a world free from nuclear weapons, democracy, modern ethics, environmental protection, women's rights, and the advancement of science. One point of contention is his support for Marxism, which he believes is morally superior due to its concept of equal wealth distribution, a notion I agree with, but question its practical implementation. Following the Tiananmen Square protests and massacre in 1989, he was awarded the Nobel Peace Prize, in part to honor the legacy of Mahatma Gandhi.

Potala Palace

52 ♦ Dagzê County, Tibet, China

The bus stopped at a police station near the edge of Lhasa. A Chinese officer who would be our chaperone for the next week sat at the front. Outside the city, the smooth roads shifted to mountainous passes. After two hours of shaking, we arrived at the base of the tallest, windiest switchback I had ever encountered, leading up to Ganden Monastery.

Founded in 1409, Ganden is one of Tibetan Buddhism's "great three" monasteries (Sera and Drepung are the others), where the 14th Dalai Lama took his final degree examination in 1958. The following year, after the rebellion that forced him to flee, eighty-seven thousand Tibetans were dead, including thousands of monks.

The Cultural Revolution (1966-1976) left the "great three" in ruins, which underwent a rebuilding in the 1980s. Following a ban on pictures of the Dalai Lama in 1996, four hundred monks rioted at Ganden. PLA troops killed two, injured more, and arrested one hundred. Previously capable of housing five thousand monks, only about four hundred remained the day I was there.

The monastery sat on the side of Wangbur Mountain. Joining me on a climb to the top was Lauren, a Canadian with long black hair, fair skin, and effervescence. We passed a police station that seemed pointless in this part of the world. The officers stationed out front glared, but let us be. I reminded myself of where I was.

We had ninety minutes to cover a vertical distance of two hundred meters (660 ft) and return. The problem was that we were already at 4,300 meters (14,100 ft), higher than the highest point of the Inca Trail. During my days of acclimation in Lhasa, one of the world's highest cities at 3,650 meters (11,975 ft), I never struggled on level surfaces, but climbing a flight of stairs left me winded. With each step up Wangbur, I could only ascend for a few seconds before stopping. After forty-five minutes of serpentine hiking, we reached the summit amid a sea of prayer flags.

Found on peaks throughout the Himalayas, these pieces of cloth connected by a string symbolize compassion, peace, strength, and wisdom. Supposedly, stepping over them brought bad *karma*, but lifting them by the hundreds became too strenuous, so I just walked on top. Only the gods know whether I had damaged my fate.

I reached the back of the mountain and followed a line of flags to a lower peak, emerging into a world of alternate hues—a cobalt sky with gunmetal clouds, a navy blue river, a beige valley floor, and chestnut mountains. Eggshell, burgundy, and mustard covered the many buildings of Ganden. Only the flags displayed the traditional colors—blue for sky and space, white for air and wind, red for fire, green for water, and yellow for earth.

Placing new flags next to old ones is believed to signify life's changing cycle of new lives replacing old ones. I tied a set I bought in the parking lot for ten yuan ($1.60) among the tattered ones, and said a prayer for Mom that spread throughout space as they flapped in the wind (M).

Lauren soon joined me and thundered, "WOW, this is the best day of my life!" I had never been with someone on such an occasion. With many to choose from, I would be hard-pressed to narrow it down to one. But this ranked near the top.

At Wangbur Mountain. Photo by Lauren Karpman.

53 ♦ Tingri County, Ri Ka Ze Shi, Tibet, China

We drove to Gyantse, Shigatse, and Sakya. With daytime highs of 5°C (41°F) dropping to –15°C (5°F) overnight, warmth became my focus with the evermore basic accommodations. Hot water was a luxury, and heat was nonexistent. I used electric blankets when available. If not, I cocooned with every layer of bedding, leaving my face exposed.

A nine-hour clattering van ride took me to Rongbuk Monastery, passing through 5,248 meters (17,217 ft), a personal altitude record I would never eclipse. Founded in 1902, like Ganden, Rongbuk was destroyed and rebuilt. At 5,009 meters (16,434 ft), it's one of the highest monasteries in the world, with oxygen levels a hypoxic 55 percent of those at sea level. I had fared well over the last week, suffering only minor stomach discomfort and labored breathing, having avoided headaches, loss of appetite, or dizziness.

The goal was Everest Base Camp, a primitive site used by trekkers at the foot of Mount Everest, the planet's tallest peak. Our guide thought it was unique to go twice, once in the evening and again in the morning. With everyone agreeing, the bus stopped at a Chinese military checkpoint before pulling into a tent village. A local bus took us the remaining few kilometers.

As much as I yearned for the Everest summit at 8,848 meters (29,029 ft), it takes months to acclimatize and costs upwards of fifty thousand dollars. With zero mountaineering experience, a hatred of the cold, and a lack of capital, base camp seemed satisfactory.

I had seen images of the more popular Nepalese version on the other side of the mountain. The Tibetan one was nothing like that. The cordoned-off area of faded prayer flags remained segregated from the distant bright tents and intrepid mountaineers, whom I had hoped to meet. I settled for cheap souvenirs and weathered signs.

With the sun setting and a chill creeping back in, we caught the local bus back to the tent village for dinner in a smoke-filled tent, where a throbbing headache set in and my vision blurred. I forced down some yak meat soup and a Coke, neither of which helped.

We returned to the monastery a few hours later. Using the light on my phone, I found the open-air toilet of pits cut into a concrete floor. I thanked Buddha that I didn't have to go number two. The sleeping dorm had wooden beds, a pile of blankets on each, a dim fluorescent light, and no heat. A fractured window let in a breeze.

I took pain meds and curled into my sleeping bag, wearing the same clothes I had been in for three days. My heart raced as it had in the Philippines. Using lessons learned, I lay motionless. After a few hours, I somehow fell asleep. I awoke and dozed off throughout the night, feeling better each time. By 7 a.m., I felt no ill effects.

The plan was to hike seven kilometers (4.3 mi) back to base camp. With an apprehensive face, our guide broke the news. Beginning that year, the Chinese enacted a rule allowing groups to visit base camp only once. My stomach sank. I intended to deem that a place for Mom after the hike. I could have the night before, but didn't feel I earned it. I had failed again.

Determined not to let the bad news ruin my day, I decided to climb the nearby hills in the barren Dzakar Chu valley (M). An hour later, my spirits were lifted as the sun warmed me, while Everest loomed in the distance. Watching the wind rip snow off the top of the world, it looked like a terrible place to be.

Rongbuk Monastery and Mount Everest

54 ♦ Dubai, United Arab Emirates

I said, "See ya' later" to Lauren and headed to the Kathmandu airport. The boarding process finished well before the scheduled 11:20 a.m. departure, but our wheels didn't leave the ground until 11:45 a.m. The captain said we would still be on time. The date was April 25, 2015.

A thin haze caught my eye during the final approach to Dubai five hours later. The man beside me, a well-dressed Kuwaiti luxury dessert designer, said it was a sandstorm. My recent contraction of aviophobia produced a sense of uneasiness as the plane punched through the wall of sand.

After an uneventful landing, I turned on my phone, and messages flooded in, asking if I was okay. I grew confused as no one knew I was traveling that morning. In the "trending news" were stories of a 7.8 magnitude earthquake, with the epicenter eighty kilometers (50 mi) from Kathmandu. My flight took off ten minutes before it struck.

My thoughts turned to Lauren, who was to leave that afternoon. I messaged her, hoping for the best and preparing for the worst. As I waited for my bag to drop off the carousel, she responded, shaken but unscathed. I caught a taxi to the hotel in the essence of time and the circumstances.

When the dust settled, the earthquake injured twenty-two thousand, left three and a half million homeless, and killed nearly nine thousand, including twenty-two at Everest Base Camp on the Nepal side. It was the country's worst natural disaster since the 1934 Nepal-Bihar quake.*

For the first time, I questioned the existence of fate—the idea that events are pre-determined. Was I supposed to leave Nepal before it was destroyed? Was there a cosmic conductor orchestrating a master plan? Had some higher power intervened?

---

* The Nepal-Bihar quake had a magnitude of 8.1, twice as strong as the 7.8 magnitude quake. It killed roughly 12,000 people.

I spent weeks looking for flights that would have kept me an extra day or two in Kathmandu. Every reasonable option got me to Cairo around 2 a.m. Given my aversion to unfamiliar places at night, I opted for a three-day stopover in Dubai. My fortuitous choice whisked me away minutes before the region was shattered. Had I remained in Nepal, I assume I would have survived. There are no guarantees.

The saying, "I believe things happen for a reason," rationalizes chaotic events, searching for a deeper meaning. As much as I wish I had found the "why" for my good fortune, I never did. Life is a continuum of events from birth to death—no more, no less. There is no rhyme or reason for an outcome, whether good or bad. There was no higher purpose why Mom got cancer and died. Fate doesn't exist. Things just happen. Sometimes, we get lucky.

I was so exhausted at this point. The past two months were an amalgamation of planes, trains, cars, boats, buses, tuk-tuks, rickshaws, and camels. Staying in one location for more than three nights was a rarity. Knowing I would need some downtime, I found an extended-stay hotel with a kitchen, washer/dryer, dedicated Wi-Fi, and proximity to the metro for $120 per night. It was expensive compared to previous locales and a bargain by Dubai's standards.

I slept late and went around the corner to a supermarket of Western foods I had sorely missed: fresh fruits and vegetables, decent bread and cheese, an aisle of chips, and an array of chocolates. As expected in this Muslim country, it lacked alcohol. I had the foresight to buy a bottle of rum before leaving Nepal, which I wasn't supposed to bring into the hotel, a detail I omitted during check-in.

I wanted to do something meaningful on my last day in the city, so I took the metro a few stops and walked to *1 Sheikh Mohammed bin Rashid Boulevard*. Built to bring prestige to the city and diversify from an oil-based economy, after five years of construction, Burj Khalifa opened in 2009. A modern take on Islamic architecture, at 829.8 meters (2,722 ft), it's the tallest structure ever created by man.

The tapered spiral streak of metal and glass featured two observation decks, one on the 124th floor and a VIP deck twenty-four levels above, the world's highest at the time. I often chose the biggest, best, and most extreme options. At 125 AED ($34), I preferred the former. The latter was quadruple the price, and my lethargy couldn't justify the expense.

The enclosed shatterproof glass created a greenhouse effect (M). Below lingered a series of yet-to-be-completed high-rises reminiscent of Las Vegas. Both cities were tourist metropolises, containing skyscrapers on either side of a central road in a desert. The main difference was that Dubai didn't promote sex, gambling, and alcohol. I'm sure these vices existed, but they weren't on every billboard.

With the money I saved, I indulged in more Western fare in the food court: a pizza covered in processed meat, French fries, Pepsi, and gelato. With a bulging stomach, I returned to my hotel and spent the afternoon at the pool.

Dubai, as seen from the 124th floor of Burj Khalifa

55 ♦ Giza, Egypt

The four-hour flight to Cairo, Egypt didn't involve mountains, earthquakes, or sandstorms. So that was nice. But the airport reminded me of Marrakech—hot, dirty, and disorderly. The rule of the road heading into the city was for every two lanes, three cars jockeyed for position.

The next day, I headed thirteen kilometers (8 mi) southwest to the Great Pyramid of Giza. Commissioned by the Pharaoh Khufu in the twenty-sixth century BCE, it originally stood 147 meters (482 ft) tall—less than one-fifth the height of Burj Khalifa—but it held the record as the tallest man-made structure for over 3,800 years. In 1311, the Lincoln Cathedral in England surpassed it by thirteen meters (43 ft).

Initially covered in polished white limestone, the unadorned exterior of car-sized blocks of local limestone ranged from light tan to dark khaki. I climbed a few stories to the doorway entrance created in the early ninth century as a robber's tunnel.

The fee of 200 EGP ($26) took me to a narrow, chest-high tunnel that descended into a smaller, rising passage with wooden plank steps, a rickety handrail, and two-way traffic jams. After a few minutes of uphill stop-and-go, my burning legs reached the King's Chamber, the presumed purpose of the pyramid.

Dark granite blocks from Aswan, over eight hundred kilometers (500 mi) away, formed the walls and high ceilings of the large rectangular room. Non-functional video cameras hung in the corners. A single light at the far end silhouetted a broken, waist-high granite sarcophagus. The thick casing lacked a top, the edges were worn smooth, and a corner was missing a chunk. At one point, this was Khufu's final resting place (M).

He was no longer there, nor was anyone else. Mom and I had been to many dead guy dedications. This was the first, besides Hitler's, that we had to ourselves. I questioned if the social unrest and terrorism threats had scared people. Maybe going to tumultuous places was the way to do it. I didn't have to fight the crowds.

The Great Pyramid of Giza

56 ♦ Luxor, Egypt

After an overnight train to Aswan, at 3:00 a.m., I linked with ten buses forming an armed convoy to venture three hours further south to the Abu Simbel temples near the Sudanese border. In the event of an attack, I welcomed being in one of the smaller vehicles, a lesser target than the luxury coaches.

I boarded a boat to cruise north along the River Nile. Stopping in Luxor, formerly the ancient city of Thebes, a millennium after the Great Pyramid was built, the carving of tombs for pharaohs and nobles began in a valley. In 1827, Sir John Gardner Wilkinson, an English Egyptologist, devised a numbering system, marking them with KV, an abbreviation for King's Valley. Starting with KV1, the list grew to KV64. Not included in the price of admission was KV62, the only pharaoh I had heard of.

Born in 1341 BCE, Tutankhamun, aka King Tut, ascended to the throne around the age of nine. The boy-king ruled for a decade before dying and being entombed. He lay undisturbed for over three millennia until Howard Carter, a British Egyptologist, discovered Tut in 1922. Robbed twice during antiquity, unlike many tombs, he avoided extensive plundering due to sediment deposited by flash floods that became further disguised by debris and workers' huts.

Carter spent a decade excavating and cataloging over five thousand objects, including the iconic gold mask, wine jars, statues, sandals, bows, model boats, and chariots. He also found two mummy fetuses, the stillborn children Tut had with his half-sister. Royal inbreeding was common. Tut's parents were siblings.

I paid the anticipated additional fee to check him out. A flight of dark stairs descended into the earth past the two security guards. Unlike the other expansive KV tombs, Tut's was the size of a hotel suite. It's possible he died unexpectedly and was buried in a grave meant for someone who wasn't royalty. Forensic science discovered he suffered genetic abnormalities and malaria-causing parasites, making him the oldest known carrier of the disease.

He resided in an environmentally controlled glass case, re-entombed eighty-five years after being discovered. Covered by a white linen sheet, he had an overbite, cleft palate, and a deformed left foot (M). It's believed he was originally 1.67 meters (5 ft 6 in) tall, but he had shrunk to no more than 1.5 meters (5 ft). Seeing what looked like a giant piece of beef jerky made me wonder: What will Vladimir Lenin look like in a few thousand years?

The Valley of the Kings

57 ♦ Alexandria, Egypt

The overnight train from Luxor pulled into Cairo, and I caught a train to Alexandria, 180 kilometers (112 mi) northwest. Founded in 332 BCE by Alexander the Great, king of the ancient Greek kingdom of Macedon, in less than a century, it grew to one of the largest, if not the largest, cities. Home to Greeks, Jews, Syrians, and Egyptians, it became the world's cultural and intellectual center, with power second only to Rome.

In the third century BCE, the successor of Alexander the Great, a Macedonian general, Ptolemy I Soter, commissioned a momentous library to showcase Egypt's wealth and acquire the world's knowledge. A well-funded campaign purchased as many texts as possible on any subject. The older, the better, as there was less chance of copying errors. The library duplicated books that came into port, kept the originals, and returned copies to the owners. At its zenith, it housed nearly half a million scrolls containing astronomy, mathematics, natural sciences, physics, poetry, cooking, and other topics. So numerous, the concept of alphabetization was introduced, likely by the first librarian, Zenodotus.

The library's decline began with the expulsion of foreign scholars in the middle of the second century BCE, causing many to flee to parts of the Mediterranean. In 48 BCE, Julius Caesar blockaded Alexandria and burned his ships. The fire spread, partially destroying the library. In the centuries that followed, not much is known after the city came under Roman rule. It's believed the library ceased to exist sometime in the third century.

In the 1970s, a professor at Alexandria University proposed a cultural center near the site of the ancient library. In 2001, the *Bibliotheca Alexandrina* opened as one of the world's great knowledge centers.

The elliptical main reading room had gray granite vertical columns supporting a sloping glass roof that peered out at the Mediterranean, surrounded by art galleries, museums, and a dedication to Nobel laureates. I had found nerd nirvana.

A few levels down resided the rare books and manuscripts. Inside the darkened room, glass cases contained the evolution of civilization from ancient Egypt, through Jewish and Christian heritage, to the Arab and Islamic ages—originals of *The Book of the Dead* (an ancient Egyptian funerary text), Torah scrolls in Hebrew, an Italian Bible, and a tenth-century Quran.

The showpiece was a re-creation of the only surviving scroll from the original library, discovered in a mummy believed to have contained documents copied in the third century BCE. (The original scroll is in Vienna, Austria.) Resembling a frayed piece of papyrus, it symbolized man's search for knowledge (M).

Learning from our mistakes, the library partnered with a San Francisco-based non-profit organization, the Internet Archive, to create a digital backup of our history. Never again will there be a loss like the original library.

Besides fortunate health, education is my greatest gift. Whether formal or informal, it has benefited me more than I could have imagined. From finding employment to open-mindedness to understanding forces of nature to writing a book. I wouldn't be who I am without it, owing a debt of gratitude to Mom for pushing me.

Re-creation of the surviving scroll from the Great Library of Alexandria

58 ♦ Wadi Rum, Jordan

I asked the airport van driver why things were different in Jordan than in the rest of the Middle East. Unlike many nations reliant on oil, he attributed his country's success to education.

I had spent the past few months mainly in male-dominated societies, where women were second-class citizens, maintaining the status quo for centuries or longer. That wasn't the case in the capital city of Amman, where women shopped at stores run by women, groups of women lunched at cafés, and the women I traveled with received fair treatment. I welcomed the change.

A five-hour drive south, covering nearly the country's length, was Aqaba. At the crossroads of Egypt, Israel, and Saudi Arabia, this Red Sea city resided on the lone twenty-six kilometers (16 mi) of Jordanian coastline. Notwithstanding its strategic location between countries that revile each other, it was a beach town of women in bright hijabs and men with shoes, pants, and long-sleeved shirts covering the shore. Though I was in an educated, progressive country, Islam still dominated. Modest attire was a way of life.

Two hours east was Wadi Rum, the "valley of sand," where four-wheel-drive trucks carried me into the desolate region to a camp of Bedouins, descendants of nomads who roamed the Arabian and Syrian Deserts. Near midday, a tribesman suggested that I climb a rock formation. Unprepared for physical activity, I had worn sandals. The red sand was pleasant near the bottom, but twenty meters (66 ft) up, the sun-scorched silica singed my feet, causing me to dash toward the tent sanctuary. The tribesman laughed and pointed to a sliver of shade that ran the entire length of the hill.

A piece of cake compared to Wangbur, I conquered the chilled sand and jagged rocks (M). Granite and limestone cliffs, pink at the top and black at the base, surrounded the plateaued peak. The sky's blue vibrancy shifted depending on where I looked. Had it been red, I would have thought it was Mars. It makes sense why it was the prime location of my third favorite film, *The Martian*.

Wadi Rum

59 ♦ Petra, Jordan

I was eight when Mom took me to see *Indiana Jones and the Last Crusade*. My favorite scene was when the dashing hero encountered a temple carved into the rock face of a valley wall. I left the theater disbelieving that such a place existed. Unlike computer graphic-reliant movies of today, this was 1989. It was real. Years later, I learned the location.

Between Amman and Aqaba lies the city of Petra, the former capital of the Nabataeans. It's unknown when they arrived, but the area thrived in the first century BCE before the Roman Empire annexed the region in 106 CE. An earthquake in the fourth century and changing trade routes led to the city's abandonment by the mid-seventh century. In 1812, the Swiss explorer, Johann Ludwig Burckhardt, rediscovered Petra.

I passed through the security gates in mid-morning and entered the *Siq*—a slender gorge split by tectonic forces, worn smooth by water. A few hundred meters further and twenty-five years in the making, I arrived at the temple sculpted out of sandstone. The two-story rose-colored structure had an overwhelming Greek style. Six vertical columns and a triangular pediment comprised the bottom story, topped by a shorter level of a similar styling.

Known as *Al-Khazneh*, it was allegedly built in the first century as a mausoleum for a Nabatean king. Nicknamed "The Treasury," one legend says pirates stored their loot there. Another claims it was the treasury of an Egyptian pharaoh. While the exterior looked as expected, the differences were the camel and donkey rides, a café falsely advertising free WiFi, and the fat "Roman soldiers" to take pictures with for a fee. If you didn't enlist their services, they would sit in front of the façade until you paid them to move, smashing my childhood expectations. I had to improvise again.

At the far edge of the city, up eight hundred stairs, sat *Ad-Deir*, "The Monastery." Nearly identical to The Treasury, but slightly larger and less preserved, a horizontal crack bisected the first story. Everything below the jagged line had eroded. Like its counterpart, it appeared in a film, *Transformers: Revenge of the Fallen*.

A set of uneven rock steps led to an outcrop (M) surrounded by mountains similar to Wadi Rum, where I watched the sunset for an hour, feeling disheartened about The Treasury but content with my consolation prize. The downside of high expectations is that they're rarely fulfilled. Life isn't like the movies.

Ad-Deir, The Monastery

60 ♦ Amman, Jordan

A forty-five-minute drive from central Amman leads to a tasteful resort with a swimming pool, an alcohol-free bar, and a buffet offering pasta and bread pudding. A long flight of stairs ended at a beach of coarse sand, where I waded into the slimy water up to my ankles. I sat down when it reached my thighs, submerging to my neck, and bobbed in the Dead Sea.

Aptly named as everything struggles to survive, there are no plants, animals, or fish—only microbes and unique algae. The world's deepest hypersaline lake boasts a salinity of 34 percent, ten times saltier than the ocean.*

I thrashed about, failing to get anywhere due to the buoyancy. I inhaled a mouthful of battery acid and gagged. A burning sensation inundated my freshly shaved neck and the gash on my foot from clipping a sharp rock in Petra. I felt sympathy for anyone who got water in their eyes.

The worst pain emanated from my nether region. I have never had chlamydia, but I imagine it was similar to that. Months earlier, I went to the travel clinic to get vaccinated for hepatitis A & B, polio, typhoid, yellow fever, and Japanese encephalitis. The nurse also prescribed doxycycline, an antibiotic and anti-malaria medication, for the Philippines. For reasons unknown, she mentioned it could treat the venereal disease.

Despite the discomfort, I paused to appreciate my situation. Weeks earlier, I battled altitude sickness near Mount Everest. A few flights and buses later, at 430 meters (1,410 ft) below sea level, I was floating at the lowest land-accessible point on the planet (M). While the past few months had their literal highs and lows, they had been the most captivating of my life.

* The Dead Sea is the world's seventh saltiest body of water.

The Dead Sea

61 ♦ Bethlehem, West Bank, Palestine

I exited Jordan and approached Israeli passport control. The girl behind the glass asked if I had been to Sudan, Iraq, Syria, and other Muslim countries. I said, "No," and she slammed her stamp into my passport. I had forgotten to get an endorsed loose-leaf piece of paper to avoid a permanent record of my visit. I had no desire to see those countries, but the barely dried ink ensured I never would until I got a new passport.

The New Zealander, Bob, had a tougher experience. He and his wife, Rachel, had traveled for nine months. His epic beard, along with stamps from African countries (none on the Israeli blacklist), caused a twenty-minute Q&A before he could pass. Due to the threat of terrorism and ISIS, the Israelis weren't taking any chances.

We arrived an hour later at a building of considerable age made of pale bricks. Small windows dotted the angular walls, tiny crosses perched on the roof, and scaffolding covered one corner. What appeared to be Eastern Orthodox Christian pilgrims streamed inside the main entrance, so we snuck into a side door and descended into a lavishly decorated cavern. Black streaks flowed through the beige marble floor, religious artwork covered the walls, and gold lanterns hung from the ceiling. A line of anxious people stretched to ground level, waiting for their moment at a silver star embedded in the floor.

My guide strolled past it and nonchalantly said, "That's where Jesus was supposedly born." My lack of religious knowledge struck again. I stood in the Grotto of the Church of the Nativity, the oldest continuously worshipped site in Christianity.

Following the crucifixion of Jesus, Christianity spread across the Middle East, the Mediterranean, Western Europe, North Africa, and the East. Early Christians faced persecution throughout the Roman Empire until Emperor Constantine I issued the Edict of Milan in 313, which legalized Christian worship.

He and his mother, Helena, commissioned a church in Bethlehem in 327 on the assumed birthplace of Jesus, which took twelve years to finish. It changed hands over the centuries and was either restored or ignored, depending on who controlled it. Earthquakes damaged it in the mid-1830s, and a power struggle among the Ottomans, France, Russia, and the Greeks led to neglect. Near the end of World War I, the British captured Jerusalem from the Ottomans and carried out repairs over the following decades.

Our small group was allowed to cut in front of the long queue. I approached the altar surrounding the 14-point silver star installed by the Catholics in 1717, confiscated by the Greeks in 1847, and replaced by the Turks in 1853. Fifteen silver lamps surrounded it—four for the Catholics, five for the Armenian Apostolic, and six for the Greek Orthodox. Each group controlled parts of the church and has been at odds for centuries.

I knelt near the Latin inscription, *Hic De Virgine Maria Jesus Christus Natus Est-1717* (Here of the Virgin Mary Jesus Christ was born-1717), and prayed for Mom, again hoping to bring her salvation, if such a thing exists (M).

Despite its slow start, tumultuous rise, schisms, and violent past, whether by choice or force, nearly one in three people affiliate with Christianity, making it the world's most popular religion. There has never been a more impactful birth in human history.

The supposed location of the birth of Jesus Christ

62 ♦ Jerusalem, Israel

My first day in Jerusalem corresponded with Jerusalem Day, commemorating Israel's repossession of the city from Jordan following the defeat of Egypt, Jordan, and Syria during the Six-Day War in 1967. Mobs of young Jewish men chanted, marched, and waved the national flag as they emulated fans in a sporting match.

The annual holiday culminates with a procession of ultranationalists through the Muslim Quarter, often leading to racial slurs and violence. I remained unafraid but kept my distance from the energized youths, seeing how the situation could spiral out of control. The one commonality, regardless of race, religion, or nationality, is that groups of adolescent males are catalysts for stupidity.

Days later, I experienced the most confusing yet enlightening hours of my life. I walked to Mount Zion Catholic Cemetery and passed through the iron gate. Tall brown grass and faded bushes surrounded rows of monotonous graves with protruding crosses. One, however, was distinctive. That of Oskar Schindler.

Born in 1908 in Austria-Hungary, the flawed man struggled with alcoholism, debt, and infidelity. He became a Nazi spy in 1936, but the Czechs arrested him for espionage two years later. Released under the Munich Agreement, which ceded parts of Czechoslovakia to Germany, he joined the Nazi Party the following year.

As a party member, the Catholic Schindler became a successful industrialist in Poland using Jewish and Polish labor during World War II. But his initial goal of profit shifted to protecting his workers, leading him to spend his fortune on bribes and black-market gifts. After the war, he emigrated to Argentina in 1949 and returned to Germany in 1958, where several failed businesses resulted in bankruptcy. He survived on donations from the *Schindlerjuden* (Schindler's Jews) until his death in 1974 at age 66.

His story became the core of the 1982 book *Schindler's Ark* and the 1993 film *Schindler's List*. I first watched the movie at age 13, during the infancy of my Holocaust comprehension. When I saw it again before visiting Auschwitz, I realized the magnanimity of his actions. I always tear up at the scene depicting a line of Jews paying tribute to him, each placing a stone on his grave, as is tradition.

His coffin-sized slab appeared just as it had on the screen. Still visible were a cross, his name, pertinent dates, and the Hebrew inscription חֲסִידֵי אֻמּוֹת הָעוֹלָם (Righteous Among the Nations), an honor bestowed upon non-Jews who risked their lives to save Jews during the Holocaust. A second inscription in German read DER UNVERGESSLICHE LEBENRETTER 1200 VERFOLGTER JUDEN (The Unforgettable Lifesaver of 1200 Persecuted Jews). With my family's history, I placed a rock on his grave.

The Temple Mount became the next objective. Jewish tradition asserts it's the site of Solomon's Temple (the First Temple), built in the tenth century BCE, which is believed to house the Ark of the Covenant, a wooden chest covered in gold containing the Ten Commandments. Destroyed in the sixth century BCE, the Second Temple replaced it until its destruction in the first century CE. Muslims assert it's where Mohammad ascended to Heaven during his Night Journey in 621.

I programmed a walking route into my phone. Bob, Rachel, and I reached the entrance, but Israeli guards with machine guns stopped us. None spoke English. After some hand signals, we ascertained that only Muslims could pass. We retraced the maze of streets and asked for directions, which led us to a narrow, elevated walkway. Halfway across the footbridge, we watched worshippers at the Western Wall, a segment of the Second Temple.

The height of many men, each level of blocks was smaller than the one below. Due to the rabbinic prayer ban on the Temple Mount, the Western Wall is the closest Jews can get. Worshippers were divided by gender. The women remained calm and orderly. The men devolved into chaos. Those with scrolls of the Torah were attacked by other Jewish men, only to have more men break up the skirmishes. These outbursts erupted multiple times within the few minutes we watched. We didn't know why.

A few steps further brought us to the Gate of Moors, the only gate of eleven open to non-Muslims. We could enter for tourism, but praying, religious texts, and religious apparel were forbidden. Despite wearing shorts covering my knees, I bought a cheap shawl to wrap around my legs. I hadn't encountered this problem since I was in Bangkok.

The Dome of the Rock, an octagonal shrine completed in the seventh century on the site of the Second Temple, occupied the courtyard's center. The gold dome installed in the second half of the twentieth century made it the city's most distinguishable landmark.

Inside sat the Foundation Stone, which, according to Jews, is where God created Adam, the first human, and Abraham almost sacrificed his son, Isaac, to prove his faith. After the Crusaders captured Jerusalem in 1099, they converted the building to a Christian church. Less than a century later, in 1187, Muslims recaptured and rededicated it as an Islamic shrine.

As non-Muslims, we couldn't enter. The best we could do is take pictures. Even that caused contention. After snapping a photo of Bob with his arm around Rachel, a guard chastised us. He took offense at the sight of a man and a woman touching.

We reemerged into the city's chaos with one last task—finish the Stations of the Cross. Though scholarly and canonical differences abound, around 30-33 AD,* following Jesus's arrest and trial by the Sanhedrin priests, he was tried and sentenced to death by Pontius Pilate, the prefect of the Roman province of Judaea. Jesus carried his cross outside the city walls, was secured to it by nails driven through his hands and feet, raised into the air, and died painfully.

The *Via Dolorosa* (Way of Suffering), an old street in the city, has the first nine stations marked by black metallic discs.

The Stations of the Cross

I. Jesus is condemned to death
II. Jesus receives His Cross
III. Jesus falls the first time under His Cross
IV. Jesus meets Mary His Mother
V. Simon of Cyrene helps Jesus to carry His Cross
VI. Veronica wipes the face of Jesus
VII. Jesus falls the second time
VIII. Jesus speaks to the women of Jerusalem
IX. Jesus falls the third time

The final five reside in the Church of the Holy Sepulchre.

X. Jesus is stripped of His garments
XI. Jesus is nailed to the Cross
XII. Jesus dies on the Cross
XIII. Jesus is taken down from the Cross
XIV. Jesus is laid in the Tomb

---

* The Gregorian calendar, the world's most widely accepted calendar, is hallmarked from the birth of Jesus. Named after Pope Gregory XIII, it was established in 1582, replacing the Julian calendar, proposed by Julius Caesar, that took effect in 45 BC. AD is an abbreviation of *Anno Domini*, medieval Latin for "in the year of the Lord." BC is an abbreviation of *Before Christ*.

Commissioned by Constantine I in 326, the year before the Church of the Nativity, walls surrounded a stone courtyard on three sides. Arched windows and domes of differing techniques exacerbated the asymmetry. The flag of the Brotherhood of the Holy Sepulcher topped a corner bell tower. A five-rung ladder rested against a second-story wall leading to a bar-covered window. Termed the "immovable ladder," it was a visual representation of the Status Quo, an agreement amongst religious groups sharing the holy sites around Jerusalem and Bethlehem. Moving it requires agreement by all six ecumenical Christian orders.

A wooden doorway adjacent to an identical one bricked up long ago served as the entrance. We passed the stairway leading to Calvary, the supposed site of the crucifixion. People kissed the Stone of Anointing, the supposed preparation site of Jesus's body for burial.

Males at the Western Wall (left) and the Dome of the Rock (right)

Inside the Rotunda, a circular domed room with a hole in the ceiling, stood the Aedicule. The boxy shrine protected the Holy Sepulchre, the supposed location of the tomb of Jesus. A line wrapped around it that we couldn't bypass this time. A group of Chinese stood before us. Eastern Orthodox women slipped in behind and nudged us forward as emotion surged through them.

Three people were allowed inside the cramped altar. Bob, Rachel, and I stepped in and knelt (M). Like other areas of the church, dim candles illuminated depictions of a crucified Christ. Per usual, I prayed for Mom and left.

Like the Church of the Nativity, it was a place she would have appreciated due to her faith. For me, it marked my last religious-inspired location.

The Aedicule

I had explored the world's predominant religions and prayed to their gods. It was always to no avail. Was I doing it wrong? Was God listening and not answering? Was anyone listening? Was there a right God? Was there a God?

Having never found any answers, I chose to have faith in myself. A belief that my successes and failures are the result of my decisions, not those of an invisible force. If God, Allah, Buddha, or Brahma exist, they gave me nothing.

63 ♦ Santorini, Greece

I arrived at the Tel Aviv airport three hours early and entered the non-Israeli passport queue behind two American girls who were questioned for half an hour. When it was my turn, a young man, barely able to shave, scrutinized every visa. He flipped forward and backward, backward and forward, fretting over the Muslim countries. He repeated the process over and over. No answer I gave satisfied him. He was stalling.

He handed my passport to his boss, a slightly older young man with a peach fuzz face, who asked what I was doing in Israel. I told him I was traveling in the Middle East. He asked to look at my pictures. I showed him. He asked why I had come to Tel Aviv. I told him this was the easiest place to fly to Greece. He asked why I wasn't going to Cyprus. I told him I liked Greece. This line of questioning went on for twenty minutes until I convinced him I wasn't a terrorist. I could now check in for my flight.

After clearing the official passport control, security halted me due to my flagged boarding pass. I emptied my bag of electronics, which were scanned multiple times and swabbed for explosive residue. I envisioned a trip to a tiny room for the rubber glove treatment. Thankfully, I didn't have to assume the position and arrived at the gate just as my flight was boarding.

My destination was Santorini, an island in the Aegean Sea, two hundred kilometers (124 mi) southeast of mainland Greece. I had spent three hours there on my first overseas trip as part of a low-budget cruise. When the ship docked in the caldera of the quarter moon-shaped island, I took a tender to shore and a cable car to the clifftop. The azure water, bright sun, and white houses manifested the most breathtaking panorama of my limited travels.

Returning four years later, I booked a one-bedroom apartment for forty dollars a night in Perissa, on the island's southeast side. I couldn't afford anything that replicated the postcards, despite being a few weeks before the tourist season. I didn't mind. I was ecstatic to be in Europe, my home away from home, where merchandise had price tags, girls wore short shorts, and cheap beer flowed. I cracked one open at 9 a.m. on the black sand beach to celebrate.

After a few days of leisure, I rented a four-wheeler, a mode of transportation I dislike more than bicycles, and set off for Oia, twenty-three kilometers (14 mi) away on the extreme northwest of the island. Becoming ever braver with the throttle, I arrived an hour later, took a quick walk, and began making my way back.

I spent hours searching for my perfect memory, only to come up empty-handed. I took side roads, hoping I might find it. Near dusk, I got frustrated and abandoned my quest. I had failed again.

Driving along the main road, a sign for a church caught my eye. Done with religion, this was more of a curiosity. I veered off the pavement onto a rough dirt path, terminating at a cliff overlooking the caldera. A set of crude, uneven stairs led down to a Greek Orthodox church big enough for a handful of parishioners.

On my ascent, I came across a hole eroded into the rock face wide enough to squeeze through. The other side presented an alternate breathtaking view of sheer bluffs dotted with white houses. I sat on the ledge, watching the island change color with the setting sun, a comforting ending to a challenging day in paradise (M).

Wanting to get back before dark, I returned to my four-wheeler. Parked nearby, a man a few years my junior sat on a similar off-road vehicle. Also named Scott, he and his new bride from Philadelphia were halfway through their two-week honeymoon.

As his first experience abroad, anti-American sentiment concerned him. I couldn't fault his anxiety. I, too, was skittish my first time overseas. I had no energy to tell him where I had been over the past three months. So I said "see ya' later" and dropped off my four-wheeler. In hindsight, I felt relieved. If I had found my spot again, I would have ruined my perfect memory. If something is flawless, leave it alone.

Santorini

64 ♦ Rineia, Greece

I went to a bar in Vlichada, on Santorini's southernmost point, approached a group that appeared to be waiting around, and introduced myself. As we talked, more travelers trickled in. By the time everyone arrived, sixteen of us had split into boats of eight.

My shipmates made me apprehensive. There was a mother and daughter from California, a young Israeli couple, a young Canadian couple just starting to date, and a middle-aged Canadian man with whom I would share a room. On the other boat, there were three married couples from the U.S. and two girls in their early 20s, whom I thought would get along better due to their homogenous makeup. I only had to endure a week if things didn't go well.

The fifty-foot vessel had four closet-sized guest cabins, three minuscule bathrooms, and a kitchen with a common area. The skipper, a 27-year-old guy from the Azores, an island chain 1,400 kilometers (870 mi) west of Portugal, who had sailed more miles than I had driven, enjoyed a cabin at the front. With no set itinerary, our path would be at his discretion and the winds.

The plan was to pull anchor in the late morning, sail, have lunch, swim, and then sail to the next port. He took us to Ios, Schinoussa, Koufonisia, and Naxos—quintessential Greece, where life moved slowly and the locals welcomed us.

I spent nearly every waking moment with my shipmates, playing games, telling stories, singing songs, or making fun of each other. I hadn't laughed that hard in a long time. Seeing how close we had become, the skipper suggested a beach barbecue for our last night on Rineia, nine kilometers (5.6 mi) southwest of Mykonos.

He dropped me on the abandoned rocky-hilled fourteen-square-kilometer (5.4 mi^2) island to gather firewood. There wasn't much to burn besides old boards and driftwood. Before Mom's diagnosis, she had booked a trip to the Greek Isles, which she never took, but hoped to visit one day. Sauntering along the empty beach, surrounded by rugged hills, dotted with dry grass and scattered stones, for a few moments, we had an island to ourselves (M).

Rineia Island

65 ♦ Pripyat, Ukraine

Sondre and I arrived at the KFC near the central train station in Kyiv, Ukraine, at 8 a.m. We sat outside as more guys our age emerged with similar confused looks. A Ukrainian girl exited a 1980s full-size conversion van. After confirming our identities, the ten of us piled in. The girl handed out paperwork and put on a movie. For the next hour, we watched the CRT television as it educated us on Chernobyl, the world's worst nuclear disaster.

The V.I. Lenin Nuclear Power Station was a group of RBMK-1000 nuclear reactors located ninety-five kilometers (59 mi) north of Kyiv. At 1:23 a.m. on April 26, 1986, a system test of Reactor 4 was conducted to assess cooling capabilities after an emergency shutdown, marking the fourth such attempt.

Like all manmade disasters, a series of unfortunate events unfolded. Fundamental design flaws, combined with human error, caused an uncontrollable chain reaction. An explosion blew the two-thousand-ton roof off the reactor. Seconds later, a more powerful blast ripped the reactor apart. Two workers died.

The Soviets didn't disclose the accident. Two days later, a nuclear plant in Sweden, 1,100 kilometers (680 mi) away, registered increased radiation levels. After confirming the release wasn't local, they deduced a severe failure had occurred in the Soviet Union, which denied the incident but eventually conceded what was already known. That evening on state TV, a brief announcement was read:

> An accident has occurred at the Chernobyl Nuclear Power Plant, and one of the reactors has been damaged. Steps are being taken to deal with the situation and aid is being given to those affected. The government has formed a commission of Inquiry.
>
> – April 28, 1986, (21:00)

The catastrophe released an estimated four hundred times the radiation of the atomic bomb dropped on Hiroshima, reaching Wales, Ireland, and Norway, with the heaviest fallout hitting Belarus, Ukraine, and Russia. Within four months, twenty-eight people, mainly rescue workers and plant personnel, had died of acute radiation sickness. Unofficial fatalities, mostly from excess cancers, range from a few thousand to tens of thousands.*

Over six hundred thousand "liquidators" were enlisted to deal with the contamination. The civilian and military personnel removed debris, dug tunnels, and exterminated animals. The costs for containment and decontamination accounted for substantial portions of the annual budgets of affected countries for decades.

Energy shortages kept the plant operational. A 1991 fire caused irreparable damage and forced the decommissioning of Reactor 2. Reactors 1 and 3 shut down in 1996 and 2000, respectively.

Every resident within a thirty-kilometer (19 mi) radius was evacuated from the Zone of Alienation. The van stopped at a guardhouse marking the entrance. Akin to a border crossing, we had our passports examined. Another checkpoint demarcated the ten-

---

* The testing of nuclear weapons during the Cold War is estimated to have released 100 to 1,000 times more radioactive material than Chernobyl.

kilometer (6 mi) zone for a second review. The girl advised us to put on long sleeves. Despite the summer heat, we obliged.

The van passed through a row of trees, rounded a corner, and parked two hundred meters (660 ft) from Reactor 4, protected by a high wall topped with barbed wire (M). By December 1986, a hastily built concrete and steel sarcophagus had been placed around the reactor, encasing the remaining uranium and plutonium. At the end of its twenty to thirty-year life cycle, rusted holes allowed rainwater to enter and radiation to escape.

The solution was the €1.5 billion New Safe Confinement (NSC). The world's largest movable structure, resembling a polished semi-circular airplane hangar, would be rolled on rails the following year to encapsulate the old one and contain the radiation for a century. The site is slated to be cleared by 2065, but the region won't be safe for human habitation for hundreds or thousands of years.

Three kilometers (1.9 mi) away lingered Pripyat. Established in 1970 to support the power plant, on the day of the disaster, its fifty thousand residents went about their routines. Within hours, dozens fell ill, complaining of headaches, coughing, and vomiting. The next day, they heard the following:

> Attention. Attention. Attention. Attention. Dear comrades, the City Counsel of the People's Deputies informs that due to an accident at Chernobyl nuclear power plant in the city of Pripyat adverse radiation levels have evolved. Party and Soviet bodies, military units are taking necessary measures. However, in order to provide complete safety for the people, especially for children, it is necessary to temporarily evacuate city residents to evacuation points in Kyiv oblast. In order to do this, to each apartment house today, April 27, starting at 2:00 p.m. buses will be provided escorted by Militsiya and members of the city's Ispolkom (executive committee). It is recommended to take with you: IDs, basic necessities, and foodstuff for the first time. Heads of enterprises and public offices have designated vital

> personnel who stay to ensure the normal functioning of the city. All apartment houses during the evacuation will be guarded by Militsiya. Comrades, while temporarily leaving your houses please, do not forget to close windows, to turn off all electrical and gas appliances, to close water taps. Please remain calm, be organized and maintain order when executing the temporary evacuation.

Under secrecy, before news spread beyond the Soviet Union, the residents were loaded onto buses and taken away. The city was emptied within hours and has stayed that way ever since.

Open to tourists for four years, but four years before the HBO miniseries, I found the sweet spot. We went hours without seeing another soul and enjoyed relative autonomy. Most of the former residents' belongings lay strewn in multi-story apartment buildings: clothes, books, beds, tables, chairs, gas masks, children's toys, medicine, alcohol, and anything not worth looting.

Inside Pripyat

From the roof of a twenty-story apartment building, Reactor 4 and the NSC featured prominently. The trees of the abandoned city had grown tall and plentiful, plants enveloped everything in their path, and grass pushed through cracks in the concrete.

The stadium, pool, hospital, fire station, theatre, and amusement park had rotting floors, peeling paint, dissolved ceilings, corroded metal, and piles of glass. Faded portraits of Soviet leaders leaned against decaying walls. One featuring Vladimir Lenin, after whom the power plant is named, stared back at his collapsed utopia.

The disaster and cover-up sparked *Glasnost*, Russian for "openness and transparency." The eighteenth-century term acquired new meaning during the mid-1980s with its adoption by Mikhail Gorbachev, the Soviet Union's eighth and final leader. In conjunction with *Perestroika,* his ill-conceived reformation of the political and economic systems, the USSR collapsed under its own weight in December 1991. The fallout from Chernobyl hammered the final nail in the empire's coffin.

Reactor 4 at Chernobyl

66 ♦ London, England

I went to Sondre's home in southeast Norway. Parting ways in China, I had promised to attend his birthday party. Beyond burnt out, I spent most of my time sleeping in preparation for the final leg, ten days in England.

One afternoon in London, I walked along the south bank of the River Thames. Passing every kind of person imaginable, each seemed to know their purpose. Whether making a business deal, parenting children, or chatting with friends, they were focused, composed, and driven. Nearly finished with my most ambitious trip, I had wrongly assumed I would have gained some clarity about my life. But the anxiety I had felt before the Philippines came rushing back in the opposite form.

Having spent the last four months mostly around people in their early 20s, I heard "I'm so jealous" more than ever. I understood their feelings and recognized my privilege. But secretly, I envied them for discovering travel at such a young age. I once again questioned my choices. Had I wasted my prime travel years working a corporate job? Should I have bought that house? Why did I wait so long to visit Europe? Why didn't I take a gap year? Nearly two-thirds through the 100 Places After, I had caught up on much of the lost time. Still, I wish I had prioritized travel earlier. When would I figure it out?

While drowning in my self-pity, I had another epiphany. Nobody truly has everything figured out. Those who appear to have the most direction are often the most lost—case in point: me. On the surface, I was living the dream, but I faced ups and downs, just like everyone else. There were days of climbing mountains and days of shitting my pants. I needed to accept that the days ahead would work themselves out, whether good or bad.

I grabbed a beer at a pop-up bar, disheartened to drink it alone. I slowly sipped as the man on the guitar started playing *Ho Hey* by the Lumineers, my theme song from New Zealand. The first few notes curled my lip into a nostalgic grin. By the song's end, I had emptied my cup.

I tossed a pound in the man's guitar case and climbed the stairs to the Hungerford Footbridge (M), a pedestrian walkway across the Thames near the London Eye and Big Ben. Aside from a bit of self-loathing, it had been a day many would have gladly lived. I had to appreciate that.

As luck would have it, I reconvened with three friends from New Zealand the next day. We drove two hours north to Cambridge to see Stacey, the girl I had visited on my first birthday without Mom. Six months earlier, her father suffered a heart attack, passing away the morning after Christmas. Having lost my parents, she asked for advice. The best I could say was that the first year would be the worst, with each day hurting a little less. Still, important days would be triggers. Her wedding would be one of those.

Stacey's nuptials fell on Father's Day. With her mum walking her down the aisle, neither could hold back their tears. The brief afternoon ceremony turned into a memorable celebration with a musical tribute to her dad, in the form of *Sandstorm* by Darude. When the party ended, I headed back to a cottage in the English countryside. Halfway there, the clock struck midnight, marking the start of my 34th year of existence, the third occurrence without Mom.

Reemphasizing my advice to Stacey, it hurt less than the first and the second. So uneventful, after a "see ya' later" to my New Zealand friends, I caught a train back to London and spent the evening alone enjoying a show on the West End. I flew home the next day, completing my voyage around the world.

On the Hungerford Footbridge

A Tale of Two Styles

67 ♦ Glengariff, Ireland

There are two ways to travel. The first is to plan every detail, creating a seamless yet regimented itinerary. The second is to go with the flow. Time, money, visas, and ease of movement determine my choice. While I lean towards the former, I'm not opposed to the latter.

A few months after England, I arranged six weeks in Europe. The first half with Jeremy was well organized and based on two specific events, which I will elaborate on later. In the meantime, we would spend a week in Ireland. With the island (including Northern Ireland) being slightly larger than South Carolina, it's possible to drive from north to south in six hours and east to west in three.

Passing through a hamlet on the way from Cork to Killarney, the navigation system led us up a twisting road. Becoming increasingly rural, the only people we saw were a pair of curious children. As we climbed, the course pavement for two cars narrowed to gravel just wide enough for one. I avoided boulders, ditches, and livestock as the smell of the overheating clutch drifted into the cabin. With no way to turn back and no signs of civilization for the past hour, I imagined spending the night in the car waiting for rescue.

We reached the summit of this 519-meter (1,703 ft) highland. A rock atop a stone pile marked the spot in Gaelic—Priest's Leap. I parked near a steel pipe cross sticking out of a boulder (M) overlooking a valley of brown and green rolling hills tumbling to a lake. Unprepared for the cold wind that never stops, we scurried back to the car. In an almost mirror image of the morning, Jeremy nervously gripped the door handle until we hit the paved road. When we arrived in Killarney an hour later, just a few days into the trip, we were already tired of each other.

Priest's Leap

68 ♦ Manchester, England

My parents signed me up for soccer when I was five, a decision that taught me about winning, losing, teamwork, and physical fitness. My father didn't witness many of these benefits, dying two years later. By default, I became the man of the house. Wanting to instill some positive male influence in my life, the summer I turned 10, Mom hosted some British soccer coaches who had come over for the summer to conduct youth camps. In return, I got free coaching.

The first to arrive were Noel, a glowing blonde from the Isle of Man, and Carl, a red-mulleted former professional goalkeeper from Telford, fifty miles (80 km) south of Manchester. I don't know how they felt about getting stuck with a widow and her young son, but they were as lovely as could be.

For the next half-decade, coaches came and went. The constant was Carl, who returned every year, staying longer each time. With his desire to remain in the U.S., Mom agreed he could live with us. The mutually beneficial arrangement meant cheap rent for him and a role model for me.

One of our pastimes was following Carl's favorite team, Manchester United, whose support was spurred by watching games with his father. Although our relationship resembled that of big brother and little brother, mimicking the origin of his fandom, I, too, supported the club of the most prominent man in my life.

As Carl built a life in Kansas, he founded a team that I played on until I went to university. I felt better knowing he would be at home while I was away. I started most matches, but I attended the school for only one year before falling out with my coach and transferring to the University of Kansas.

As life isn't static, after nearly a decade, Carl moved out and married a wonderful woman. We stayed in touch, often spending holidays together and discussing Manchester United. He was ecstatic to hear I would be attending a game, the first event in the planned timeline.

As one of the year's prime matches against their greatest rival, Liverpool FC (the two clubs are the most successful in English football), I used the secondary market to buy tickets, the most expensive I had ever purchased. We met our contact at a hotel bar near the stadium, shook hands, and he handed me an envelope worth more than some people's rent.

We had seats twenty rows up (M), in line with the penalty spot. To our right sat the Liverpool supporters, partitioned by security guards in every row. Dubbed the *English Disease* in the 1960s, hooliganism has stigmatized the sport ever since. The posturing felt no different than American football, fraught with intoxicated zealots.

The match kicked off at 5:30 p.m., and the seventy-five thousand fans erupted with chants and songs, neither of which I knew. The first forty-five minutes ended dull and scoreless. Having played and followed the sport for three decades, I knew that could be the final result. My fear subsided with goals from Manchester United in the 49th, 70th, and 86th minutes, and a stunner from Liverpool in the 84th. The 3-1 storybook ending was worth the price of admission.

The Manchester United game

69 ♦ Paris, France

The purpose of the Organization is to contribute to peace and security by promoting collaboration among the nations through education, science and culture in order to further universal respect for justice, for the rule of law and for the human rights and fundamental freedoms which are affirmed for the peoples of the world, without distinction of race, sex, language or religion by the Charter of the United Nations.

— Constitution of the United Nations Educational, Scientific and Cultural Organization (1945)

Little things turn into big things. The tension with Jeremy started in the car in Ireland. The lack of separation worsened over four days in Scotland, three days in London, and four days in Paris.

On our penultimate day in the City of Lights, my request for some time apart angered him due to his so-called inability to navigate without a map or a phone. As we walked past a newsstand, I bought the most extensive map available, threw it at him, and said,

"Problem solved." It was a dickhead move, but I had dual intentions. First was the need for time by myself. There are only a few people I can always be with. He wasn't one of them. Second, I wanted him to learn how to get around on his own, hoping it might be a first step toward solo travel. Hiking the Inca Trail was at the top of Jeremy's bucket list. I sensed his disappointment about not being included, but I needed to do that alone.

One of my strongest recommendations is to take a solo trip. Start small, but go somewhere new. Step outside your comfort zone. You will make mistakes, but the best part is nobody will know about them. Come home and evaluate. You may decide you never want to do it again, or maybe you discover your adventurous spirit. While I often faced loneliness, traveling alone forced me to devise a plan, execute it, and solve problems as they came up, which instilled the confidence to do it again. If I had waited for someone to join me everywhere, I wouldn't have gone anywhere.

With the reprieve from my shadow and a spring in my step, I aimed to get Mom to the top of the Eiffel Tower. I left my apartment in the 5th arrondissement and walked northwest for an hour. Initially exuberant, with each step closer, the knot in my stomach tightened. The foul-smelling mud in the open field next to the tower intensified my intestinal quandary.

I had two options to reach the top of the iron lattice icon with concave sides tapering to a point: multiple elevators or stairs plus an elevator. Still energized by my newfound autonomy, I climbed seven hundred steps to the second level without stopping. Forced to buy an elevator ticket to the third, I grew restless in the queue and debated forfeiting the six euros. I crammed into the elevator for the ascent, stepped off, completed one lap, and returned to the second level. I raced down and away without looking back. To this day, I can't explain why I felt such disdain.

I checked my phone and saw an email response from the United Nations Educational, Scientific and Cultural Organization (UNESCO), requesting to join a group tour of their world headquarters. None were available that day, but they invited me to view an art exhibit. I had my ticket into one of the world's great humanitarian organizations.

During World War II, European countries fighting the Nazis and their allies met in the United Kingdom to rebuild the educational system after the war. The idea gained momentum and spread to more countries, which held a London conference in November 1945 to establish an organization promoting a culture of peace.

A brisk fifteen-minute walk got me to the World Heritage Center at *7 Place de Fontenoy*. I orbited the gated perimeter, stopping at an exhibit dedicated to the Schengen Area. In 1985, Belgium, France, West Germany, Luxembourg, and the Netherlands signed an agreement in Schengen, Luxembourg, allowing borderless travel between them. This gesture of trust spread to more of Europe. As of 2015, it included twenty-six countries, encompassing more than four hundred million people.

I took a moment to appreciate photos of mundane activities at borders without walls. A man rode his bike along a mountain pass between Austria and Switzerland. Rowboats were beached between Bulgaria and Romania. A woman held her child in a field between Hungary and Slovakia. A young couple lay on a hill between France and Italy. These snapshots displayed the continent's progress since its evisceration during the first half of the twentieth century.

After passing security, I exchanged my ID for a visitor's badge. My shorts and T-shirt drew puzzled looks from the professional men and women. Hidden in a quiet corner, the art gallery showcased a few paintings and handmade jewelry featuring a stone endemic to the Dominican Republic. As the only visitor there, the artist approached and asked what I did. I told him I was a traveler. With vigor, he said he was, too. We chatted for a few minutes, extolling the merits of exploration, until he insisted I watch a video of the poem "Ithaka," narrated by Sean Connery (yes, that Sean Connery).

I left the artist with a handshake and went outside to a grass courtyard containing the Square of Tolerance. The gift from Israel honored Yitzhak Rabin, the country's fifth prime minister. He received the Nobel Peace Prize in 1994, along with Shimon Peres, the Foreign Minister of Israel, and Yasser Arafat, the leader of the Palestine Liberation Organization, for their efforts to promote peace in the Middle East. A year later, an Israeli ultranationalist opposing the initiative assassinated Rabin in Tel Aviv.

An olive tree stood before a white concrete wall engraved with the preamble of UNESCO's Constitution in English, French, Chinese, Spanish, Hindi, Italian, Portuguese, and Russian. Hoping for peace in the Middle East, Arabic and Hebrew were next to each other at the top. In English, it read:

> SINCE WARS BEGIN IN THE MINDS OF MEN,
> IT IS IN THE MINDS OF MEN THAT THE DEFENSES
> OF PEACE MUST BE CONSTRUCTED

As I stood in front of this wish for the world, all negative feelings from earlier vanished, replaced by a sensation I had been searching for over a year since Oslo—hope (M).

I left UNESCO and went back to the apartment to see that Jeremy had survived. I was proud of him, and he seemed proud of himself. We had cooled off and were better for it. Ironically, a few years later, he got a job with extensive domestic travel. However, his dream of hiking the Inca Trail remains just that—a dream.

The UNESCO World Heritage Center

70 ♦ Munich, Germany

I correctly assumed that my best mate and I would be at odds, so I coordinated our *Oktoberfest* arrival to coincide with some friends, our second planned event. The origins of the world's largest *Volkfest* (People's Fair), date back to the October 12, 1810, with the marriage of Crown Prince Ludwig I to Princess Therese of Saxe-Hildburghausen in the fields near the Munich city gates. The area was named *Theresienwiese* (Therese's Meadow) to pay homage to the new princess, and a series of horse races ensued.

The city repeated the festivities the following year and established it as an annual event in 1819, except during years affected by war, disease, or other calamities. Despite being called *Oktoberfest*, the celebration takes place in late September, with a few days spilling into October. The dates moved forward at some point to utilize the better weather.

Amid flashing lights, buzzers, carnival rides, and thousands of people, we entered *Theresienwiese* (M) at 11 a.m. and met up with Annalise, a German native attending her tenth consecutive *Oktoberfest*.

We walked into one of the many makeshift beer halls, hoping to find a table for eight. Nearly the entire six-thousand-person capacity was elbow-to-elbow with partygoers standing on benches, singing, and pounding beers.

We moved to a quieter tent and snagged an empty table where casual drinkers had come to grab a bite. The waitress brought a few liters of transparent lager as we waited for the others to arrive. With real estate disappearing, we maneuvered empty glasses to appear like the others were in the bathroom. Folks asked if they could sit. They didn't like hearing "*nein*." Annalise got into heated arguments. I didn't understand the language, as usual, but I knew what they were saying.

The friends arrived around noon, delayed by hangovers and one shower at their remote accommodation. Our apartment, within walking distance, costing triple the usual price, was worth it. After a string of apologies, we brushed off the morning's issues.

As the afternoon turned into evening, the energy grew, and the liters tumbled. I take partial responsibility for suggesting Kings Cup, aka Circle of Death, an ill-advised drinking game. Sitting and chatting shifted into standing and singing.

Jeremy left around 8 p.m. Worried about finding his way back, he wasn't happy I stayed. But by 10 p.m., I could barely stand on my bench, clutching whoever I could. With only one key between us, I feared he would pass out, leaving me to wander the streets. With a missed turn here and there, I stumbled back.

71 ♦ Bohinjsko jezero, Slovenia

I awoke feeling like death warmed over. Alcohol was the primary culprit, but the cold Jeremy gave me compounded my misery. Excluding food poisoning, I had never been sick while traveling. My good fortune had run out.

The next day, I said, "See ya' later," to him. Still struggling to navigate, he went the wrong way on the metro and almost missed his flight. I could only laugh. Things were still cold between us, but I knew we would be fine.

Hours later, I met up with Jason (Niagara Falls, September 11th Memorial, Mount Vernon), his brother, and their buddy—three seasoned veterans who go wherever the wind takes them. They proposed renting a car in Munich, driving through the Balkans, and then returning to Munich. We didn't realize the difficulty of this fly-by-the-seat-of-your-pants idea.

Rental companies wouldn't let their cars leave the Schengen Area. To make matters worse, the Syrian Civil War spawned an exodus of refugees. The unrest in the region shut down all trains as they were too complicated to monitor. We settled on a bus to Ljubljana, Slovenia.

At this point, my cold was in full swing. Sitting in the back, the heat from the engine and vents coalesced. Unable to open the windows, my temperature skyrocketed, my head filled with fluid, I couldn't pop my ears, and blowing my nose was futile. Including the border crossing, the drive took five hours. I had done longer, more demanding rides. None had been as miserable. I talked with others at the hostel over breakfast. My illness had spread across Europe. It took one girl three weeks to recover. I still had two more to go.

We had zero expectations of Slovenia, but it turned out to be clean, affordable, with good food and friendly people. We liked it so much that we stayed an extra day to catch a bus two hours northwest to Lake Bohinj, the country's largest permanent lake.

We arrived at midday and rented some bikes. My first time on one since Cotopaxi, I faked enthusiasm. After half a kilometer, we stopped for a picnic lunch, where I sat on a park bench (M), enjoying fine bread, meat, and cheese amid a world of reflective glass—nearly perfect dual images of an overcast sky and rocky hills covered in lush green forest. The stones of the shoreline, visible through the shallow translucent water, created the only variation. Regardless of how bad I felt, there was zero tension with these guys.

Lake Bohinj

72 ♦ Sarajevo, Bosnia

I was nine when the U.S. led the charge of the Gulf War in 1990, waged against Iraq after invading their oil-rich neighbor, Kuwait. The U.S. and its allies claimed an overwhelming victory in less than seven months. Too young to understand the purpose, I only remember the *Operation Desert Storm* T-shirt my paternal grandma bought me and the non-stop TV coverage, earning it the nickname the *Video Game War*.

A year later, the Socialist Federal Republic of Yugoslavia (SFRY) began disintegrating. The carnage was more extreme, but I don't remember seeing it on TV. With my country not spearheading the campaign, displaying technological military dominance, it's not surprising. As my time in the Balkans went on, it became impossible to avoid *The War*, a term I had associated with World War II that took on a different meaning in the former Yugoslavia.

Following World War II, the SFRY formed, comprised of six socialist republics:

1) Bosnia and Herzegovina
2) Croatia
3) Macedonia
4) Montenegro
5) Slovenia
6) Serbia, including two autonomous provinces—Kosovo and Vojvodina. Serbia's largest city, Belgrade, served as the capital.

Josip Broz Tito, the principal designer of the SFRY and leader of the Communist Party of Yugoslavia, rose to power in 1953. Born to a Croat father and Slovene mother, the authoritarian quashed nationalistic sentiments. The peace lasted until Tito died in 1980, shadowed by an ethnic nationalism that swept through the country in the latter part of the decade. Devoid of federal leadership, with each republic having relative autonomy and political influence, Serbia attempted to assert authority over the others.

Upset with the ever-tightening Serbian stranglehold, Croatia and Slovenia declared independence in 1991, sparking the *Croatian War of Independence* and the *Ten-Day War*, respectively. The former lasted four years, while the latter lasted ten days, as the name indicates. Both wars involved local forces fighting the Yugoslav People's Army (JNA), which aimed to preserve Yugoslavia by defeating the seceding governments. However, the Serbian government attempted to use the army to create a greater Serbian state, causing the JNA to lose members from other ethnic groups, essentially becoming a Serb army.

In March 1992, Bosnia and Herzegovina declared independence and received international recognition of its sovereignty on April 6, the same day their war began, involving three belligerents:

1) Bosnians for the Republic of Bosnia and Herzegovina.
2) Croats for the Croatian Republic of Herzeg-Bosnia and Croatia.
3) Serbs for the Republika Srpska and the Federal Republic of Yugoslavia.

Most of the combat occurred between the predominantly 1) Muslim Bosniaks and 2) Catholic Croats against the 3) Orthodox Serbs.

Arriving in the Bosnia and Herzegovina city of Mostar, it had been two decades since the fighting stopped. We asked the owner of our hostel, a 28-year-old man who lived through it as a boy, why it started. He didn't have an answer, but all we had to do to see remnants was walk across the city.

We encountered Stari Most, a pedestrian bridge commissioned in 1557. In the middle of the *Bosnian War*, the *Croat–Bosniak War* broke out from October 1992 to February 1994, marked by sporadic fighting between the two allies. Croat forces destroyed the bridge in November 1993, but thanks to a group of international organizations (headed by UNESCO), it was rebuilt and reopened in 2004. Locals now use it for diving twenty-nine meters (95 ft) into the icy river for a tip.

The city center had an eclectic mix of buildings, from immaculate to derelict. I wouldn't call it a bad neighborhood, but the hair on my neck stood up. An eight-story building lacking a definable shape stuck out like the sorest thumb. The best I can do is a rhombus and a square made a baby. Off-limits to the public, we tread lightly to avoid detection from residents in nearby apartments. I doubt anyone paid attention.

The other side of the tall wall resembled Chernobyl, devoid of doors, windows, or people. Only broken glass, trash, and graffiti remained in the concrete skeleton. We climbed a staircase without handrails and went up a rusty fire escape to the roof. As the tallest structure in the area, it provided a 360-degree view for snipers.

A storm was closing in. We hurried down as a lightning bolt tore through the sky, unleashing an apocalyptic downpour. We took shelter in a pub to discuss our next move. Over a game of darts, we decided to head straight into the heart of the conflict, Sarajevo.

We again befriended our hostel owner, an older man with a gruffness, weathered skin, and stained teeth from smoking. A teenager at the time, too young to fight, he conveyed a more cynical attitude. Still bitter about the subject, he drove us to a coffee shop in the hills surrounding the city, where Serb forces attacked with artillery, tanks, and guns. In the spring of 1992, they blockaded Sarajevo, cutting off food, medicine, and utilities.

On May 22, Bosnia and Herzegovina became a United Nations (UN) member state. The following month, the UN established a security zone on the city's edge, including the airport, which the Serbs controlled but handed over in response to a UN ultimatum. Airlifts of supplies could now help counter the siege, but they weren't enough.

In March 1993, Bosniak workers started building a secret tunnel beneath the airport. Without official plans, they dug nonstop with shovels and pickaxes from opposite ends. Four months later, the eight-hundred-meter (2,600 ft) Sarajevo Tunnel linked the siege zone to the outside world, making it easier to smuggle in food, fuel, cigarettes, alcohol, and black-market embargo-defying weapons.

As the siege and violence continued throughout 1994, the UN called for increased military involvement from NATO in response to Serb atrocities. Combined with the resurgence of the Bosniak-Croat alliance, the Serb army's position became unsustainable. In late 1995, the constituent parties reached a peace accord in Dayton, Ohio, and later signed it in Paris. They agreed to coexist within a single sovereign state made up of two territories, one for Serbs and one for Croat-Bosniaks.

It took our hostel owner two days to cross the city during the siege to reach the tunnel, hoping to find medicine for his brother. For us, it was a twenty-minute ride from the coffee shop to a two-story home with holes ranging from a fingernail to a head. Now it's a museum, with a strip of yellow tape in the backyard bearing the word "MINE" blocking a patch of unexploded ordnance. Our hostel owner swore under his breath between cigarette drags as he looked at a plaque showing the disparity in military power.

Only twenty meters (66 ft) of the tunnel remained. I admired the simple sophistication of the humid lifeline. Barely wide enough for a person, logs supported boards that formed the floor, walls, and ceilings. A metal track guided push carts. Soft electric lighting ran throughout. Besides delivering supplies, it allowed thousands to escape, earning the nickname the *Tunnel of Hope* (M).

The Siege of Sarajevo ended in February 1996. Lasting nearly four years, it was the longest siege of a capital city in modern history. The Bosnian War overall displaced over two million people, making it the largest humanitarian crisis in Europe since World War II. With a death toll of roughly one hundred thousand, a large percentage of whom were Bosniaks, it was the most brutal Yugoslav War, marred by ethnic cleansing, genocide, and crimes against humanity, including mass rape and sexual assault.

It's funny how my country came to the defense of the Muslim Kuwaitis but didn't show such support for the Muslim Bosniaks. It helps to have lots of oil.

The Sarajevo Tunnel

73 ♦ Budapest, Hungary

The guys had to get to Munich for their flights home. I needed to get to London and didn't feel like the extra travel, so I gave them a "see ya' later" and stayed in Budapest.

I finally shook off my cold. Feeling energized, I walked south along the Danube on the Pest side, crossed over to Buda, and found a path leading up to the Citadella, a former fortress built in 1851. A reminder of my most shameful incident, the Széchenyi Chain Bridge, appeared in the distance. I had never felt like such a hungover loser in pursuit of 100 Places After as I did that day.

Mom had been to sixty more places in the two years since. Most I was proud of, or apathetic at worst. I had no intention of returning to Budapest, but life gave me a second chance. I walked to a road that ran along the river, arriving at the bridge half an hour later. As I had to cross it anyway, I finally reached the midpoint (M).

A far cry from before, there was no pool party and no Jeremy. I missed him and wished he were there for his Budapest redemption. As much as he annoyed me, we were friends for over half our lives. He was one of the people who helped me the most after Mom passed. For that, I am forever grateful.

74 ♦ Anvers Island, Antarctic Peninsula

I have often marveled at the thin line which separates success from failure.
— Sir Ernest Shackleton, *South* (1919)

Four months later, I arrived at a hotel lobby in Punta Arenas, Chile, one of the world's southernmost cities. At the end of summer, it was freezing. I boarded a bus with sixty others for the half-hour ride to the airport. Waiting in a terminal with only a few gates, I was surprised that most of my fellow travelers were in their 30s and 40s. I had expected an older crowd.

We flew to the Falkland Islands, an autonomous British overseas territory five hundred kilometers (300 mi) off the southeastern coast of Argentina. After changing hands among European powers during the late eighteenth and early nineteenth centuries, Argentina claimed sovereignty in 1820, only to lose it to Britain thirteen years later. On April 2, 1982, Argentina invaded and occupied the islands, but a British expeditionary force regained control within ten weeks, ending the brief Falklands War.

We landed at Royal Air Force Mount Pleasant, a British airfield built after the war to bolster regional defenses. An hour bus ride through a landscape resembling the Scottish Highlands took us to the port town of Stanley. The capital and largest city (population 2,100) felt like 1970s England, with quaint streets, charming buildings, and placidity. I grabbed a pint at a pub emblazoned with Union Jacks to escape the English-like rain.

The *Akademik Sergey Vavilov*, a 117-meter (384 ft) Finnish science vessel for polar exploration and Russian aquatic research, anchored in the harbor. Its ice-strengthened hull could hold 155 passengers and crew. Rudimentary by cruise ship standards, it featured a spa, wellness center, and a bar with panoramic views.

A year earlier, I bought the cheapest option, a triple room with a shared bathroom. A few weeks before leaving, I received a free upgrade to a private room with a porthole and a personal bathroom. To put things in perspective, I estimated the room's value at three thousand dollars and the single supplement at six thousand. It was easy to see why the cost of these two weeks rivaled my four months traveling around the world.

We set off in the late afternoon, heading south toward the Drake Passage, eight hundred kilometers (500 mi) of water with no significant land mass anywhere along the passage's latitude. Imagine placing your finger on a globe just south of South America and spinning it. You won't touch land. This geographic phenomenon gives rise to the Antarctic Circumpolar Current, a west-to-east flowing current around the continent characterized by high winds and gut-wrenching swells. I struggled to eat the bland broth at dinner and returned to my cabin, forgoing the main course and dessert. I slapped a motion sickness patch behind my ear and didn't leave my bunk for the night.

We pressed on south for two days at the mercy of the winds and seas, the limiting factors for success. "Weather-dependent" became the foremost phrase in the Antarctic lexicon.

The first stop was supposed to be Elephant Island, nine hundred kilometers (560 mi) south of the Falklands. Nearly a century earlier, polar explorer Ernest Shackleton and his crew sought refuge there after an unsuccessful attempt to cross Antarctica on foot. Their survival is one of the most extraordinary feats of endurance, demonstrating man's ability to overcome insurmountable odds in the face of death. It's where I desired to go most on this trip, but my arch-nemesis, *failure*, reared its ugly head again.

Our weather-dependent timing couldn't have been worse. We encountered a storm with winds gusting up to forty knots (46 mph, 74 kph), which set us back a day. In my uninformed opinion, we skipped Elephant Island due to our hard arrival at Palmer Station, a U.S. Antarctic research base established in 1968. With only about ten to twelve civilian ships stopping there each year, tardiness wasn't an option.

Able to accommodate forty-four people, the station focused on function over form—steel buildings, tanks, piping, antennae, and cables nestled in a cove on one of the few patches of rock. A pole in the center of town had arrows pointing in different directions (M).

PALMER STATION – LAT 64.46 S LONG 64.03 W
MCMURDO SCOTT STATION BASE – 2480 MILES
SOUTH POLE – 1744 MILES
PUNTA ARENAS – 837 MILES
STONINGTON CT – 7319 MI
MOSS LANDING – 6673 NM[*]

I had been further from home, but never anywhere this remote.

Palmer Station

* Palmer Station is named after Nathanial Palmer, the first American to see Antarctica in 1820. McMurdo Scott Station Base is a U.S. Antarctic research center. Stonington CT (Connecticut) is the birthplace of Nathaniel Palmer. Moss Landing is a city in California popular for marine research.

75 ♦ Hovgaard Island, Antarctic Peninsula

The weather calmed the next day for my solitary chance at camping, an activity I detest. Call me soft, but I prefer a roof, a bed, a flushing toilet, and temperature controls. In the spirit of 100 Places After, I had to.

Those interested in sleeping under the Austral stars gathered for a reality check on the outer deck. The woman giving the pep talk summed it up. There are two types of fun in this world. *Type 1 Fun* is the kind you have while doing the activity. *Type 2 Fun* is the kind you have when telling the story. Camping would be Type 2 Fun.

I layered on all my warm clothes: two pairs of socks, four layers on my lower body, six on my upper body, two pairs of gloves, one hat, and one hood. As I stepped onto Hovgaard Island, I received four items: a sleeping bag, a sleeping bag liner, a thin mat, and a single-person waterproof shelter. I set up camp on an ice-covered hill surrounded by rugged mountains shrouded in clouds that looked like fog.

To minimize our human impact, everyone must follow the rules: cleaning shoes when entering or leaving the ship, no food on land, and no human waste. A plastic bucket named "Mr. Yum Yum" served as our toilet. I limited my liquid intake and ate a light dinner.

After a quick number one, I wedged into my sleeping bag, closed my eyes, and began perspiring. Fearful of waking in a pool of chilled sweat, I unzipped my jacket and took off my gloves. I got cold again and put everything back on. I repeated this several times until I finally fell asleep around midnight.

I awoke to light tapping around 4 a.m., thinking it was a curious penguin. I peeked out to see gentle snow falling. I was annoyed I hadn't slept longer, but this turned out to be a blessing in disguise. I shoved my bare, red, throbbing hands back into my gloves, made fists, and pressed them between my thighs, where they stayed until I woke a few hours later to the rustling of everyone packing up. Blinded by the bright white world, I loaded my gear and left (M). Antarctic camping was undoubtedly Type 2 Fun.

Hovgaard Island

76 ♦ Neko Harbour, Antarctic Peninsula

The zodiac sped toward Neko Harbor as the stench of penguin crap wafted from a kilometer away. A mix of trash dump and decaying flesh, my eyes watered, and my nose started to run.

Hundreds of Gentoos frolicked on the beach. The adults, about half my height, had white bellies, black backs and heads, orange beaks and feet, and a white streak above each eye. I did my best to avoid slipping in their gooey pink mess and found a poo-free spot for (M) among calving glaciers sending thundering waves across the bay.

At some point in my search for 100 Places After, I vowed to get Mom to all seven continents, the only firm goal I made. I had debated the *New 7 Wonders of the World,*[*] but every continent seemed loftier. As all previous Antarctic excursions had been to islands of an archipelago, in the way Hawaii is part of the U.S., it's

* The *New 7 Wonders of the World* are the Great Wall of China, Petra, Christ the Redeemer, Machu Picchu, Chichén Itzá, the Colosseum, and the Taj Mahal. The Great Pyramid of Giza is an honorary candidate.

not "America." I wanted to stand on the landmass considered the fifth-largest continent. A feat I incorrectly assumed was unique.

Half of the sixty tourists on the boat completed their quest for number seven that day. One man in his late 20s, traveling for fourteen months, had the ambition of visiting every country in the world. He had been to seventy-five so far. I was content with my fifty-two.

The hard part is figuring out how to count a country. I often see stories about someone becoming the first "blank" to visit every country or doing it in a "blank" way. Usually, it was a speed run for a passport stamp at an airport or dipping their toe in.

I don't believe there's a set amount of time someone must spend in a place to consider having been there. But I think you need to gain an understanding to check it off the list.

A person can reach almost anywhere in a few days. It just requires desire and resources. Had Mom not taken care of me financially and given me her wish, I wouldn't have gone to such lengths on my own.

Neko Harbour

77 ♦ Cierva Cove, Antarctic Peninsula

The plan for kayaking was one or two weather-dependent paddles a day. Apart from the brief lull, conditions had been mediocre, and I had forgone multiple outings.

On my last morning, the sky was its usual dark smoke, and the sea was far from glassy. If it had been our first time, we wouldn't have gone out. Having overindulged at the bar the night before, I felt unenthusiastic about exerting any energy.

I donned one-third of my camping gear, thin rubber boots, and a dry suit. I climbed into the slender red plastic craft with a skirt to keep the water out and set off into Cierva Cove, pushing through frozen minefields that rose and fell with the swells.

I had seen enough ice to last a lifetime, but as I approached a monolithic berg from an alien moon with spikes, curves, and rough walls, for a brief moment, I wasn't cold. Finding synergy with one of nature's most inhospitable environments made the twelve-thousand-kilometer (7,450 mi) trip worthwhile (M). For the first time kayaking in Antarctica, I experienced Type 1 Fun.

Cierva Cove

HOMESICK

78 ♦ Potosi, Bolivia

No matter how dreary and grey our homes are, we people of flesh and blood would rather live there than in any other country, be it ever so beautiful. There is no place like home.

— Frank Baum, *The Wonderful Wizard of Oz* (1900)

The boat docked at King George Island two days later, the largest of the South Shetland Islands, 120 kilometers (75 mi) north of the Antarctic Peninsula. We used the bar as a makeshift airport lounge, waiting for news that our plane had left Punta Arenas with passengers making the trip in reverse.

For the first time in a week, the sun appeared. I went outside to feel it on my face. Minutes later, a storm rolled in. We weren't going anywhere. I got cellular service from a Chinese tower, sent a message home, and had my flight to Bolivia rescheduled for two days later.

I had been on the road for months at a time over the past three years. Occasionally, I wanted to click my ruby slippers together, say, "There is no place like home," and wake up in my bed. Food poisoning or a hangover were often the culprits, and those thoughts dissipated once I felt better. I had only been away for two weeks, but I had already burned out.

After sixteen hours and four flights crisscrossing South America, I arrived in La Paz at 6 a.m., having managed only one hour of sleep in the past twenty-four. Going from sea level to the world's highest *de facto* capital, at 3,650 meters (11,975 ft), compounded my tiredness. I awoke in the afternoon, still fatigued, before boarding an overnight bus to Sucre, where I again only got one hour of sleep.

Upon arrival, I was hit by a series of chills, worsened by the hotel's lack of heat. I showered in the hottest water I could stand and put on my Antarctic camping gear. It still wasn't enough, so I pulled out my thermometer (yes, I travel with one), revealing an exhaustion-induced fever.

Years earlier, I had a similar experience traveling from London to Amsterdam to Berlin to Prague, having consumed too many cocktails and getting too little sleep. The remedy was medicine, water, and rest. Aside from going to the grocery store, I stayed in my room for thirty-six hours. I considered going home, but didn't want to pay to rearrange everything.

I arrived in Potosi feeling about 70 percent. At an altitude of 4,100 meters (13,450 ft), it was the lowest elevation I would be at for a while. Founded in 1545 as a mining town, it became one of the largest cities in the Americas due to the silver-infused veins running through *Cerro Rico*—Rich Mountain.* From the sixteenth to the eighteenth century, it produced vast amounts of the world's silver, providing immense wealth for the Spanish. As the silver dried up, the focus shifted to tin.

With little to do, I signed up for a mine tour. I received a helmet with a light, a jacket, pants, waterproof boots, and a surgical mask. As a kind gesture, I could buy gifts for the miners. There were two options:

1) Sugary drinks, cigarettes, coca leaves, and a small bottle of 96 percent alcohol.
2) Dynamite (invented by Alfred Nobel) and a three-minute fuse.

Both cost twenty bolivianos ($3). I chose Option 1.

The mine's periphery resembled a post-apocalyptic landscape of garbage and indiscernible stenches. Hole-riddled, rusted sheds processed materials. A narrow building with several doors, peeling paint, and barred windows served as living quarters.

* *Cerro Rico's* maximum height is 4,782 meters (15,689 ft).

Housing (left) and a miner at Cerro Rico (right)

An angled rock wall with a weathered-board door marked the entrance. A rickety wooden ladder led to the underworld. More miserable than above, trash-filled water pools dampened the air, and distant explosions filled it with dust.

Miners chipped the walls and pushed rock-filled carts. I gave them goodies as they passed, coveting the alcohol and coca leaves. On average, they earned eighty bolivianos ($12) per day. Many would succumb to silicosis, an irreversible lung disease caused by inhaling crystalline silica dust. With a life expectancy of 40, *Cerro Rico* has earned its nickname, “The Mountain That Eats Men.”

Back on the surface, it took minutes for my eyes to adjust to the sun. Realizing my unjustified homesickness, I had found another place where the plight of others put things in perspective (M).

The mine at Cerro Rico

79 ♦ Uyuni, Bolivia

A three-hour bus ride southwest and a four-wheel-drive SUV brought me to Salar de Uyuni, the world's largest salt flat (M). Distant mountains surrounded the vast margarita-like salt beneath a cloudless sky. Pools of rainwater created mirrors on top of the murky sludge. Every surface reflected the sun.

After a few hours, I headed to town for lunch, ordered a pizza, and went to wash off the white crust. Inside the piss-covered bathroom, I saw my flaming red face, neck, hands, and legs. I knew the sun would be intense at 3,656 meters (11,995 ft), but I had done a half-assed job applying sunscreen. Stupid, stupid, stupid!

I faced the full extent of the damage in the morning. My ears, already not small, had swelled to twice their normal thickness. My bright crimson legs, so inflamed, had developed cankles—where the calf merges into the foot—making it difficult to discern the presence of an ankle. Unlike my ears, I take pride in my nicely tapered legs. I felt less than sexy. I don't know how much radiation I received, but I'm guessing it was a hell of a lot more than at Chernobyl.

Salar de Uyuni

80 ♦ San Pedro de Atacama, Chile

Three days of riding through the Atacama Desert, one of the driest places on Earth, brought me to some of the most majestic landscapes. I struggled to enjoy them due to the pain and focused on avoiding the sun. I repeatedly awoke to warring temperatures at night—chills on my upper half and fire on my lower. I had slept better camping in Antarctica.

My spirits lifted in the low-elevation town of San Pedro de Atacama, Chile at an altitude of 2,400 meters (7,900 ft). I went to the pharmacy for some after-sun gel and didn't attempt my lousy Spanish. The pharmacist saw what I needed. The burnt areas were still red and warm to the touch, but the swelling had subsided.

Thirteen kilometers (8 mi) west was *Valle de la Luna* (M), named due to its resemblance to our nearest celestial body. The lifeless gorge, with its crevasses, peaks, sand mountains, and dry riverbeds, had areas that hadn't seen rain for hundreds of years. Unlike our grayscale Moon, it was a soft reddish-brown with mineral deposits resembling snow. Watching a sunset that stung my skin, I once again found myself somewhere I couldn't fathom was on our planet. Still, there was only one place I wanted to be.

Valle de la Luna

81 ♦ Buenos Aires, Argentina

Reminiscent of getting to Spain from Morocco or Greece from Israel, my despondent demeanor changed in Buenos Aires, Argentina. Located at sea level, the "Paris of South America" offered cafes, neighborhood canals, baroque architecture, exquisite wine, and world-class steaks. For the first time in a long while, I found somewhere I didn't want to leave. To add to my serenity, my ears and ankles were their usual size. My skin had stopped burning and was peeling. Life was good enough.

Reveling in contentment, I commenced one of my more obscure pastimes, walking among the dead. I had been to cemeteries on all seven continents, most recently a collection of headstones at an old Antarctic whaling port. While it might sound odd, I have grown to enjoy them. Not just for their mystique and beauty. They remind me that as long as my heart beats, my lungs breathe, and my legs move, I can go anywhere. All were fortunes I had forgotten.

The grandest in Buenos Aires was La Recoleta. The city's first public cemetery, completed in 1822, was filled with thousands of mausoleums, including those of Argentine presidents, Nobel laureates, military figures, artists, and Napoleon's granddaughter.

The most prominent flashed a polished dark mirror finish with bright flowers covering a cross on an elaborate door. Above it read FAMILIA DUARTE. Inside was arguably the most famous Argentine, Eva Perón, more commonly known as Evita.

Born in 1919, she was the youngest of five children of Juan Duarte, a wealthy rancher, and his mistress, Juana Ibarguren. When Eva was one, her father abandoned them to be with his first family. The only things he left behind were poverty and his name.

At 15, she moved to Buenos Aires to pursue a career in acting, achieving moderate success in radio and film. Her life changed in 1944 at a charity event when she met the 48-year-old widower, Colonel Juan Perón, an ambitious military officer and politician. Although she was half his age, the couple married a year later.

Perón was elected president in 1946, and Eva became an influential political figure. She established a charity, led the Ministries of Labor and Health, played a vital role in securing women's suffrage in 1947, and founded the Female Peronist Party, the country's first large-scale women's political organization. Her association with the *descamisados* (shirtless) made her popular among Argentina's underprivileged, though she was equally controversial among the country's elite.

Urged to run for vice president in 1951 alongside her husband, fierce opposition from the military and upper class, combined with her declining health, forced her to withdraw. Diagnosed with cervical cancer the year prior, despite a hysterectomy and being the first Argentine to utilize chemotherapy, she continued working until succumbing to her illness on July 26, 1952, at age 33.

Flags flew at half-mast for ten days, and lines to see her stretched for weeks. Despite never holding political office, she received a state funeral. A statue of a *descamisado* was to be larger than the Statue of Liberty, where her embalmed body would be displayed like Lenin's.

Before the statue was finished, a 1955 military coup overthrew her husband, who fled the country. The new dictatorship disbanded the Peronist Party and made it illegal to possess the couple's picture or utter their names. The *de facto* president, General Pedro Eugenio Aramburu, vowed to keep Eva "outside politics." Her body disappeared, and its whereabouts remained unknown.

Argentina held general elections in 1958, and Aramburu stepped aside, retiring from the military. Twelve years later, a left-wing Peronist guerrilla organization kidnapped, interrogated, and executed him. He had left a letter with his lawyer detailing the whereabouts of Eva, stipulating it be delivered four weeks after his death to whoever was president. A year later, a covert military operation found her in a crypt in Milan, Italy. Her relatively intact body was taken to Spain and reunited with her husband.

Juan Perón emerged from exile in 1973, returned to Argentina, and was elected president for a third time, only to die the following year. His third wife and vice president, Isabel, succeeded him, becoming the first female president of a country. She had Eva laid to rest in the Duarte family tomb in 1976 (M).

In my pursuit of uniqueness, I checked two new boxes. One, this was the first place dedicated to a cancer death (if you don't count Hiroshima or Chernobyl). As impactful as it has been in my life and the lives of others, it has always existed.

The first account and case trace back to ancient Egypt. However, it wasn't until the sixteenth and seventeenth centuries that autopsies gained acceptance, leading to broader hypotheses about the causes.

In 1775, the British physician Percivall Pott linked the disease with an environmental carcinogen after observing the high rate of scrotal cancer among chimney sweeps. During that century, the microscope led to a breakthrough in the understanding of metastasis through the lymph nodes.

The initial treatment was surgery, which had low survival rates. The discovery of radiation in the late nineteenth century led to the first non-surgical treatment. In the twentieth century, chemotherapy, hormonal therapy, adjuvant therapy, immunotherapy, and targeted therapy emerged.

The problem is that cancer is a numbers game. Half of men and one-third of women will develop it, making cancer the second leading global cause of death, behind cardiovascular disease. As a friend of mine who lost his father said, "Everyone gets cancer. You hope you get a good kind."

The other checked box was finding a place dedicated to a meritorious woman. There had been an American president, a Chinese emperor, a Japanese Buddhist monk, a Muslim dynastic founder, a Spanish pauper architect, the last tsar, his communist successors, a demagogic Nazi, the father of evolution, a pacifist Hindu, Egyptian pharaohs, and the purveyor of the world's largest religion. The commonality was the dangly bit between their legs.

You could argue that the Taj Mahal memorialized a woman. At no fault of Mumtaz, her circumstances, like those of many women, didn't allow for much beyond the miraculous feat of motherhood. Eva had a more prominent social role, but the paradox is that a man elevated her status. I suppose everyone needs a kingmaker, or in this case, a queenmaker. But she made the most of it. She played the man's game and won. It's a shame she died so young.

I never paid much attention to gender while searching for 100 Places After. I should have. Maybe that's an indictment of me? Or perhaps it reflects society's suppression of women? Why are there so many "Fathers of a Nation" and so few "Mothers"? Whatever the reasons, I visited these male-inspired locations because a woman gave me life, raised me as a single parent, and secured my financial well-being after she died. I did her a disservice by not including women more. It's one of the few regrets I have about this book.

The tomb of Eva Peron

THE SEARCH FOR CLOSURE

82 ♦ Berlin, Germany

The Chief of the Security Police and the SD (SS-Obergruppenführer Reinhard Heydrich) then gave a short report of the struggle which has been carried on thus far against this enemy, the essential points being the following:

a) the expulsion of the Jews from every sphere of life of the German people,

b) the expulsion of the Jews from the living space of the German people.

—Wannsee Protocol (January 20, 1942, translation)

In my final year of high school, I read an article in *The New Yorker* by comedian Steve Martin about closure, which became the most impactful piece of literature of my adolescence. From then on, I went to great lengths to attain satisfying conclusions in many areas of life. In the summer of 2016, I started my search for closure of 100 Places After.

The month in Antarctica and South America was one of my toughest. I had traveled to the end of the Earth only to feel a longing for home. Hesitant to hit the road again, three months after Argentina, I returned to my comfort zone—Berlin.

I took the S-Bahn southwest for an hour, exited at the *Berlin Wannsee* station, and walked along the waterfront to *Am Großen Wannsee 56–58,* where a cobblestone path cut through trees surrounding a multi-story stone villa with a circular driveway and an awning. I went to a room at the back of the house with tall windows offering views of the Havel River. It was here, seventy-four years earlier, that the Nazis answered the Final Solution to the Jewish Question.

In 1940, they proposed the Madagascar Plan to relocate one million Jews each year for four years to the island nation off the east coast of Africa, assuming many would perish under harsh conditions or at the hands of the SS, who would control it as a police state. The idea ceased after the German Air Force failed to gain air superiority against Britain, along with a British naval blockade. To create a Jew-free society, the Nazis devised a more practical scheme.

On January 20, 1942, fifteen senior Nazi officials convened in the Berlin suburbs. The meeting began with *SS-Obergruppenführer* (equivalent to lieutenant general) Reinhard Heydrich discussing European Jewish affairs. Over half a million Jews had emigrated from Germany. But with further emigration prohibited, the problem became the remaining eleven million throughout the continent.

Attendees received a list. The "A" group was under German control, while the "B" group was either allied, neutral, or a combatant. Not listed was Poland, which the Nazis and Soviets had already mutilated.

Heydrich disseminated the combing of Europe from west to east and "evacuating" Jews to transit ghettos before transporting them further east. Austria, Germany, and the Protectorate of Bohemia and Moravia got priority to free up space for displaced Germans and imported laborers.

Next came the simple determination of who would and wouldn't be "evacuated." Jews who had suffered injuries in World War I, earned the Iron Cross in World War I, or were over 65, might be sent to an old-age concentration camp. The more complex issue arose of what to do with the "Mischlinge"—mixed-race persons.

On September 15, 1935, the Nuremberg Laws stripped Jews of various rights. The *Law for the Protection of German Blood and German Honour* forbade Jews from marriage or extramarital sex with Germans, employing German women under 45 in Jewish households, and displaying the Reich's flag or colors.

.	Country		Number of Jews
A	Altreich		131,800
	Ostmark		43,700
	Eastern Territories		420,000
	Generalgouvernment		2,284,000
	Bialystok		400,000
	Protectorate of Bohemia and Moravia		74,200
	Estonia - free of Jews -		
	Latvia		3,500
	Lithuania		34,000
	Belgium		43,000
	Denmark		5,600
	France / occupied territory		165,000
	unoccupied territory		700,000
	Greece		69,600
	The Netherlands		160,800
	Norway		1,300
B	Bulgaria		48,000
	England		330,000
	Finland		2,300
	Ireland		4,000
	Italy, including Sardinia		58,000
	Albania		200
	Croatia		40,000
	Portugal		3,000
	Roumania, including Bessarabia		342,000
	Sweden		8,000
	Switzerland		18,000
	Serbia		10,000
	Slovakia		88,000
	Spain		6,000
	Turkey (in Europe)		55,500
	Hungary		742,800
	USSR		5,000,000
	Ukraine 2,994,684		
	Byelorussia without Bialystok 446,484		
	Total: over		11,000,000

The *Reich Citizenship Law* stated that only Germans (or those with related blood) could be citizens. Anyone else would be considered a state subject devoid of citizenship rights. A person with three or more Jewish grandparents was classified as a "Jew," regardless of their religious practice or personal identity. Those with one or two Jewish grandparents were labeled as "Mischlinge," assuming they were born before the marriage date of September 15, 1935. Those born after would be considered Jews.

Using the Nuremberg Laws as a guide, the Wannsee Conference attendees discussed various scenarios: Jews or Mischlinge who were married to Germans, did or didn't have children, and their appearance or behavior. Generally, the outcome was evacuation.

The meeting lasted about ninety minutes, including discussions on sterilization, logistics, avoiding the evacuation of Jews critical to the war effort, and not alarming the general populace. At the conclusion, *SS-Obersturmbannführer* (equivalent to lieutenant colonel) Adolf Eichmann, head of "Jewish affairs" and responsible for much of the deportations, produced a summation.

Each participant received a copy of the Wannsee Protocol. Most were destroyed, but number 16 of 30 was discovered after the war and used as evidence in the Nuremberg Trials—military tribunals to prosecute high-ranking Nazis for war crimes, crimes against humanity, and crimes against peace.

Now a memorial, I strolled the meeting room's periphery. The men's biographies, photos, and a colorful European map hung on the wall. Documents in a protective case had replaced the table where they sat (M).

The Wannsee Conference attendees didn't start the genocide. Death squads were already committing mass murder since the invasion of the Soviet Union, generally by shooting, which became psychologically traumatic to those pulling the trigger. These men established a new method of killing—gassing.

Little-known names of occupied Polish villages became synonymous with death. In December 1941, Chełmno tested vans with redirected exhaust fumes. In 1942, the purpose-built Bełżec,

Sobibór, and Treblinka became operational under *Operation Reinhard,* using the exhaust of captured Soviet tanks. The converted labor camps of Auschwitz and Lublin/Majdanek used Zyklon-B.

By killing tens of thousands daily, within two years, Bełżec, Sobibór, and Treblinka became unnecessary. They were dismantled, the mass graves dug up, the bodies cremated, the remains reburied, and buildings erected to make the areas appear as innocuous farms. Auschwitz alone could handle the extermination capacity. The combined death toll of the camps was more than 2.7 million—180,000 for each man at the Wannsee Conference.

I had taken Mom to the deadliest implementation of the Final Solution. I had taken her to where the unremarkable man most responsible for it met his demise. In my first step towards closure, it seemed fitting that she found her way to its practical origin.

The Holocaust killed six million Jews, roughly two-thirds of Europe's Jewish population. Combined with Soviet prisoners of war, the disabled, Roma (Gypsies), Jehovah's Witnesses, criminals, and homosexuals, the total rises to eleven million. What the Nazis failed to realize is how hard it is to eradicate an idea, some decades old and others millennia. Ironically, Nazism lasted twenty-five years.

Am Großen Wannsee 56–58

83 ♦ Berlin, Germany

A few days earlier, I received a message from Victoria, a Canadian living in Poland whom I had met in Cambodia. She had spent the last few weeks at a yoga retreat in Thailand but was leaving because she contracted Dengue Fever, a mosquito-borne disease common in tropical regions. Instead of heading home like some people would, she was going to Berlin for a Coldplay concert. I'm not their biggest fan, but I had all their albums. When she asked if I wanted to join, I bought my ticket within minutes.

On a perfect summer evening, we took the metro to the city's western edge to *Olympiastadion*, a former Nazi relic intended to symbolize the Third Reich's grandeur during the 1936 Summer Olympics. To capitalize on the propaganda opportunity, the purpose-built stadium had a capacity of 110,000, including a special stand for Hitler. In a blow to the "master race," Jesse Owens, an African American, won four gold medals there.

We passed through the seventy-seven-meter (250 ft) tall stone towers that once hoisted the Olympic rings and descended a long staircase below ground level. At 9 p.m. sharp, the band took the stage, and the sixty-eight thousand fans erupted. They opened with *A Head Full of Dreams*, *Yellow*, *Every Teardrop Is a Waterfall, The Scientist*, *Birds,* and *Paradise*. With each song, my anticipation grew.

In 2004, the lead singer, Chris Martin, wrote *Fix You* for his wife at the time, Gwyneth Paltrow, whose father had passed away from cancer. After Mom, the song always struck a painful chord in me (forgive the bad pun). If I heard it on the radio, I changed the station. If it came on at a friend's house, I exited the room. I couldn't leave *Olympiastadion*. From the first unmistakable note, my grin eroded to a solemn stare, and my eyes filled. After each refrain, I fought tears from streaming down my face.

I often turned to music during tough times, whether it was getting over a girl, dealing with tragedy, or losing Mom. More recently, I always had something playing on those days while walking the streets of whatever city I was in, waiting at the airport going from one continent to the next, or sipping a beer in a rented apartment. Certain songs reminded me of places. *One* from *A Chorus Line* for Las Vegas, *Ho Hey* by the *Lumineers* for New Zealand, *Lazaretto* by *Jack White* for Greece, *2 Heads* by *Coleman Hell* for Ireland, and *Ein Prosit* for Munich. After that night, *Fix You* for Berlin.

When the four minutes of catharsis ended, my shirt sleeve was wet. I peered over at equally hot-messed Victoria. I didn't know her reasoning. I didn't ask. We shared a moment of unspoken solace (M). When the music stopped a half hour later, I had found more closure.

The Coldplay concert at Olympiastadion

84 ♦ Ayia Napa, Cyprus

The day before the Coldplay concert, gunmen with bombs and automatic weapons killed more than forty people and injured more than two hundred at Istanbul, Turkey's main airport. Sondre and I had rolled the dice many times in supposedly dangerous places, only to realize how overblown the threat was. For the first time, we changed our plans because of terrorism.

We made the right choice to visit the Romanian capital of Bucharest for a few days as conditions in Turkey worsened. Weeks later, a faction of the army tried to overthrow the government in a failed coup. We wouldn't have been in the country, but it illustrated their troubles.

Our ultimate destination was Ayia Napa, located in the southeastern corner of Cyprus. I didn't know much about the city, aside from its reputation as a beach town with vibrant nightlife. I should have realized something was off when I told people where I was headed, and they responded with an eyerolling, "Oh boy."

The city was a British teen haven akin to spring break in Mexico. A few weeks earlier, I celebrated my 35th birthday and had no business mingling with people half my age. We made a mistake.

For the next few days, we lounged around the pool or watched soccer. One morning, to stave off my boredom, I pulled up a map on my phone. After a few taps, I settled on a walk to Cape Greco, a national park in the southeastern tip of the country, nine kilometers (5.6 mi) away.

I set out a little after 8 a.m. to beat the heat, carrying two liters of water, snacks, sunscreen, a power bank, and toilet paper (you never know). After a kilometer, I encountered a manicured stone path hugging the rocky coastline and followed it for the ocean breeze.

Halfway to my destination, the trail vanished into a hotel with a miniature golf course and greasy sun-magnets sipping tropical drinks. It briefly restarted, only to be replaced by a minefield of jagged rocks akin to sea coral. Luckily, I was wearing the same shoes I had hiked the Inca Trail in, with thick rubber soles.

To extricate myself from the porous razor blades, I found an inland road. Annoyed to take it due to the heat, I had no choice. I followed it for a few kilometers to a fork. The left led down to the ocean, while the right went up to the "KAVOS" VIEW POINT. I went right.

After another dusty kilometer, I could go no further. I approached an abstract metal sculpture with eight birds—probably doves—attached to vertical poles atop a sphere (M). The irony of this artwork is its location in the eye of a storm of violent lands.

At my twelve o'clock was Syria, a country torn apart by civil war for the past five years, with hundreds of thousands dead and millions displaced. At one o'clock was Lebanon, controlled by the terrorist organization Hezbollah. At two o'clock was Israel, plagued by ongoing religious struggles since its founding. At three o'clock was Egypt, home to sporadic acts of terrorism. At nine o'clock was Turkey, amid a coup. At six o'clock was a dichotomous party town.

I rested in a shelter, ate a granola bar, guzzled water, and reapplied my sunscreen. With the heat near 35°C (95°F) and a similarly long walk back, I took the quicker interior road to avoid the rocks, arriving at the hotel two hours later. Although my time in Cyprus wasn't what I expected, it brought closure to one topic. I'm too old for this.

The "KAVOS" VIEW POINT

85 ♦ Zizur Mayor, Spain

Walking the Great Wall of China, Steve told me to watch *The Way*, a 2010 film about a man who scatters his son's ashes along the *Camino de Santiago*, an ancient European pilgrimage route leading to the supposed final resting place of Santiago (Saint James the Great), one of the first apostles of Jesus Christ and the patron saint of Spain. With the end of 100 Places After in sight, I sought more closure.

I headed to Paris for a night to drop off anything I didn't need, aiming to get my bag down to 10 percent of my body weight. I pared it down to the bare essentials: one pair of shorts, one pair of pants that zip into shorts, two pairs of underwear, two tank tops, one T-shirt, two pairs of socks, one rain poncho, one hat, one long-sleeve shirt, sunscreen, toiletries, and a first aid kit. I ended right on the mark at 6.5 kilograms (14 lbs).

A pilgrim can set off from anywhere and walk their own path, creating countless ways. The most popular route, as shown in the film, begins in Saint-Jean-Pied-de-Port (St. Jean for short) in southwest France near the Spanish border.

I arrived there after 10 p.m. during unseasonably hot weather and spent the next day gathering supplies for the journey: a water bottle, a walking stick, and my *credencial*, the pilgrim's passport. Along the way, I would encounter *albergues*, hostels open only to pilgrims, where, like a real passport, the *credencial* would be stamped, proving I had completed that segment.

I didn't sleep much and awoke wide-eyed and nervous before the screech of my alarm. Waiting for sunrise, I pondered the road ahead. Would I meet new and exciting people? Would I find a rejuvenated outlook on life? Would I get closer to closure? At twenty to thirty kilometers (12 to 19 mi) per day, I anticipated completing the 780 kilometers (485 mi) in about a month.

I entered the empty streets on the far side of St. Jean but left the town within minutes. From everything I had heard, the first eight kilometers (5 mi) were the worst. As I climbed the never-ending hill, more pilgrims appeared. The ants go marching one by one.

I reached the village of Orisson two hours later. In desperate need of a bathroom and breakfast, I grabbed a pastry, a Coke, and a glass of fresh-squeezed orange juice. I sat on the terrace and conversed with a towering Danish man named Henrik. A head taller than me, with a full beard and a booming voice, he would have made an incredible Viking if he had been born a millennium earlier. He was tackling the *Camino* for the third time, having completed smaller sections but never conquering it from St. Jean.

We stayed together for the rest of the day, covering the twenty-five kilometers (16 mi) to Roncesvalles, where I paid six euros for a bunk. After a shower, sink laundry, and a mediocre dinner, I was in bed by 10 p.m.

Before sunrise, I was out the door and told Henrik I would see him in Zubiri, twenty-two kilometers (14 mi) away. As daylight broke, a twinge developed where my leg and pelvis connected, growing worse with each step. I stopped every kilometer or two and uttered, "F*** you, *Camino*."

I hobbled into Zubiri around 1 p.m., entered the first *albergue* I could, grabbed a bed, and lay motionless. The shops hadn't closed for their afternoon *siesta*, so I found a pharmacy with a bandage big enough to fit around my hips and inner thigh. Minus another wretched dinner, I didn't move.

My leg felt a bit better in the morning. The first few kilometers were touchy but not as painful. My meticulous wrapping paid minor dividends. I encountered an outdoor café to get my usual sugar-filled *Camino* breakfast. Before I could sit, I received a thunderous "HELLO!" and a friendly wave. My spirits lifted as I pulled a chair next to Henrik and his elevated bare feet. He, like many others, suffered from blisters. I didn't know who had the more urgent problem.

We reunited again, though much slower, and completed the twenty-one kilometers (13 mi) without incident, arriving in

Pamplona early in the afternoon. Lacking the revelry of San Fermin, I needed all the rest I could get, a prospect easier said than done.

To get quality sleep, I need cold, dark, and quiet. The *albergues* lacked all of these. There were hotels, but they cost more and sterilized the camaraderie. Maybe I should have splurged? Each night, I slept no more than three to four hours, largely due to the snoring Korean. No matter which hostel I stayed in, some with over a hundred beds, he was never far away, beleaguering me with his bed-rattling rumble.

Henrik and I set off early on Day 4 with the morning's goal of *Alto de Perdón* (Mount of Forgiveness) at 735 meters (2,411 ft). We encountered our first bout of rain, transforming the trail into thick mud. At the top stood forty windmills and metal cutouts depicting pilgrims walking and on horseback, fighting the prevailing wind, set against a backdrop of rolling hills with sporadic dark trees (M). An engraving read *Donde se cruza el Camino del viento con el de las estrellas* (Where the way of the wind meets the way of the stars.)

I recognized this place from the film. Only a few days in, I had found my first spot on the *Camino* in the search for closure. I wondered how many there would be along the way. Only time and a lot of walking would tell.

Donde se cruza el Camino del viento con el de las estrellas

86 ♦ Santiago de Compostela, Spain

Henrik and I finished the day's twenty-three kilometers (14 mi) to Puente la Reina without any setbacks. My hip hurt but held. Day 5 was another twenty-two kilometers (14 mi) to Estella. Day 6 was supposed to be an easy twenty-two kilometers (14 mi) to Los Arcos, but I could barely walk when I arrived. To alleviate stress on my hip, I overcompensated with my other leg, resulting in an ever-increasing shin pain.

On the morning of Day 7, my leg resembled a camel's back with humps of hard tissue that had appeared out of nowhere. I limped the twenty-eight kilometers (17 mi) to Logroño and spent the evening massaging, icing, and popping acetaminophen to no avail as the pain and swelling worsened. The only solution was rest. I had walked 163 kilometers (101 mi).

A few days earlier, I had befriended four Irish girls on a two-week holiday who planned to end in Logroño and take a bus to the seaside town of San Sebastián. That evening over drinks and tapas, they invited me to join them. I hesitantly accepted. Taking a break should help physically, but it also meant saying "see ya' later" to Henrik. We had grown close over the past week, and it saddened me to part ways.

I spent five days on the beach enjoying exquisite food, a life I could have lived indefinitely. However, the girls had to go back to Ireland, and I had a decision to make: restart from where I left off or cheat. With my leg in roughly the same condition, I took a train across most of the country to Sarria, a common starting point 108 kilometers (67 mi) from the finish.

I walked twenty-one kilometers (13 mi) to Portomarín, twenty-five kilometers (16 mi) to Palas de Rei, twenty-five kilometers (16 mi) to Arzúa, and nineteen kilometers (12 mi) to O Pedrouzo. These segments differed from the beginning due to the weekend warriors packing the restaurants and *albergues*. Entire towns were booked by the time I hobbled in. I began reserving everything online or befriending Spanish speakers who would call ahead to secure a spot for me. I missed the carefree nature of before. With Henrik and the Irish girls hundreds of kilometers away, it felt like I was starting over. I didn't invest much effort into anyone and hated myself for taking the easy way. This was much harder than the Inca Trail.

Pilgrims clogged the last hundred kilometers (62 mi) for good reason. Anyone who walked it or biked the final two hundred kilometers (124 mi) was eligible for a *Compostela*, a certificate that served as an indulgence, reducing the punishment for their sins. I didn't believe in the concept, but thought it couldn't hurt to have one.

On my final day, my hip twinged, my shin swelled, and I had tweaked my knee the day before. Eager to finish by early afternoon, I powered through my last twenty kilometers (12 mi). As I approached the finish line, I listened to *Fix You*. The song ended as I entered the square of the *Cathedral of Santiago de Compostela*, a towering combination of Romanesque, Gothic, and Baroque architecture. Alone and in a foul mood, I went to the pilgrim office around the corner, waited in line for an hour, and received my hollow *Compostela*.

The next morning, I entered the queue to pay my respects to Santiago. When my turn arrived, I knelt, faced the shiny silver coffin, faked a prayer, and moved on (M).

I had waited two years to walk the *Camino*, which was supposed to be about closure. My satisfaction was proportionate to the distance I covered, 273 kilometers (170 mi), just over a third of my goal. Meeting badasses who had walked from Germany and England added to my shame. I wish I could come up with a clever excuse like "the real failure would have been not trying at all." But that's bullshit. I was pissed at my lack of physical preparation, pissed I didn't have a life-altering experience, and pissed at my worst failure of 100 Places After. I had no one to blame but myself. Life isn't like the movies.

A few weeks later, Henrik finished his journey. At least one of us found closure.

Cathedral of Santiago de Compostela

87 ♦ Ngorongoro District, Arusha Region, Tanzania

I returned to Paris to collect my belongings. My lumpy shin and twinging knee limited me to only a few stairs at a time. Meeting Sondre in Dublin, Ireland, two weeks later, I passed as semi-normal. Over beers, I told him about my search for closure and how I planned to go to Africa. Yes, I know Morocco and Egypt are technically in Africa, but I wanted "Africa" Africa.

Five months later, it took me twenty-four hours to fly to Nairobi, Kenya, 145 kilometers (90 mi) south of the Equator. Like other developing countries, I arrived at a hot, dirty, chaotic airport. My pre-booked transfer never showed. With loads of men vying for taxi fares, I quickly found a replacement.

I embarked on a three-week camping trip. Have I mentioned I dislike camping? After an arduous Day 1 drive south, we pulled into a modest site on the edge of Arusha, Tanzania, set up our tents, made dinner, and washed the dishes in buckets of various chemicals. A well-stocked bar with Western spirits and local beers served as the evening's highlight. I felt rather good by bedtime, but the heat and stale air made for a mediocre sleep. My saving grace was a USB-powered fan attached to a battery bank.

Before dawn, I dispatched a few bugs in the cleanest bathroom stall before my morning confessional. Too tired to use bottled water, I brushed my teeth with the tap. I had my trusted ciprofloxacin, just in case. After breakfast, we packed our bags, broke down the tents, air-dried the dishes until damp, and continued south.

We stopped at a village of the Maasai Mara, an ethnic indigenous group of southern Kenya and northern Tanzania who had grazed livestock in the region for two centuries. A tale like many natives removed from their lands, the British relocated them in 1959 from the Serengeti to the 8,300 square kilometer (3,200 mi^2) Ngorongoro Conservation Area (NCA). Decades later, new legislation restricted further human settlement, paving the way for hotels—tourists proving more profitable than natives.

The slender villagers wore bright clothes and decorative beaded jewelry. Some sported shiny wristwatches, and many had shaved heads. Only warriors could keep their long hair. Huts made of woven sticks, earthen walls, dirt floors, and animal skin-covered beds delineated the village perimeter. Tables of overpriced trinkets comprised the center. Hell, it cost twenty dollars just to get into the village. But I couldn't fault the price gouging. They were reciprocating the best they could.

A campsite a few hours further and a few thousand meters higher brought cooling relief. As luck would have it, I had arrived during the start of the Great Migration, an annual affair of over two million wildebeest, zebras, gazelles, and the usual cast of African characters making their way from the NCA to the Maasai Mara reserve in Kenya.

With my torso poking out of the four-wheel drive vehicle, I wandered through the Ngorongoro Crater (M), the largest caldera in East Africa, roughly the size of Tallahassee, Florida. Interspersed amongst acacia forests, fresh lakes, and savannas were elephants, Cape buffaloes, lions, leopards, hyenas, vultures, Marabou storks, warthogs, wildebeests, zebras, hippos, giraffes, gazelles, and honey badgers. Only the rhinoceros eluded me. I had a decent start to African closure.

The Ngorongoro Crater

88 ♦ Zambia-Zimbabwe Border

The bus passed Mount Kilimanjaro, the continent's highest point. As it blinked into view, a measure of remorse arose. I had mapped out plans to climb the dormant volcano years earlier, but never pulled the trigger. I told myself I had done enough in pursuit of 100 Places After. Instead of standing on top of Africa, a blurry picture and a daydream had to suffice.

I continued through Tanzania, Malawi, Zambia, and Zimbabwe, logging over 4,700 kilometers (2,900 mi). For reference, the drive from New York to Los Angeles is 4,500 kilometers (2,800 mi). I never found another place during those two weeks. Arriving in Victoria Falls, I was relieved to be out of the bus and the tent. Full disclosure: I cheated a few times, renting the occasional hut to escape the heat or torrential downpours.

Sondre met me, having spent the last few days across the border in Livingstone. Months earlier, we enjoyed beers in our eleventh country together, having crossed borders by car, bus, boat, plane, train, and on foot. Our plan for the twelfth and thirteenth was the most elaborate yet.

We walked to Zambia via the Victoria Falls Bridge, a single-span steel crossing constructed in 1904-1905, to a shed that offered ziplining. We tried going tandem to cement our platonic bromance, but our combined weight exceeded the 120-kilogram (265-lb) allowance. We had to go solo.

The operator hooked my dual cables onto a thick, singular line stretching across the gorge. I slunk until my feet dangled, and the harness crunched my groin. After a gentle nudge, I was cruising one hundred meters (330 ft) above the murky, rapid-laden Zambezi River. The water's power generated dual rainbows spanning the chasm, with lush forest stretching to the horizon.

Thirty seconds later, I coasted to a stop in Zimbabwe and waited for Sondre. I bought beers for us back in Zambia as we sat in the sun watching people bungy jump for an hour before returning (M) to Zimbabwe for another beer. We concurred that this was our favorite border crossing.

Crossing the Zambezi

89 ♦ Cape Town, South Africa

Our apartment near the Cape Town, South Africa city center came with views of the windswept Table Mountain. Wanting to get up there sometime during the week, the term "weather-dependent" reemerged. A waiter offered the best advice: "If there are no clouds in the morning, you should go. If there are, you shouldn't."

I awoke to an empty sky and hesitated to disturb my late-rising roommate, but I figured it was worth the risk. By the time we had finished breakfast an hour later, a wispy haze had rolled over the mountain. I would have hiked to the top in my earlier days and deemed it a consolation for Kilimanjaro. Lacking time and desire, we opted for the cable car.

Unlike most mountains that rise to a point, Table Mountain is a three-kilometer (1.9 mi) plateau with vertical cliffs.* We walked half a kilometer over the undulating rocky surface and grabbed a seat overlooking the sprawling, unplanned metropolis with crammed streets running in all directions. The conical-peaked Lion's Head Mountain bisected the center from the coastal suburbs. Two water reservoirs landmarked the foreground, as did the fifty-five-thousand-seat Cape Town Stadium in the distance.

A guy in front of us had hopped onto a secluded outcropping. Wanting to outdo him for some silly reason, I sought to keep searching. Sondre said, "Sometimes you need to appreciate the view you have."

In my search for 100 Places After, whether a few steps this way or that, I never settled until I found perfection. Some instances required specificity, such as those relating to Jesus, the Great Pyramid, the Wannsee Conference, or Mom's house. In the grand scheme, the vicinity was good enough. But I sometimes missed the moment, like spending too much time behind the camera.

* The highest point of Table Mountain is 1,086 meters (3,563 ft).

I had known Sondre for three years, and two since he lost his stepbrother, Jan Ove. Since then, I shared experiences with him that I wouldn't have with anyone else. In doing so, I like to think I helped fill some of his loss, and in a way, he became like a brother to me.

I never thought a chance encounter in China would lead to a friendship that spanned the globe. Appreciating everything we had been through, I chose this generic spot on a mountain (M) before sharing a beer with my friend in our fourteenth country.

Me and Sondre at Table Mountain. Photo by fellow traveler.

90 ♦ Cape Town, South Africa

"white person" means a person who in appearance obviously is, or who is generally accepted as a white person, but does not include a person who, although in appearance obviously a white person, is generally accepted as a coloured person.

"native" means a person who in fact is or is generally accepted as a member of any aboriginal race or tribe of Africa.

"coloured person" means a person who is not a white person or a native.

— Population Registration Act, 1950

The one constant on the long rides from Kenya to Zimbabwe was impoverished Black Africans. These were some of the poorest places yet, rivaling Cambodia and India. As the bus slogged along, men in plastic chairs or women balancing heavy bags on their heads stared with confusion, disdain, envy, or a combination. Children waved with bright eyes and enthusiastic smiles, curious about the bus people. I don't know at what age their optimism turned to pessimism. I'm guessing around puberty. Smiles seem harder to come by as we get older.

Cape Town was different—a mix of races coexisting in relative harmony. A vast economic disparity persisted, but it was a far cry from anywhere I had been in the past few weeks. It was hard to fathom that less than a quarter-century earlier, the city and country were engulfed in racism at the highest levels.

The systemic issue stretched back to the mid-seventeenth century when the Dutch established the Cape Colony, a way station for ships traveling to the East Indies and the first European settlement in South Africa. Due to labor shortages, slaves were imported.

In the late eighteenth century, the Dutch, French, and British engaged in a series of wars, with control of the colony changing hands multiple times until the British gained decisive command in 1814. The empire passed the *Slavery Abolition Act 1833*, superseding all slave laws in South Africa and ending the practice. But over the next century, local laws denied suffrage, limited land ownership, required registration and documentation, and regulated the employment of non-whites.

South Africa became a sovereign state in 1934. During World War II, Black migrant workers flocked there to fill jobs due to a scarcity of white labor amidst rapid economic growth. The government failed to adjust to the migration, resulting in overcrowding and higher crime.

The ensuing cynicism led to the rise of the Herenigde Nasionale Party (National Party, or NP), a political party founded in 1914, comprised of mainly Dutch-descended Afrikaners and English-speaking whites. Running on a platform of nationalism and promises to ensure continued white supremacy, the NP gained control of parliament in 1948.

They believed South Africa wasn't one nation but four distinct racial groups: White, Black, Indian, and Coloured (mixed ancestry). To ensure the races didn't mix, the NP instituted legislation that became known as *apartheid* (apartness).

Anyone over 18 was categorized, often arbitrarily,* and required to carry an identity card. This segued into separating the races by area and the forcible removal of millions into *Bantustans*, a group of aside homelands, which the NP hoped would become independent nation-states not part of South Africa. Municipal areas were segregated, often with "whites only" signs in places far superior. Blacks could only work or operate businesses in white areas with a pass. Those caught without one were often arrested and prosecuted. Marriage or sex of whites and non-whites was illegal, communism was banned, education was separated, government representation was limited, and voting rights were restricted.

Unlike armies that defeated the Nazi's racial ideology, the fight against the NP was a methodical legal battle spearheaded by a man from the humblest of upbringings, who, by sheer willpower, sacrifice, and compassion, toppled those who sought to destroy him.

Born in 1918, Rolihlahla Mandela was the son of a polygamist chief. His pious Christian mother sent him to a Methodist school where he was baptized and given the name Nelson. In 1943, he finished his BA from the University of South Africa and pursued law at the University of the Witwatersrand, where he encountered racism as the only Black student.

His political activism began when he joined the African National Congress (ANC), a social-democratic political party formed in 1912, and he became a member of the national executive in 1950.

---

* One test, the "pencil test," involved sticking a pencil in someone's hair and having them shake their head. If it fell to the floor, they passed and were classified as white. If it stuck, they failed and were coloured or black.

Skeptical of a united multi-racial fight, his views changed with his embrace of communist ideologies, including those of Marx, Engels, Lenin, Stalin, and Mao Zedong.

The ANC launched the Defiance Campaign in June 1952, inspired by Gandhi's* non-violent *satyagraha.* Volunteers wore armbands, burned passbooks, and used "whites only" facilities. Thousands were arrested and incarcerated, but the campaign grew the ANC. Mandela's influence skyrocketed, making him a government target.

A month later, he and other ANC leaders were arrested, convicted of "statutory communism," and given nine months of hard labor. Thus began the legal cycle that dominated most of Mandela's adult life.

Following the violent suppression of demonstrators, particularly the Sharpeville Massacre in 1960 that left sixty-nine dead, he shifted toward armed resistance, hoping to exert pressure by targeting infrastructure for communication, transportation, and electricity with minimal casualties.

In preparation for a guerrilla war, he spent the early part of 1962 fundraising, speaking, and studying in Africa and London. Upon his return to South Africa in August, he was arrested and charged with inciting strikes and leaving the country without permission. The following year, police uncovered documents detailing plans to sabotage the government. Mandela's trial garnered international attention, prompting calls for his release. But he and two others were found guilty and sentenced to life in prison, narrowly avoiding the death penalty.

The convicted were sent to Robben Island in 1964, seven kilometers (4.3 mi) off the coast of Cape Town. Mandela broke rocks into gravel or toiled in the lime quarry during the day. At night, he worked on his Bachelor of Law (LLB) degree through the University of London. As a D Group prisoner, the lowest level, he was allotted one visitor and one letter every six months.

---

* Gandhi was murdered four years earlier.

His situation improved when he transferred to Pollsmoor Prison in suburban Cape Town in 1982. Suffering from tuberculosis, he was relocated to Victor Verster Prison on the Western Cape in 1988 and received his best conditions yet—a private house, a personal cook, visitors, and was allowed to complete his LLB.

Throughout the 1980s, the bloodshed in South Africa increased. With a civil war looming, Mandela was offered release multiple times if he denounced the violence. He rejected the proposal, arguing, what good is his freedom if the people aren't free?

The leader of the NP, Pieter Botha, suffered a stroke in 1989 and was replaced by F.W. de Klerk, a man with differing views who instituted sweeping reforms amid pressure from the international community. He rescinded bans on anti-*apartheid* groups, restored freedom of the press, and released political prisoners, including Mandela. After twenty-seven years of incarceration, he was freed without conditions on February 11, 1990.

Elected president of the ANC, he traveled the world, meeting politicians and heads of state. With *apartheid* declining and a new government approaching, the ANC and NP entered negotiations but distrusted each other. To stem the violence, de Klerk and Mandela agreed to a multi-racial general election and a constitutional convention. In 1993, the two men received the Nobel Peace Prize for their efforts.

On April 27, 1994, South Africa held its first fully democratic general election. The ANC won 63 percent of the vote, and Mandela was elected president, making him the first Black chief executive in the country's history.

He inherited a country in shambles. Significant portions of the Black community suffered from a lack of electricity, sanitation, clean water, illiteracy, and unemployment. He installed programs to increase welfare spending and provided free healthcare for children and pregnant women.

The new constitution allowed him to serve two consecutive five-year terms. He chose only one and retired in 1999, shifting his focus to combating HIV/AIDS, a problem he had underperformed on during his presidency. He took a significant step back from the public eye in 2004 but continued to advocate for causes worldwide. He succumbed to a respiratory infection in 2013 at 95.

Sondre and I boarded the ferry at the *Nelson Mandela Gateway To Robben Island*, arriving forty-five minutes later at an arid wasteland of shrubs and trees. An un-air-conditioned bus drove us past the primary school, guards' houses, church, and the quarry where Mandela toiled. A colony of penguins frolicked at the island's southern end. Cape Town and Table Mountain were visual reminders of how close he was to the world he once knew.

The Maximum-Security Prison, constructed in the 1960s by political and common law prisoners, closed in 1991, a year after Mandela's release. The inside was a somewhat better version of Auschwitz I. The bathrooms had concrete floors and white tile walls. Cells lined the narrow hallways. I didn't know which was Mandela's. A former political prisoner-turned-guide said it was "the one with the stuff in it." Reconstructed to its 1964 appearance, it had a thin mat, a few blankets, a table with a cup and plate, and a bucket (M). Gandhi enjoyed far superior possessions.

Nelson Mandela's cell on Robben Island

Mandela spent eighteen years in this elevator-sized cage of racism and nationalism, unfounded beliefs that being born with a certain skin tinge or on a particular piece of dirt makes a person superior. Like a whack-a-mole, the toxic combination pops its head up every so often in some corner of the world and wreaks havoc. For over four decades, the majority of his countrymen were oppressed by the minority, but Mandela's unending sacrifice ushered in a new South Africa, making him another "Father of the Nation."

THE LAND OF THE FREE? THE HOME OF THE BRAVE?

91 ♦ Plymouth, Massachusetts, USA

O say can you see, by the dawn's early light,
What so proudly we hail'd at the twilight's last gleaming,
Whose broad stripes and bright stars through the perilous fight
O'er the ramparts we watch'd were so gallantly streaming?
And the rocket's red glare, the bombs bursting in air,
Gave proof through the night that our flag was still there,
O say does that star-spangled banner yet wave
O'er the land of the free and the home of the brave?

—Francis Scott Key,
"The Star-Spangled Banner," stanza one (1814)

Before every major sporting event in my country, the crowd rises and faces the American flag. They remove their hats, some place their right hands over their hearts, and military members salute. The first stanza of the national anthem, "The Star-Spangled Banner," is sung.

The lyrics originated from the Defence of Fort McHenry, a 1814 poem by Francis Scott Key, who witnessed British ships assault the fort during the War of 1812. Like many traditions rebranded by America, the music is the official tune of the Anacreontic Society, an eighteenth-century English gentleman's club of amateur musicians named after the Greek poet Anacreon, famed for his drinking songs. Maybe that's why everyone gets so drunk.

It had been four years since my U.S. East Coast road trip. Since then, the views of my country had changed. Living in this tumultuous present, I examined my past.

My upbringing was inundated with the non-evidence-based belief that we were the greatest country ever created. Every morning in elementary school, I was propagandized by the Pledge of Allegiance.* History books focused on our virtues and glossed over our faults. Military commercials advertised our immense strength. The overwhelming theme throughout is our most coveted pride—freedom. It's a concept we love more than anything, so thick you can choke on it and be grateful you had the sovereignty to do so. What made us this way? Why did we think we were special? Was America the land of the free? Was it the home of the brave? Mom and I were going to find out.

My country's story is a geographic one. In 1507, fifteen years after Christopher Columbus's discovery of the New World, the German cartographer Martin Waldseemüller created a world map. As a tribute to the Italian explorer, Amerigo Vespucci, he named the lands in the Western Hemisphere *America.* Over the next century, European settlers made landfall on the Atlantic Coast, expanding westward over generations until they reached the Pacific Ocean. It seemed logical for me to follow a similar route.

A few months after Africa, I visited my family in Massachusetts and drove thirty minutes to Plymouth. Often referred to as "America's Hometown," it felt like a good starting point.

In the late sixteenth and early seventeenth centuries, English Separatists fled to Holland from England, seeking religious freedom. Fearing the loss of their language and heritage, combined with economic hardship, they embarked from Plymouth, England, in September 1620, bound for America. On board were 102 passengers (73 men and 29 women), with just over one-quarter being Separatists. The one-hundred-foot (30 m) *Mayflower* crew numbered twenty-five to thirty.

---

* U.S. Code 2011, Title 4, Chap. 1, Sec. 4 - "I pledge allegiance to the Flag of the United States of America, and to the Republic for which it stands, one Nation under God, indivisible, with liberty and justice for all."

Following a turbulent crossing, land was spotted off the coast of Cape Cod in November. The *Mayflower* attempted to sail south toward its intended destination in the Virginia Colony. But conditions and inadequate provisions forced it to dock in Provincetown. Failing to reach their objective and lacking legal authority to settle the area, some non-Separatists felt their contracts didn't bind them. An agreement, known as the *Mayflower Compact*, was drafted to maintain order and establish a framework for governance. Signed by forty-one free white men, it decreed that issues would be resolved by voting, thus setting the tone for American democracy.

The Pilgrims settled in Plymouth Harbor and faced a brutal winter that claimed nearly half their population. With assistance from local tribes, they learned to survive the harsh New England climate. Sadly, the peace wouldn't last.

In the summer of 1622, new English settlers established the community of Wessagussett. A year later, word reached Plymouth that Natives planned to attack both settlements. The claim proved false, but Myles Standish, a military officer, decided to strike first. He gathered some militiamen, lured three Natives into a home under the pretense of sharing a meal, and closed the door. Standish killed one, and his men killed the others. Four more Natives were executed outside. Hearing about Standish's actions, locals fled their homes, and the fur trade that the Pilgrims depended on dried up.

Things worsened for the Natives in the area and throughout the New World. Like most indigenous cultures touched by colonialism, their population declined due to war, disease, slavery, and territory confiscation. Conversely, Plymouth flourished as the oldest municipality in New England.

I pulled into the city of fifty-six thousand people, with an ethnic makeup of 92 percent white and 0.1 percent Native. Grey shingled roofs topped white houses, and magnificent boats filled the harbor. American flags adorned local shops, displaying fifty white stars representing the states and thirteen alternating red and white horizontal stripes for the original colonies.

I parked by a rock wall lining the shore and walked the main thoroughfare, Water St., towards an out-of-place house-sized portico with Roman columns. Below street level was a sandy pit with black metal bars exposed to the ocean. In the middle sat Plymouth Rock (M), the celebrated location where the Pilgrims supposedly disembarked in 1620, despite no supporting evidence.

In a prophetic metaphor for the USA's fractured future, the ten tons of Dedham granite split in half after the townspeople moved it in 1774. They left the bottom behind, transferred the top to the town meeting house, and then relocated it to Pilgrim Hall in 1834. The two pieces were reunited near the waterfront in 1880, and the date *1620* was etched into it.

The Rock ranked near the bottom of the 100 Places After. It would have been a waste of time if I had gone out of my way. It gave me something to do on a Tuesday. Despite the dullness, its symbolism is indisputable.

Through sheer determination and a bit of luck, the Pilgrims overcame adversity, illness, pain, and death. They bravely risked everything to pursue the American Dream before it even existed. It's a shame their freedom came at the decimation of others. Often, that's how freedom works.

Plymouth Rock

92 ♦ Boston, Massachusetts, USA

I caught a bus to downtown Boston and walked to Boston Common, the country's oldest city park. Dating back to 1634, it marks the start of the Freedom Trail. Envisioned in 1951 by a local journalist, the two-and-a-half-mile (4 km) route highlights the birth and rise of the U.S. from the seventeenth, eighteenth, and early nineteenth centuries.

I followed the double-brick path in the concrete, resembling the outline of the Berlin Wall, and stopped at the Old State House, the oldest surviving building in Boston. Less exciting than Plymouth Rock was a round emblem of cobblestones set into the ground with thirteen spokes intersecting at a central star (M). A brass ring on the periphery read SITE OF THE BOSTON MASSACRE - MARCH 5, 1770.

British taxation without representation in the 1760s, combined with troops stationed in Boston since 1768, had angered the colonists. On March 5, 1770, a confrontation erupted outside the Custom House when an angry crowd of colonists taunted and threw objects at a group of British soldiers. The situation escalated, and amid the chaos, the soldiers fired into the crowd, killing five colonists, including Crispus Attucks, a man of African and Native descent, often seen as the first casualty of the American Revolution.

The incident caused outrage throughout the Colonies, with Patriot leaders using it as propaganda against British authority. The soldiers involved were put on trial, with John Adams, the future second U.S. president, serving as their defense attorney. While most were acquitted, two were convicted of manslaughter and given reduced sentences.

The night of March 5, 1770, was hardly a massacre. Five deaths were insignificant. Still, it became a crucial event in the growing split between Great Britain and the Colonies' fight for freedom. John Adams summed it up: "On that night, the foundation of American independence was laid."

The site of the Boston Massacre

93 ♦ New York, New York, USA

On the shore dimly seen through the mists of the deep
Where the foe's haughty host in dread silence reposes,
What is that which the breeze, o'er the towering steep,
As it fitfully blows, half conceals, half discloses?
Now it catches the gleam of the morning's first beam,
In full glory reflected now shines in the stream,
'Tis the star-spangled banner - O long may it wave
O'er the land of the free and the home of the brave!

—Francis Scott Key,
"The Star-Spangled Banner," stanza two (1814)

A four-hour bus ride west took me to New York City, where I reunited with Sondre. I was last there in 2013 during the government shutdown. In search of more closure, we loaded onto a ferry bound for the Statue of Liberty, aka Liberty Enlightening the World.

Following the Union's victory in the American Civil War, Édouard René de Laboulaye, an abolitionist and president of the

French Anti-Slavery Society, proposed a statue to commemorate the country's centennial, reasserting the foundations of liberty and democracy. The U.S. government agreed that if the French paid for the statue, the U.S. would provide the pedestal on which she stood.

A fundraising campaign ensued in 1882. Emma Lazarus, a descendant of one of the first Jewish families to emigrate to America in the mid-1600s, was asked to donate a poem for auction. Her 1883 submission of *The New Colossus* gave hope to the oppressed seeking the American Dream.

The New Colossus

Not like the brazen giant of Greek fame,
With conquering limbs astride from land to land;
Here at our sea-washed, sunset gates shall stand
A mighty woman with a torch, whose flame
Is the imprisoned lightning, and her name
MOTHER OF EXILES. From her beacon-hand
Glows world-wide welcome; her mild eyes command
The air-bridged harbor that twin cities frame.

"Keep, ancient lands, your storied pomp!" cries she
With silent lips. "Give me your tired, your poor,
Your huddled masses yearning to breathe free,
The wretched refuse of your teeming shore.
Send these, the homeless, tempest-tost to me,
I lift my lamp beside the golden door!"

In 1885, Joseph Pulitzer, famous for the Pulitzer Prize and publisher of the New York World, initiated a fundraising drive to raise one hundred thousand dollars. In a shrewd business tactic to boost newspaper sales, he published the names of all those who had donated. Within five months, he had raised the target amount.

With sufficient funds, the pedestal was finished in April 1886, and the statue reassembly commenced. It had been built in France by Gustave Eiffel (the man who designed the Eiffel Tower), dismantled, shipped over, and waited in New York for nearly a year.

The final product signified the Roman goddess Libertas, the embodiment of liberty. Flowing robes draped the copper icon. Above her nondescript face sat a crown of seven-pointed rays, representing the seven seas and seven continents. Her right hand thrust a torch above her head, symbolizing enlightenment. Her left hand held a tablet inscribed with JULY IV MDCCLXXVI, the date of the U.S. Declaration of Independence. A broken chain at her feet embodied the nation's abolition of slavery. She provided the first glimpse of America upon arriving at Ellis Island, the busiest immigration gateway to the New World.

Despite her revered status, like many of my country's landmarks, her ironic symbology brought controversy. Most visibly was the depiction of a woman. On October 28, 1886, the island hosted a dedication ceremony attended by two thousand males, presided over by U.S. President Grover Cleveland. Only two females attended. The organizers asserted they couldn't guarantee a woman's safety amidst the crush of people. Angry suffragists aboard a boat got as close as possible and gave speeches promoting women's right to vote. (American women wouldn't attain universal suffrage until the passage of the Nineteenth Amendment in 1920.)

At the same time, millions of African Americans faced segregation, disenfranchisement, and racial violence under Jim Crow laws. The statue's symbolism represented liberty for some, but not for all.

Those seeking their American Dream via the Pacific faced similar hardships. The Chinese Exclusion Act of 1882, passed four years before the dedication ceremony, banned Chinese laborers from immigrating to the U.S. and severely limited the rights of Chinese Americans. Notwithstanding the statue's welcoming message on the other side of the country, Asian immigrants were often denied entry, subjected to racist policies, and frequently detained at Angel Island (the West Coast equivalent of Ellis Island, located in San Francisco), sending a clear message that freedom and opportunity were reserved mainly for Europeans.

From 1892 to 1924, nearly eighteen million people immigrated to the U.S. from the Eastern Hemisphere. Ninety-six percent were European, with the Statue greeting more than half. The government implemented an immigration quota system in the early 1920s based on each nationality's proportion of the 1920 U.S. population. Since most migrants were from Europe, the majority of future immigrants would also come from Europe. The quota system lasted until 1965, when it was modified at the height of the Civil Rights Movement.

One hundred thirty years after the dedication ceremony, Sondre and I disembarked on the back side of Liberty Island. The place buzzed with English and non-English speakers of all genders. I had never seen so many selfie sticks, symbols that the intended ideals of Liberty Enlightening the World had somewhat replaced the long-forgotten contempt of the unrepresented.

We passed a solitary American flag atop a tall pole and followed the tree-lined path to my country's most emblematic representation of freedom (M). Perched on a granite pedestal on an eleven-pointed star, she greeted ships entering New York Harbor from the Atlantic Ocean. As a born and bred multi-generational American, I can only imagine the optimism she infused in the tired, poor, huddled masses, yearning to breathe free.

Liberty Enlightening the World

94 ♦ Philadelphia, Pennsylvania, USA

And where is that band who so vauntingly swore,
That the havoc of war and the battle's confusion
A home and a Country should leave us no more?
Their blood has wash'd out their foul footstep's pollution.
No refuge could save the hireling and slave
From the terror of flight or the gloom of the grave,
And the star-spangled banner in triumph doth wave
O'er the land of the free and the home of the brave.

—Francis Scott Key,
"The Star-Spangled Banner," stanza three (1814)

We picked up our rental car near LaGuardia Airport, arriving in downtown Philadelphia a few hours later. It was late afternoon, and we needed a drink. A beer garden in the middle of the Independence National Historical Park, nicknamed "America's most historic square mile," would suffice.

Doing what we swore we wouldn't, a final beer turned into a final final, which led to a final final final. Enjoying my tasty beverages amongst the catchy music, I gazed across the street at another inaccessible locale in 2013. Wanting more closure, the following morning, we shuffled towards the most important building in my country's history.

In the wake of the Boston Massacre, relations between Britain and the Colonies deteriorated further. In general, the British Parliament passed legislation taxing, limiting, or punishing the colonists who defied the acts, leading to more legislation.

The cycle came to a head on April 19, 1775, when British soldiers from Boston attempted to seize Colonial ordnance in Concord, Massachusetts. The two forces clashed as the sun rose over the nearby town of Lexington. The minor Patriot victory inflicted low casualties on both sides, with the British tactically retreating to Boston. The American Revolutionary War had begun.

In May, the Second Continental Congress convened at the Pennsylvania State House, the *de facto* seat of the American government. A year later, Thomas Jefferson drafted the Declaration of Independence, a proclamation declaring the Colonies to be sovereign states no longer subject to British rule.

On July 4, 1776, the ratified document paved the way for the United States of America with the infamous line, "*We hold these truths to be self-evident, that all men are created equal.*" The document continued by listing King George III's "repeated injuries and usurpations," denounced the British people, and concluded that the Colonies were free.

On September 3, 1783, the war ended with the Treaty of Paris, which asserted United States sovereignty. Patriot deaths from battle, POWs, disease, or other causes numbered around twenty-five thousand. Britain and its allies lost about fifteen thousand. Paltry numbers for the wars to come. But unlike other British colonies that gained independence a century or two later, often through political means, this confirmed that blood would be the price of American freedom.

Congressional delegates convened at the Pennsylvania State House in May 1787, hoping to establish a new government. Over the course of four months, the United States Constitution materialized, becoming the supreme Law of the Land on March 4, 1789. The new country would operate as a republic, a theme reflected in the first three words of the preamble, "*We the People*."

Sondre and I arrived at the two-story red brick building with a steepled bell tower half an hour early for our 1 p.m. entrance and sat on a shaded bench as alcohol seeped from our pores in the suffocating heat. We had exercised our freedom to be hungover. When it was our turn, we filed into the rebranded Pennsylvania State House—Independence Hall.

Restored to its original appearance, the Assembly Room (M) featured a desk and chair at the far end, bordered by two grand fireplaces. Two rows of tables, arranged in a semicircle, covered the remaining floor space with quill pens, books, paper, and candles. A crystal chandelier hung from the ceiling, sparkling in the sunlight streaming through the windows with half-drawn, translucent green drapes. It was here that the Declaration of Independence and the Constitution were debated, adopted, and signed. Depending on who you were, these two documents defined your American freedom.

Independence Hall

95 ♦ Gettysburg, Pennsylvania, USA

O thus be it ever when freemen shall stand
Between their lov'd home and the war's desolation!
Blest with vict'ry and peace may the heav'n rescued land
Praise the power that hath made and preserv'd us a nation!
Then conquer we must, when our cause it is just,
And this be our motto - "In God is our trust,"
And the star-spangled banner in triumph shall wave
O'er the land of the free and the home of the brave.

—Francis Scott Key,
"The Star-Spangled Banner," stanza four (1814)

"*We hold these truths to be self-evident, that all men are created equal.*" Never has a more promising yet hypocritical statement been penned. After Thomas Jefferson completed his draft of the Declaration of Independence, John Adams and Benjamin Franklin made several edits. One was removing the condemnation of slavery, a decision that haunted the country, but was unsurprising.

American slavery began in 1619, the year before the Pilgrims set sail, when the first enslaved Africans arrived at the Virginia Colony. Over time, the practice expanded, becoming legal in all thirteen colonies. During the Constitution's drafting, the enslaved comprised one-fifth of the population, with over 90 percent concentrated in the South due to its agrarian-based economy. With nearly half of the convention's fifty-five white male delegation enchaining people, some Southern delegates would only join the Union if slavery was allowed. Concessions alleviated the stalemate.

Although "slave" or "slavery" weren't explicitly used, euphemized guidelines defined certain people's freedom. The infamous *Three-Fifths Compromise* counted "three fifths of all other Persons" and added them to the residing states' population, strengthening their political power through Congressional representation, taxation, and Electoral College votes. Other articles banned the importation of slaves starting January 1, 1808, and prevented states from freeing escaped slaves, ensuring they were returned to their owners.[*]

All Northern states had abolished slavery by 1804; however, it took decades to phase out in some.[†] The South had no intention of ending the "necessary evil," fearing emancipation would do more harm to the economy and society than perpetuation. Going a step

---

[*] Article I, Section 9, Clause 1 and Article IV, Section 2, Clause 3, respectively.

[†] Vermont was the only northern state in the 1830 census to not have slaves.

further, some considered it a "positive good," arguing Southern slaves had better lives than "wage slave" white Northerners dependent on money.

Despite the 1808 Constitutional ban, illegal smuggling persisted, but it was of little concern. There were already more than enough slaves. From 1810 to 1860, the slave population nearly quadrupled as slaves birthed more slaves, often with offspring resulting from owners taking sexual liberties. The child inherited the status of the mother, not the father.

Slaves numbered nearly four million by 1860, making up one-third of the Southern population and one-eighth of the entire country. Slavery was so deeply embedded in America that ten of the first twelve presidents owned slaves, eight while in office.* A more fitting statement would have been, *"We hold these truths to be self-evident, that all land-owning white men are created equal."*

In November 1860, the former Illinois congressman Abraham Lincoln was elected the sixteenth president, running on a platform aimed at preventing the expansion of slavery into new territories. Fearing the destruction of their economy and a reduction of governmental power due to the further unbalancing of free and slave states, seven Southern states—South Carolina, Mississippi, Florida, Alabama, Georgia, Louisiana, and Texas—seceded from the Union, emerging in February 1861 as the unrecognized country, the Confederate States of America.

Despite Lincoln's efforts to prevent armed conflict, on April 12, Confederate forces attacked Fort Sumter in South Carolina, igniting the American Civil War. Shortly after, four more states—Virginia,

---

* Presidents who owned slaves (CAPS denote ownership while president): GEORGE WASHINGTON (1), THOMAS JEFFERSON (3), JAMES MADISON (4), JAMES MONROE (5), ANDREW JACKSON (7), Martin Van Buren (8), William Henry Harrison (9), JOHN TYLER (10), JAMES POLK (11), ZACHARY TAYLOR (12). John Adams (2) and his son John Quincy Adams (6) never owned slaves.

Arkansas, Tennessee, and North Carolina—seceded and joined the Confederacy, splitting the nation in half.

Both sides bolstered their armies with new recruits, followed by the unpopular conscription. In July 1861, each army numbered fewer than two hundred thousand soldiers. By January 1863, the Union's forces grew to over six hundred thousand, roughly double the Confederacy's.

Further augmenting the Union's advantage, on January 1, 1863, Lincoln issued the Emancipation Proclamation, liberating the three and a half million Confederate slaves. Once they entered Union territory, either by escape or military advancement, they were free and eligible to join the Union Army. (The Emancipation Proclamation didn't free the half a million slaves in non-rebellious areas or those already under Union control.)

On July 1, 1863, the opposing primary forces of the Eastern Theater converged on the town of Gettysburg, Pennsylvania, a confluence of roads and a population of 2,400. For three days, ninety-four thousand Union soldiers of the Army of the Potomac clashed with seventy-one thousand Confederates of the Army of Northern Virginia using cannons, bullets, bayonets, sabers, stones, and hands. When the smoke cleared, Union casualties totaled twenty-three thousand and Confederate casualties twenty-eight thousand. Although it wasn't clear at the time, the Union victory is often described as a turning point in the war.

Two hours after leaving Independence Hall, we arrived at Gettysburg. The next morning, we drove from one preserved battlefield to another, passing rolling fields, period-correct wooden fences, and oxidized cannons the color of Liberty Enlightening the World. The heat was worse than the day before. It was mid-July, the same month the battle raged 154 years earlier.

I parked in a field and assured Sondre that this was our last stop. After the battle, the deceased approached eight thousand, making it the deadliest of the war. The rotting corpses were placed in hastily dug graves or left unburied. Appalled by the situation, Pennsylvania Governor Andrew Curtin commissioned a cemetery for the Union soldiers. Four months later, the process of relocating three and a half thousand bodies began. (Confederate soldiers weren't buried in Gettysburg. Efforts in the 1870s relocated them to the South.)

Abraham Lincoln, who was asked to make "a few appropriate remarks" at the cemetery's dedication, in 272 words, encapsulated the war, paid homage to the fallen, and offered hope to the living. It became one of my country's greatest legacies.

The Gettysburg Address

Four score and seven years ago our fathers brought forth on this continent, a new nation, conceived in Liberty, and dedicated to the proposition that all men are created equal.

Now we are engaged in a great civil war, testing whether that nation, or any nation so conceived and so dedicated, can long endure. We are met on a great battle-field of that war. We have come to dedicate a portion of that field, as a final resting place for those who here gave their lives that that nation might live. It is altogether fitting and proper that we should do this.

But, in a larger sense, we can not dedicate -- we can not consecrate -- we can not hallow -- this ground. The brave men, living and dead, who struggled here, have consecrated it, far above our poor power to add or detract. The world will little note, nor long remember what we say here, but it can never forget what they did here. It is for us the living, rather, to be dedicated here to the unfinished work which they who fought here have thus far so nobly advanced. It is rather for us to be here dedicated to the great task remaining before us -- that from these honored dead we take increased devotion to that cause for which they gave the last full measure of devotion -- that we here highly resolve that these dead shall not have died in vain -- that this nation, under God, shall have a new birth of freedom -- and that government of the people, by the people, for the people, shall not perish from the earth.

Abraham Lincoln
November 19, 1863

Memorials dedicated to Lincoln's speech covered the Gettysburg National Cemetery. Unsure which was legitimate, I asked a volunteer for clarification. He said none of them. Since the speech was so brief, nobody knew the exact location. It wasn't until 1952 that a librarian at the National Archives and Records Administration uncovered the only known photo of Lincoln on a platform surrounded by a crowd. Decades later, further analysis identified the location within the adjacent Evergreen Cemetery, which served as a Union artillery platform during the battle.

We walked along a concrete path that circled a doghouse-shaped mausoleum to where the volunteer had directed us. There were no plaques or monuments. It was all guesswork (M).

Lincoln never saw his belief that "*all men are created equal.*" Six weeks after the start of his second term, on April 15, 1865, he was assassinated in Washington, D.C. by John Wilkes Booth, a Confederate sympathizer and anti-abolitionist. Less than one month later, on May 9, the Confederacy surrendered, ending the American Civil War. In its wake were 1.1 million casualties, including over 650,000 dead soldiers—more than all other U.S. wars combined. Depending on their stance, they gave their lives either in the pursuit of or in the denial of freedom.

The approximate location of the Gettysburg Address

96 ♦ Memphis, Tennessee, USA

When our land is illumined with Liberty's smile,
If a foe from within strike a blow at her glory,
Down, down with the traitor that dares to defile
The flag of her stars and the page of her story!
By the millions unchained, who our birthright have gained,
We will keep her bright blazon forever unstained!
And the Star-Spangled Banner in triumph shall wave
While the land of the free is the home of the brave.

— Oliver Wendell Holmes, Sr.
"The Star-Spangled Banner" unofficial fifth stanza (1861)

Despite the Union's victory and a reunified country, anti-Black resentment ran rampant in the South. Various political maneuvers prevented Blacks (and, to a lesser extent, poor whites) from registering to vote and denied political representation.

During this period of disenfranchisement, the Jim Crow system of discrimination and racial segregation emerged. An antecedent to *apartheid*, though not as widespread, state and regional laws mandated segregation in public facilities, schools, transportation, and housing. Racial violence, lynchings, and economic oppression reinforced the system, keeping African Americans in a subordinate position.

In 1892, seeking to challenge a Louisiana law that required "white," "black," and "colored" to ride in separate rail compartments, Homer Plessy, who was seven-eighths white and one-eighth Black, bought a first-class ticket and sat in the white section. Arrested after refusing to move to the colored area, *Plessy v. Ferguson** (1896) made it to the Supreme Court, which ruled 7 to 1 that segregation was legal under the "separate but equal" doctrine.

---

* *Ferguson* refers to John Howard Ferguson, the Louisiana judge who originally ruled that racial segregation was constitutional.

Segregation remained the law of the land for over half a century until, in 1951, Oliver Brown tried to enroll his daughter in the closest school to their home in Topeka, Kansas (the state capital and about an hour west of my home). Denied entry, she rode a bus to an all-Black school farther away. The Browns and other Black families filed a class-action lawsuit. *Brown v. Board of Education of Topeka* reached the Supreme Court in 1954, which ruled 9 to 0 that "separate but equal" was unconstitutional, overturning *Plessy v. Ferguson*, at least regarding education. Unsurprisingly, the South didn't welcome desegregation.

On December 1, 1955, a seamstress and secretary for her local chapter of the National Association for the Advancement of Colored People (NAACP) rode a bus in the "colored" section in downtown Montgomery, Alabama. When the "white" section filled up, the driver instructed her and the other Black riders to move to the back. After the others complied, Rosa Parks slid into the window seat. The bus driver threatened to have her arrested if she didn't get up. Parks stood, or rather, sat her ground. True to his word, the driver called the police.

Parks was found guilty of disorderly conduct on December 5. On that day, leaflets were distributed to the Black community, urging them to refrain from riding the buses and instead carpool, take a cab, or walk. That evening, Black ministers and community leaders gathered to discuss future boycott strategies. The newly formed Montgomery Improvement Association elected 26-year-old neophyte and recent Boston University graduate with a Ph.D. in Systematic Theology, Dr. Martin Luther King Jr., as their president.

King organized the Montgomery bus boycott using similar strategies to those on the day of Parks's arrest. The lack of Black riders disrupted the city's economic and social fabric, leading to the Supreme Court ruling in *Browder v. Gayle*[*] (1956) that Alabama's

---

* *Browder v. Gayle* refers to Aurelia Browder, a Montgomery woman arrested eight months before Rosa Parks for sitting in the white section of a public city bus, versus W. A. Gayle, the mayor of Montgomery.

segregation laws were unconstitutional. Montgomery passed an ordinance allowing Blacks to sit wherever they wanted, ending the 382-day boycott. The victory propelled King into the spotlight.

In 1957, he, prominent Black religious leaders, and civil rights advocates founded the Southern Christian Leadership Conference. Inspired by Mahatma Gandhi, they emphasized nonviolent protests, often organizing sit-ins, kneel-ins, and marches. Aiming for media coverage to highlight the struggles of southern Blacks and gain public sympathy, the strategy saw mixed success.

King's most triumphant demonstration came one century after the Emancipation Proclamation with the *March on Washington for Jobs and Freedom*. On August 28, 1963, a quarter-million predominantly Black protesters descended on Washington, D.C., walking from the Washington Monument to the Lincoln Memorial. As the final speaker of the day, King entered the throes of American oratory lore with his "I Have a Dream" speech, referencing the Pilgrims, the Declaration of Independence, the Constitution, the Emancipation Proclamation, and the Gettysburg Address.

The following year, he attended the signing of the Civil Rights Act of 1964, outlawing discrimination based on an individual's "race, color, religion, sex, or national origin" in public accommodations. At 35, King became the youngest recipient of the Nobel Peace Prize. Watching "I Have a Dream" at the Nobel Peace Center in Oslo three years earlier, I saved a place for him.

We arrived in Memphis, Tennessee, on a gentle Monday afternoon. The streets were nearly barren in a city teetering on the edge of gentrification, yet unable to decide. Quaint shops struggled to attract customers alongside abandoned, windowless buildings. Gated apartments were around the corner from dilapidated lots. I didn't want to walk around there at night.

We parked near the former Lorraine Motel, a sixteen-room motel that catered to Black clientele during the segregation era. On the evening of April 4, 1968, as King stood on the balcony in front of Room 306, James Earl Ray, an anti-Black segregationist, pulled the trigger of a high-powered rifle from across the street. The bullet entered King's cheek, shattered his jaw, traveled down his spinal column, and lodged in his shoulder. Unconscious but with a pulse, he was rushed to the hospital, where he died an hour later at age 39.

His death sent shockwaves across the country. Riots erupted in over one hundred cities, including some of the largest in Baltimore, Chicago, Kansas City, and Washington, D.C.

A week after the assassination, President Lyndon B. Johnson signed the Civil Rights Act of 1968, expanding the legislation from four years earlier and making it illegal to discriminate in housing based on a person's classification.

The Lorraine Motel transformed into low-income residential use. A group of local businessmen purchased it and converted it into the National Civil Rights Museum, which opened in 1991.

The white curtains were drawn in every room. The same pale green of Liberty Enlightening the World and the Gettysburg cannons covered the doors. A white '59 Dodge and a white '68 Cadillac were parked out front. Room 306 on the second floor had been cordoned off, with plexiglass replacing one wall. Two beds had beige blankets, one with a corner turned down. From the window (M), I saw the balcony with a white wreath where the dreamer was slain.

Where the dreamer was slain

97 ♦ White Sands Missile Range, New Mexico, USA

Note: The following story is the only one not in chronological order due to its geographic location in the context of this chapter.

Perhaps my factories will put an end to war sooner than your congresses: on the day that two army corps can mutually annihilate each other in a second, all civilized nations will surely recoil with horror and disband their troops.

— Alfred Nobel (1891)

A few months before Plymouth Rock, Jeremy and I flew to Albuquerque, New Mexico, roughly three-fourths from Boston to Los Angeles. On a frigid April morning, we took Interstate 25 an hour south, stopping to fill up on gas and provisions. Another hour south, the roads shrank to one lane each way as we approached the middle of nowhere and turned onto a secluded thoroughfare, stopping behind a line of vehicles cresting in the distance. I inched forward, parked, waited a few minutes, and repeated this for another hour.

We approached the entrance to the White Sands Missile Range, a U.S. military testing ground, and presented IDs before continuing along asphalt without lines and a lane's width of sand on either side. Wispy, knee-high, faded green plants dotted the desert, stretching to the mountains. Arriving in the middle of nowhere, I pulled into a gravel lot. We walked a quarter mile (0.4 km) into an oblong fenced-off area, roughly the size of a football field, with a black lava-rock obelisk twice my height (M). An attached plaque read:

TRINITY SITE
WHERE
THE WORLD'S FIRST
NUCLEAR DEVICE
WAS EXPLODED ON
JULY 16, 1945

In 1938, German chemists Otto Hahn and Fritz Strassmann discovered nuclear fission, splitting an atom's nucleus into smaller parts. Fearing that the Germans would develop an atomic bomb first, the U.S. created the secret Manhattan Project in 1942.

Leadership fell to General Leslie Groves, a U.S. Army Corps of Engineers officer overseeing the construction of the Pentagon. He chose J. Robert Oppenheimer, a theoretical physicist and professor of physics at the University of California, Berkeley, as director to manage design and production.

It was a curious decision as Oppenheimer lacked organizational experience and a Nobel Prize, the latter an assumed requisite. Other Nobel laureates had been considered for the role, but none were sparable due to their importance in other projects.

Adding to security concerns were Oppenheimer's close ties with members of the Communist Party—his brother, his wife, and his girlfriend. Able to persuade Groves that he was the right man, the security requirements were waived, and Oppenheimer obtained the necessary clearance.

The next issue was the location. The original consideration was Oak Ridge, Tennessee, a site for enriching uranium and plutonium. Favoring a more remote location, Oppenheimer recommended the area near Albuquerque, where he owned a ranch. The easily accessible site had a mild climate, a low population, and was far enough from enemy attacks. The area around Los Alamos became the site of Project Y.

Research began in 1943. Oppenheimer assembled chemists, physicists, engineers, and other scientists from the U.S. and Britain. By the end of the year, Los Alamos's population had grown to three and a half thousand and nearly tripled over the next three years.

Anticipating a functional bomb design, Groves approved Oppenheimer's request to conduct a full-scale test in March 1944. The requirements included an unpopulated area, minimal wind to reduce fallout, and flat terrain to lessen the secondary effects. He selected a site in the northern part of the Alamogordo Bombing Range (renamed White Sands Missile Range in 1958).

On July 16, at 05:30 Mountain War Time, Trinity detonated with an energy equivalence of twenty-one kilotons (42 million pounds) of TNT. The fireball vaporized the one-hundred-foot steel mounting tower and transformed the sand into radioactive green glass, dubbed trinitite. A mushroom cloud rose seven miles (11 km) into the atmosphere, the cruising altitude of a passenger jet. Less than three weeks later, an atomic bomb destroyed Hiroshima, marking the start of a new, cataclysmic era of war.

In producing dynamite, Alfred Nobel hoped to create something so devastating that waging war would become unthinkable. He never witnessed the first half of the twentieth century, lowlighted by two world wars. The first was contemporaneously called "the war to end all wars." The second repositioned the benchmark for humanity's deadliest conflict.

I struggle to weave the underlying concepts of freedom and bravery into the prospect of nuclear weapons. The best I can do is elaborate on what Nobel hypothesized as the unnamed concept of Mutually Assured Destruction (MAD), a strategy in which two (or more) sides eradicate each other, regardless of the aggressor.

The problem with Nobel's logic—dynamite wasn't destructive enough. MAD wouldn't be coined or become possible until the Cold War, when the U.S. and the Soviet Union entered a nuclear arms race. In the decades to come, more countries attained the bomb, and concepts such as nuclear proliferation, nuclear warfare, nuclear fallout, and nuclear holocaust emerged. Humans discovered a new way to end humanity.

Despite Nobel's misguided judgment, his idea was sound. With the advent of MAD, conflicts in the second half of the twentieth century were less deadly than those in the first half, typically more localized civil wars or revolutions. There have been instances where this apocalyptic knife-edge balance was nearly upset. For humanity's sake, cooler heads prevailed. But as we can't put atomic weapons back in Pandora's box, the threat of global annihilation always remains.

Trinity was one of the most remarkable engineering achievements in human history, symbolizing what my country could accomplish. In the seven years since the discovery of nuclear fission, we harnessed the power of the atom and jolted the world into the Atomic Age, bringing various benefits.

Nuclear commercial applications, such as radioluminescence (a method of making things glow in the dark) and distinctive smoke detectors, became widespread. Nuclear medicine developed, enabling new imaging techniques. The arsenal to fight various cancers and blood disorders expanded with radionuclide therapy. Nuclear power provides a cleaner alternative energy source compared to fossil fuels, though it hasn't been without incidents.

The Trinity Site held its first open house in 1953. Open to the public on the first Saturdays in April and October, our options were limited, hence the non-chronological order of this story.

The Trinity Site

After seventy years, radiation levels were ten times higher than those of the normal background. One hour was equivalent to two to four times the daily average or one-quarter of a cross-country flight.

The black obelisk marking the hypocenter was as unimpressive as Plymouth Rock. But by taking Mom there, I found closure on my nuclear trinity—Hiroshima, Chernobyl, and the middle of nowhere.

98 ♦ San Francisco, California, USA

In the aftermath of Trinity and World War II, the United States emerged as the yin to the Soviet Union's yang. We were the self-appointed gatekeeper to halt the spread of communism, unified against a common enemy, proudly conveying the title as the leader of the "free world." But with the collapse of our nemesis, we needed a new adversary. Lacking an international bogeyman, we turned our attention inward and embarked on a new war, one not fought with guns, bombs, and tanks. It was a war of cultural ideology against ourselves.

We nitpicked at each other for a decade until a group of Islamic terrorists filleted our complacency. In the wake of September 11th, as America tends to do, we united when attacked externally, putting our internal issues on hold. But with each passing year, our minute differences pried us apart. We became divided on nearly every issue—economics, religion, abortion, guns, politics, and science. The buzzword *polarized* dug its way into the everyday vocabulary.

As I traveled west, discovering both the admirable and abhorrent aspects of my country, so did my polarization. I was proud of our founding principles but ashamed of our initial flaws. Proud of our ideals but ashamed of how we practiced them. Proud of our achievements but haunted by the costs. I was proud to call myself American, yet at times ashamed of America. I loved my country but loathed what it had become. Now, we lacked a middle ground. Compromise was a memory. We had mutated into a perilous dichotomy of left vs. right, blue vs. red, liberal vs. conservative, and me vs. you. We were anything but united.

January 21, 2017, another unforgettable day of division. I was in Africa during one of the long bus rides. I pulled out my phone and started reading about the *Women's March on Washington*, inspired by Martin Luther King Jr.'s 1963 non-violent protest. Through the power of social media, the demonstration epicentered in my nation's capital sparked the largest single-day protest in U.S. history and spread to every continent.

Protesters marched for women's rights, LGBTQIA rights, reproductive rights, racial equality, immigration reform, environmental protection, and other hard-earned, yet threatened freedoms. Reading about these demonstrations, I was glad to sit alone. No one saw me dry my prideful eyes. With 100 Places After nearing its end, I kept one in reserve to symbolize why America is the land of the free and the home of the brave.

Five weeks after my U.S. road trip, I flew to Berkeley, California, to see my paternal uncle, Curt. I would visit him every summer as a teenager when he lived in nearby San Francisco. Another world from the Anglo heteronormativity of my life, the city offered my first experience with diversity, a byproduct of its multicultural past that defines America.

Following its defeat in the Mexican-American War, Mexico relinquished California to the U.S. in 1848. That same year, gold was discovered in the northern part of the region, drawing hundreds of thousands of fortune-seekers. With some finding their riches and many not, the boom fast-tracked California to statehood in 1850.

As the easily accessible gold dried up, Native Americans were forced off their lands or slaughtered. Chinese and Latino miners suffered racism and violence at the hands of whites. With the end of the gold rush in the mid-1850s, San Francisco diversified into a banking center due to the influx of capital, only to be devastated by a 7.9-magnitude earthquake in 1906.

It served as a hub for the war in the Pacific during World War II while witnessing the mass internment of Japanese residents by presidential decree. In 1945, it hosted fifty governments to draft the United Nations Charter, seeking to maintain peace, promote international relations, and preserve human rights.

The 1950s saw the emergence of the Beat Generation and the San Francisco Renaissance. The 1960s experienced the rise of the hippies and the Black Power movement. The 1970s marked the start of the gay rights movement. The 1980s saw an increase in high-rise construction, accompanied by a surge in homelessness, and ended with the 6.9 magnitude Loma Prieta earthquake. The 1990s featured the dot-com boom and gentrification. The 2000s dealt with the burst of the dot-com bubble, paving the way for the explosion of social media and the rise of tech companies in the 2010s.

My favorite thing to do there was hiking the Marin Headlands, a hilly coastal peninsula located on the other side of the Golden Gate, a one-mile (1.6 km) strait separating San Francisco Bay from the Pacific Ocean. Starting in the 1820s, the most practical way to reach it was by ferry. However, as the city's growth lagged behind other major American cities, San Francisco needed a better solution. After years of legal battles and fundraising hurdles, construction on a bridge began in 1933. Finished in just over four years, the 1.7-mile (2.7 km) Golden Gate Bridge was the longest and tallest suspension bridge in the world at that time.

On a Sunday morning, Curt and I headed north from Berkeley, passing around San Francisco Bay, past San Quentin prison and Angel Island, into a parking lot for twenty cars. We descended a flight of stairs amid a lattice of beams and rivets. The six lanes of traffic roared above us. We emerged on the east side. Two tall towers supported thick cables with hundreds of ropes reaching the roadway. A dull, dingy shade of International Orange, it hadn't been painted in a while. The atmospheric haze made the Bay Bridge, the financial district, and Alcatraz Island barely visible. A dozen sailboats roamed the bay. We stepped on steel plates stamped with "USA" to the midpoint (M).

In the distance lay San Francisco, my relative utopia, representing the spectrum of humanity chasing their American Dreams. Aware that my utopia was a fantasy—as all utopias are—this one had crime, poverty, and a checkered past. What made it utopic was that it represented our progress.

The hardest thing for a person or society to do is to change. New is frightening, different thinking is counterintuitive, and blaming others is easier than looking in the mirror. This fear of new, fear of difference, and fear of losing power was the core of American division. But in understanding how my country has evolved over the centuries, transformation is not only possible, it's inevitable.

Religious Separatists sowed our roots. Colonists bled for independence. Immigrants crossed oceans, yearning to breathe free. The right to own people ripped us apart. We spent a century putting ourselves back together, losing one of our greatest dreamers along the way—all of it, every sacrifice, for freedom.

My country is far from perfect. It's full of those trying to deny the liberties of anyone who looks, sounds, worships, lives, and loves differently from them—a problem that has permanently plagued America. But since our founding, while it hasn't been a smooth journey, we have gradually pursued our asymptotic utopian goal where not "*all men are created equal*," but where "*all are created equal*." Where differences are embraced, not excluded. Where hate is abhorred, not applauded. Where acceptance triumphs over division. Where hope trumps despair.

The path ahead would be arduous, like it always has been, filled with setbacks, pain, and death. But as we have proven time and time again, the bravery of those willing to fight for their freedom and the freedom of others will prevail. We would emerge stronger, like we always had. That's why America was the land of the free. That's why it was the home of the brave.

The Golden Gate Bridge and my relative utopia

Closure

99 ♦ Maui, Hawaii, USA

I flew to Maui, the second largest of the Hawaiian Islands and the site of my favorite childhood vacation. Working a second job, Mom spent most of her expendable income on an oceanside luxury hotel with waterslides.

Stepping off the rental car shuttle bus, my silver sedan awaited in spot 100. I smirked at the number's coincidence. Maybe fate does exist? As much as I would have liked to stay at the opulent resort of my youth, I couldn't justify the cost. In part due to my cheapness. More so due to my continued lack of employment.

Like most who came into money, I was lax with it. I indulged in expensive activities, attended festivals where everything cost triple, visited some of the wealthiest countries, and had big nights out. I'm unrepentant about these expenses, as Mom had allotted the money for such purposes. But as my timeline extended, the more flights I took, the longer I traveled, the tighter my purse strings tightened. I scoured for cheap tours, stayed in crappy hostels, and spent more time at home. Being so close to 100 Places After, I could have splurged. Still needing to write this book, knowing my return to the working world wasn't imminent, I rented a tiny room with a mini fridge and twin bed on the island's western edge. I would clean it before leaving to save money.

A restaurant dinner served as my lone indulgence. I walked to a bar, ordered a Mai Tai and an ahi tuna burger, and watched surfing on TV. Next to me sat a middle-aged married couple finishing their meals. I overheard the husband comment on how much his wife had eaten. I glanced at a half-empty plate in front of a gaunt face and a scarf-covered head. She appeared to be in the final stages of cancer.

I'm guessing they were on a last trip together, a final hoorah before her end. It reminded me that time is our greatest commodity.

My alarm sounded at 2 a.m. Groggy and grumpy, I packed a cooler with water, soft drinks, and a sandwich. I reached the entrance to Haleakalā National Park an hour later, where the pristine highway grew steeper as I ascended the shield volcano, making up three-quarters of the island. The sweeping bends turned into blind switchbacks, and the air grew colder with each turn. Just after 4 a.m., I reached the end of the road—a cul-de-sac parking lot near the summit, with half of the forty spots already filled. You would be hard-pressed to find an easier way up a volcano.

A slight headache set in. I had been higher but never ascended so quickly from sea level to ten thousand feet (3,050 m). I emerged a shade before 6 a.m. The icy wind sliced through my T-shirt, hiking pants, and sweatshirt. I used a towel as a makeshift blanket and walked to a nearly enclosed octagonal shelter filled with gawkers jockeying for prime real estate next to an east-facing window. I wasn't in the mood, so I relocated to a nearby hilltop.

The summit sits above one-third of the troposphere, the lowest atmospheric layer where nearly all weather occurs, making it ideal for astronomical research. The Moon shone so brightly it cast shadows, and the stars pulsated. As the Earth rotated, light emitted eight minutes earlier from a sphere of burning plasma warmed my face and illuminated the nearly lifeless crater of conical mounds and lava rock. Mauna Kahalawai appeared in the distance, a volcanic peak half the height of Haleakalā, forming the rest of the island. Below it, dark water and forests sandwiched narrow beaches.

Haleakalā means "house of the sun." Legend has it that the demigod Maui climbed the volcano to lasso the sun, thus extending the length of a day. Whether it was rising early at Angkor Wat or Varanasi, the midday rays at any beach, a glimpse in Antarctica, or watching it set at Moulay Idriss, Petra, or Santorini, I never got enough sun, minus Salar de Uyuni. Partly for selfish reasons, but there was more.

An hour after Mom died, I packed her belongings and left the hospital. The rays of the sunrise erupted behind the clouds in a way I hadn't seen before. I took it as a sign she had arrived in the afterlife. Whether there was one or not, I didn't know. I searched for any way to rationalize what happened. Since that morning, whenever the sun popped out, though I knew it wasn't real, I associated it with her saying hello. I stood atop Haleakalā (M) until she waved from high in the sky, having attained my penultimate piece of closure.

Sunrise over Haleakalā

100 ♦ Maui, Hawaii, USA

It took Mom a long time to reenter the dating world after losing my father. Her lifelong struggle with being overweight made her self-conscious. During my teenage years, she garnered the courage to get back out there, but nothing materialized for a long time.

She eventually met a guy who was nothing like me, but he was reliable and made her happy enough. He could have left after her diagnosis and never looked back. He didn't. He comforted her, did the dirty work, held her hand during chemo, and watched her take her last breath. But with our lynchpin gone, I lost contact with him. We weren't friends and never progressed beyond a cordial relationship. I'm grateful for his care and comfort. That's as far as my affection went.

Together for over a decade, they maintained the status quo of boyfriend and girlfriend. In a way, I relished that they never married. It removed the guesswork from her healthcare, finances, and funeral arrangements. While I appreciated his input, he had no real authority. Still, part of me wished they had gotten married.

With her low self-esteem, his inability to commit made her feel inadequate. There's no question he loved her. But it's something that will stay with me. After she got sick, in a "shit or get off the pot" moment, she vowed they would marry on the beach in Maui at sunset upon a cancer-free declaration.

I left Haleakalā and returned to my room. In the late afternoon, I drove north along the coast towards the island's northwestern edge. I parked in a garage adjacent to a high-end tourist shopping center and walked through it until my toes touched the ocean. I strolled along the beach in front of the luxury hotel of my youth. The place looked the same except for some wear and tear.

Not wanting to be late for the imaginary wedding, I arrived well before sunset and sat on the beach. I thought about how the past few days reminded me of my journey. Scenic drives were reminiscent of those in New Zealand and Australia. The beaches resembled those in the Philippines. Haleakalā recapped Cotopaxi, the trails of the Galápagos, the landscape of San Pedro de Atacama, the crazy switchback roads in Tibet, and waiting for the sun's warmth near Everest. I couldn't believe it was ending.

A light rain fell, and a stiff breeze whipped up the sand. Far from the perfect setting, I feared a deluge would ruin this hypothetical weather-dependent ceremony. In a moment of serendipity, the overcast sky parted, allowing me to watch the same sun I saw rise that morning dip below the opposite horizon as I completed my search for 100 Places After on the fifth anniversary of Mom's death (M).

Melancholy washed over me. It wasn't the ending I had envisioned, but it was the one I had. As much as she wanted an enchanted wedding day, her greatest regret was not witnessing mine. It broke my heart, but I was never in such a position. There were a few romances in my life. Most never progressed beyond a fling. Or the rare case of falling in lust, which faded over time. I had yet to find soul-quenching love with anyone I considered spending the rest of my life with.

From the onset of my travels, I imagined meeting the girl of my dreams in a distant corner of the world. We would lock eyes and fall head over heels. She would join me as we gallivanted to exotic locales. After Mom's faux nuptials, number 100 would be my wedding. An idyllic backdrop. A romantic kiss. Cue the music. Fade to black.

As I have learned many times, life isn't like the movies. There are no slow-motion musical montages. The quarterback doesn't always throw the last-second touchdown. Not everyone lives happily ever after. This fairy-tale ending wasn't meant to be. At least not yet.

After returning from Africa, I met a girl in a chance encounter that blossomed into the most fulfilling relationship of my life. A few years younger and half a head shorter than me, she had long brown hair, green eyes, fair skin, and a great smile. Oddly enough, she had grown up just a mile from me. We had even been to some of the same concerts and might have crossed paths. The yin to my yang, she hadn't traveled much, didn't watch sports, and was free-spirited.

While our personalities differed, the little things strengthened our bond. We liked the same food and TV shows, shared a dark sense of humor, and enjoyed a cocktail with breakfast. We spent evenings out with friends. Evenings at home involved new recipes, eating them in bed, savoring wine, and cuddling.

Having never experienced love, I was unsure what it truly was. I couldn't explain why I always missed her, did things for her that I wouldn't do for anyone else, or placed her well-being above my own. It took some time, but I realized I had fallen for her—the girl whose contagious laugh made me laugh, to whom I told my secrets, whose overly generous heart softened me, and whose foot I would touch with mine as I fell asleep. I loved her. Sitting on the beach, wishing she were with me to watch the sunset, I thought of everything I wouldn't have done if Mom hadn't given me her final wish.

I wouldn't have conquered adventure sports. I wouldn't have found natural beauty. I wouldn't have witnessed extreme poverty. I wouldn't have studied genocides. I wouldn't have been scammed. I (hopefully) wouldn't have shit my pants. I wouldn't have pursued those who have done the most to benefit humanity. I wouldn't have run with bulls. I wouldn't have biked down a stratovolcano. I wouldn't have hiked the Inca Trail. I wouldn't have seen the top of the world. I wouldn't have learned about different religions. I wouldn't have completed my atomic trinity. I wouldn't have found freedom and bravery. I wouldn't have discovered hope. I wouldn't have made worldwide friendships. I wouldn't have found my love. I wouldn't have failed as much as I did. I wouldn't have succeeded as much as I did. I wouldn't have lived as much as I did.

Maybe someday I could take Mom to every country in Europe or South America. Or travel around Australia or Central America. Or finish the *Camino*. Maybe this book will sell a copy or two, and I could visit another hundred places. Maybe the girl I fell in love with would join me.

When would it be enough? When would I consider the wish fulfilled? Most likely, I would stop once I physically couldn't do it anymore. Until then, there would always be a temple, mountain, museum, or massive man-made thing to seek out. A tourist hotspot, an untouched gem, or a dead man or woman dedication. Whatever the future held, whether it was in the hands of God, Allah, Buddha, Brahma, luck, fate, or mine, going to 100 Places After was the most rewarding achievement of my life. It's a debt I can never repay to the woman who made it possible.

Closure

THE END AND THE BEGINNING

Mom had the ascites drained a few days after meeting with the minister, and the delicate dance of chemo, infusions, drugs, and scans resumed. Wanting a reprieve from the depression, she and her boyfriend went to a lake in central Missouri, three hours from home. She worsened each day as the refilling ascites distended her stomach and morphed her feet into swollen anchors.

Besides death, her biggest worry was being a burden. She feared not being able to go to the bathroom alone, feed herself, or climb the stairs. Those days had arrived. She had fallen in public, unable to lift her leg up a single step, embarrassing her beyond words. The cancer had stripped her health. It was finishing off her pride.

They cut the trip short by a day and went to the hospital, where my father died. I received a call from her boyfriend, who told me her vital signs dropped after the paracentesis. She was in the emergency room.

I hurried to find her connected to an oxygen cannula and other tubes. She greeted me with a smile. I reciprocated and hugged her. A nurse entered and said one of Mom's levels was low, and drinking milk was the easiest way to raise it. Mom hated milk, but it was better than chemo. She took a few sips. I pushed her to drink more. I thought she was being obstinate. She leaned over and vomited. Erring on the side of caution, the hospital admitted her.

A doctor emerged hours later. The unalarmed man recommended fluids and thought she would go home in a day or two. Covering all options, he asked what to do if her heart stopped. She adamantly said they should take extreme measures.

Her boyfriend stayed with her. I went to my place for a few hours of sleep and returned early in the morning. Not much had changed. Being prone for the past twelve hours made Mom fussy, and she wanted to sit in the chair beside the bed. The nurses got her upright, but an erratic heartbeat arose, so the hospital moved her to the cardiac unit for closer observation.

Mom's best friend for over twenty years, Amy, who was like my second mom to me, stopped by. Her presence brought optimism as they talked and joked until Mom fell asleep. I discussed the situation with Amy as tears filled my eyes, and I turned away in shame. I had been stoic until then, but I couldn't hold back the flood. Amy embraced me as I sobbed, shuddered, and spasmed. I apologized. She responded, "For what?" I felt terrible that I got her shirt wet.

We debated what to do about my Aunt Karen, who knew Mom was in the hospital but didn't realize how fast things were deteriorating. None of us could believe it. We thought it was best she come out. When she arrived the next day, Mom mumbled, "What are you doing here?!" recognizing how serious things must be for her sister to show up. I told the partial truth that she came to give me a hand.

I moved into the hospital, attending to every need I could: water, repositioning, and feeding. Mom had managed two spoonfuls of pudding since her admission. The nurses handled things outside of my purview. None of it mattered. She wasn't improving. As her health declined, the mystery of why increased. The assumption was she would make it at least to Christmas. It was early September. The hypothesis was the ascites. The problem was that no one had saved any fluid for testing. Mom needed another paracentesis.

Nurses moved her onto a gurney. All she could say was, "Ow, ow, ow!" She returned an hour later, again saying, "Ow, ow, ow!" The tests showed a severe infection. We don't know how it started, but it explained why everything was spiraling out of control. Gasoline had been dumped on an inferno.

Her speech worsened the next day as she slurred and struggled to form sentences. She became angry, unable to complete even the simplest tasks. Around midday, she had a hot flash and started sweating. I ran to get a fan. When I returned, she was breathing heavily, and her lips were blue. I asked what was wrong. She mustered "cold" as a debilitating agony erupted in her stomach. I called a nurse, who gave her pain medication. Until then, she had only taken acetaminophen.

I was pulled aside and told the outlook—less than twenty-four hours. I called her friends to give them a chance to say goodbye. To gain closure for both them and Mom, though she didn't know it. Visitors filled the hallway, awaiting a final conversation. I stood at the end of the corridor and watched the sunset.

When everyone had left, I tried sleeping in a chair while holding her hand. Around 3 a.m., I noticed a change in her breathing. The rhythmic slumber had shifted into an agitated groan. Her lips were blue again, and she had lost all ability to speak. I looked into her eyes and saw terror. Something had ruptured. I ran into the hallway and found a nurse who did what she could. Strong medication required physician approval. But within a half-hour of the morphine, Mom fell asleep for the last time.

I discussed the final stages with a doctor and asked that we keep her comfortable without extreme measures. He agreed and suggested transferring her to the cancer unit, which is better equipped for end-of-life care. A nurse attached a DO NOT RESUSCITATE bracelet before wheeling her to the older section of the hospital. I sensed death in the dank air.

The twenty-four-hour deadline passed. Sedated with a morphine drip, it became a waiting game. No longer on monitoring equipment, I didn't know what was happening. A nurse asked about organ donation. I said there was nothing worth giving. More friends came to pay their respects. I sometimes asked everyone to leave the room so I could hug Mom and tell her I would be fine. There would be no more pain. It was OK to go. She never responded.

Around 5 a.m., her breathing became a laborious, throaty gasp as she bit the air. The death rattle had begun. Sitting in the chair, holding her hand, I felt a mix of emotions. I was exhausted in every way a person could be and wished for this all to end. But when it did, she would be gone. I sat and waited until the gulping slowed. I stood up. She gasped and paused, gasped and paused, gasped and paused. At 5:26 a.m., she took her last breath, her face went limp, her head fell, and her color drained. I clutched her, burst into tears, and wailed a sound I had made one other time. Cancer had won.

I slunk into the chair beside her. A bizarre cold sensation washed over me, unlike anything I had felt before, lasting only a few seconds. I don't know if the soul is real. If it is, Mom hugged me one last time. I told her "goodbye."

I composed myself, packed up, and left the room. I looked away as a man wheeled her out in a black bag. Karen and I exited the hospital just before 7 a.m. The piercing rays of a sunrise greeted us.

The next day, I told the funeral director that Mom desired cremation. Not long after, her ravaged body and the cancer were set ablaze. When the fire was extinguished, all that remained was a silver urn with her ashes and a memory. One month later, I opened the lid and prepared to take my first small step toward fulfilling her final wish. I wondered where she would take me.

Mom and I
Top left and bottom left photo by Karen Lewis.
Top right photo by Curt Hall.

ACKNOWLEDGMENTS

There are many people I would like to thank. Jeff, for his consummate advice and the "aha" moment of taking Mom to 100 Places After. Jeremy, for always being there and joining me on many adventures despite our tiffs. Lauren, for taking the great cover photo. Carl, for being my little bro. Aunt Karen for her help in the hospital. Uncle Curt, who encouraged my unemployment. Steve, for having me watch *The Way*. Sondre, for meeting me in the far corners of the world, doing whatever we do during the day, meeting for dinner, and trying not to travel on Sundays. Hannah for being my shadow, loving me unconditionally, and smelling everything on our w-a-l-k's. Amy for always being there for her bonus son. Debbie for helping with the book, coming up with ideas, allowing me to execute them, and letting me tell her I love her every day. And Mom, who brought me into this world, raised me, suffered more than a person should, and allowed me to live my dreams.

THANK YOU

100 Places After was about more than just the miles traveled. It was about honoring a wish, finding meaning in unexpected places, and holding onto the moments that shaped me.

If this book moved you, inspired you, or gave you something to carry forward, I would be grateful if you shared your honest thoughts in a review. Your feedback not only helps other readers discover this story but also supports me in bringing more journeys to life.

If you would like to continue traveling with me, I invite you to explore my guidebook, *How to Travel the World*. It's filled with the lessons, tips, and insights that I gathered along the way.

Thank you for joining me on this journey.

BIBLIOGRAPHY

Aarvik, E. (n.d.). *The Nobel Peace Prize 1989 Presentation Speech*. (Nobelprize.org) Retrieved October 7, 2022, from https://web.archive.org/web/20080906163726/http:/nobelprize.org/peace/laureates/1989/presentation-speech.html

AJ Hackett. (n.d.). *How one man from New Zealand brought Bungy Jumping to the world!* Retrieved August 17, 2020, from https://web.archive.org/web/20080917012328/http://www.ajhackett.com.au/history.html#info

Allilueva, S. (2016). *Twenty letters to a friend: A Memoir*. New York: Harper Collins.

Argyle, C. (1980). *Chronology of World War II*. London: Marshall Cavendish Books Limited.

Aries, E., Andersen, R., Hsiang-Ching, K., Murphy, S., & Kochanek, K. (2003). *Deaths: Final data for 2001. National vital statistics reports; vol 52 no 3*. Hyattsville, Maryland: National Center for Health Statistics.

Armatta, J. (2010). *Twilight of Impunity: The War Crimes Trial of Slobodan Milosevic*. Durham, NC: Duke University Press.

Atomicarchive.com. (n.d.). *Radiation at Trinity Site*. Retrieved February 15, 2023, from https://www.atomicarchive.com/history/trinity/radiation.html

Auschwitz-Birkenau State Museum. (2020). *Early concepts*. Retrieved December 28, 2020, from http://auschwitz.org/en/history/auschwitz-ii/early-concepts

Ball, T., & Dagger, R. (2019, November 13). *communism*. (Encyclopedia Britannica) Retrieved August 17, 2022, from https://www.britannica.com/topic/communism

Baum, L. F. (1900). *The Wonderful Wizard of Oz*. Chicago: Geo. M. Hill Co.

BBC. (2011, March 10). *Profile: The Dalai Lama*. Retrieved October 7, 2022, from https://www.bbc.com/news/world-asia-pacific-12700331

BBC News. (2014, December 10). *World's 'first' bungee jump on film*. (BBC) Retrieved August 17, 2020, from https://www.bbc.com/news/av/uk-england-29819029/world-s-first-bungee-jump-in-bristol-captured-on-film

Boddy-Evans, A. (2018, August 15). *Timeline: Enslavement in the Cape Colony*. (ThoughtCo) Retrieved December 8, 2022, from https://www.thoughtco.com/timeline-slavery-in-the-cape-colony-44550

Bradford, W. (1901). *Bradford's History "Of Plimoth Plantation."*. Boston: Wright & Potter Printing Co.

Braun, D. (2012). *National Geographic Tales of the Weird: Unbelievable True Stories*. National Geographic Socieity.

Britannica, The Editors of Encyclopaedia. (2021, December 6). *Alfred Nobel*. (Encyclopedia Britannica) Retrieved February 23, 2022, from https://www.britannica.com/biography/Alfred-Nobel

Britannica, The Editors of Encyclopaedia. (2021, November 1). *Chinese Civil War summary*. (Encyclopedia Britannica) Retrieved August 17, 2023, from https://www.britannica.com/summary/Chinese-Civil-War

Britannica, The Editors of Encyclopaedia. (2022, August 26). *Temple of Jerusalem*. (Encyclopedia Britannica) Retrieved October 11, 2022, from https://www.britannica.com/topic/Temple-of-Jerusalem

Britannica, The Editors of Encyclopaedia. (24, June 2024). *Battle of Gettysburg*. (Encyclopedia Britannica) Retrieved June 26, 2024, from https://www.britannica.com/event/Battle-of-Gettysburg

Britannica.com. (2020, November 10). *Toward the "second Revolution": 1927–30*. Retrieved June 13, 2022, from https://www.britannica.com/place/Soviet-Union/Toward-the-second-Revolution-1927-30#ref42055

Britannica.com. (2022, Mar 1). *The Soviet Union: Atomic weapons*. Retrieved June 13, 2022, from https://www.britannica.com/technology/nuclear-weapon/The-Soviet-Union

Broomfield, M. (2017, January 23). *Women's March against Donald Trump is the largest day of protests in US history, say political scientists*. Retrieved from Independent: https://www.independent.co.uk/news/world/americas/womens-march-anti-donald-trump-womens-rights-largest-protest-demonstration-us-history-political-scientists-a7541081.html

Brown, J. (1906). *The Pilgrim Fathers of New England and Their Puritan Successors.* London: The Religious Tract Society.

Browning, C. R. (2004). *The Origins of the Final Solution.* Lincoln, Nebraska: University of Nebraska Press.

Buckley, M. (2012). *Tibet.* Guilford, Connecticut: The Globe Pequot Press Inc.

Casson, L. (2001). *Libraries in the Ancient World.* New Haven: Yale University Press.

Castellar-Gassol, J. (1999). *Gaudi: The Life of a Visionary.* Barcelona, Catalonia: Edicions de 1984.

Central People's Government of the People's Republic of China & Local Government of Tibet. (1951, May 23). The Agreement of the Central People's Government and the local government of Tibet on Measures for the Peaceful Liberation of Tibet.

Chan, A. (2001). *Mao's Crusade: Politics and Policy Implementation in China's Great Leap Forward.* New York: Oxford University Press.

Chernow, R. (2010). *Washington: A Life.* New York: The Penguin Press.

Clodfelter, M. (2008). *Warfare and Armed Conflicts: A Statistical Encyclopedia of Casualty and Other Figures, 1494-2007.* Jefferson, North Carolina: McFarland & Company, Inc.

CNN Library. (2018, September 3). *Ground Zero Memorial and Rebuilding Fast Facts*. (CNN) Retrieved May 5, 2021, from https://www.cnn.com/2013/07/27/us/ground-zero-memorial-and-rebuilding-fast-facts/

Colic-Peisker, D. V. (2003). *Bosnian refugees in Australia: identity, community and labour market integration.* Geneva: United Nations High Commissioner for Refugees.

Crowe, D. (2004). *Oskar Schindler: The Untold Account of His Life, Wartime Activities, and the True Story Behind the List.* Cambridge, MA: Westview Press.

Dalai Lama XIV. (1990). *Freedom in Exile: The Autobiography of the Dalai Lama.* New York: Harper Collins.

deadsea.com. (2020). *10 Most Important Facts about the Dead Sea*. Retrieved September 27, 2022, from https://deadsea.com/articles-tips/travel-tips/10-most-important-facts-about-the-dead-sea/

Desmond, A., & Moore, J. (1991). *Darwin: The Life of a Tormented Evolutionist.* New York: Warner Books.

Dickey, E. (2007). *Ancient Greek Scholarship: A Guide to Finding, Reading, and Understanding Scholia, Commentaries, Lexica, and Grammatical Treatises, from Their Beginnings to the Byzantine Period.* Oxford: Oxford University Press.

Diebelius, G. (2016, January 5). *Mount Everest had its highest death toll ever in 2015 with 22 climbers killed (and NOBODY reached the summit)*. (Dailymail.com) Retrieved September 15, 2022, from https://www.dailymail.co.uk/travel/travel_news/article-3385160/Mount-Everest-highest-death-toll-2015-22-climbers-killed-reached-summit.html

Documentation Center of Cambodia. (2007). *A Hisotry of Democratic Kampuchea (1975-1979).* Phnom Penh, Cambodia: Documentation Center of Cambodia.

Documentation Center of Cambodia. (2007). *A History of Democratic Kampuchea (1975-1979).* Phnom Penh, Cambodia: Documentation Center of Cambodia.

Documentation Center of Cambodia. (2007). *A History of Democratic Kampuchea (1975-1979).* Phnom Penh, Cambodia.

Duignan, B. (2022, May 11). *Plessy v. Ferguson.* (Encyclopedia Britannica) Retrieved February 13, 2023, from https://www.britannica.com/event/Plessy-v-Ferguson-1896

Encyclopedia.com. (2019). *Little Red Book.* Retrieved September 23, 2021, from https://www.encyclopedia.com/social-sciences/applied-and-social-sciences-magazines/little-red-book

Engels, F., & Marx, K. (1848). *Manifesto of the Communist Party.* Moscow: Progress Publishers.

Esposito, J. L. (1999). *The Oxford History of Islam.* Oxford: Oxford University Press.

Eustache, D. (2012). *Idrīs I.* (Encyclopaedia of Islam, Second Edition) Retrieved January 19, 2022, from https://referenceworks.brillonline.com/entries/encyclopaedia-of-islam-2/idris-i-SIM_3492?s.num=0&s.rows=20&s.f.s2_parent=s.f.book.encyclopaedia-of-islam-2&s.q=Idris+I

Ferling, J. (2009). *The Ascent of George Washington: The Hidden Political Genius of an American Icon.* New York: Bloomsbury Press.

Figes, O. (1997). *A People's Tragedy : The Russian Revolution 1891-1924.* London: Pimlico.

Fischer, L. (1964). *The Life of Lenin.* New York: Harper & Row.

Fleming, F. (2000, November 3). *Cliffhanger at the top of the world.* (Guardian News & Media Limited) Retrieved April 6, 2021, from https://www.theguardian.com/books/2000/nov/04/historybooks.books

Fowler, J. D. (1997). *Hinduism: Beliefs and Practices.* Brighton: Sussex Academic Press.

Fraser, N., & Navarro, M. (1996). *Evita: The Real Lives of Eva Perón.* London: André Deutsch.

Gandhi, M. (1940, December 24). *Letter to Adolf Hitler.* Retrieved from mkgandhi.org: https://www.mkgandhi.org/letters/hitler_ltr1.php

Gandhi, M. (1962). *Last Glimpses Of Bapu.* Agra: Radhey Mohan Agarwala.

Gandhi, R. (2007). *Gandhi: The man, His People, and the Empire.* Berkeley: University of California Press.

Ghose, T. (2017, May 7). *Happy Birthday, Dynamite: Interesting Facts About the Explosive Material.* (LiveScience) Retrieved February 23, 2022, from https://www.livescience.com/59000-interesting-facts-about-dynamite.html

Government of Nepal. (2015). *Incident Report of Earthquake 2015.* Retrieved September 15, 2022, from https://web.archive.org/web/20150629024928/http:/drrportal.gov.np/incidentreport

Groves, L. R. (1962). *Now it can be told: The Story of the Manhattan Project.* New York: Harper & Row.

Hakeda, Y. S. (1972). *Kūkai: Major Works.* New York: Columbia University Press.

Hantel, A. (2017, November 29). *How cancer affects men and women differently.* (Edward-Elmhurst Health) Retrieved November 18, 2022, from https://www.eehealth.org/blog/2017/11/how-cancer-affects-men-and-women-differently/#:~:text=Statistics%20show%201%20in%202%20men%20will%20develop,men%20are%20prostate%2C%20colon%2C%20lung%20and%20skin%20cancers.

Harris, J. (1985). *A Statue for America: The First 100 Years of the Statue of Liberty.* New York: Macmillan Publishing Company.

Hemingway, E. (1923). *Pamplona in July: World's Series of Bull Fighting a Mad, Whirling.* Toronto: Toronto Star Weekly.

History.com Editors. (2021, August 4). *American bomber drops atomic bomb on Hiroshima.* Retrieved 7 2021, December, from https://www.history.com/this-day-in-history/american-bomber-drops-atomic-bomb-on-hiroshima

History.com Editors. (2023, January 10). *Ellis Island.* (History) Retrieved January 16, 2023, from https://www.history.com/topics/immigration/ellis-island

Hitler, A. (1925). *Mein Kampf.*

Hitler, A. (1945, April 29). *My political testament.* (Hitler.org) Retrieved August 10, 2022, from https://en.wikisource.org/wiki/My_Political_Testament

Independent Electoral Commission. (2022, May 31). *Elections '94.* Retrieved December 8, 2022, from https://web.archive.org/web/20080628132254/http:/www.elections.org.za/Elections94.asp

Ingrao, C., & Emmert, T. A. (2013). *Confronting the Yugoslav Controversies: A Scholars' Initiative.* West Lafayette, Indiana: Purdue University Press.

Interfax-Ukraine. (2010, January 4). *Chornobyl nuclear power plant site to be cleared by 2065.* (KyivPost) Retrieved October 26, 2022, from https://web.archive.org/web/20121005150746/http:/www.kyivpost.com/content/ukraine/chornobyl-nuclear-power-plant-site-to-be-cleared-b-56391.html

International Atomic Energy Agency. (1996). *Ten Years After Chernobyl: What Do We Really Know?* Vienna.

International Atomic Energy Agency. (2022, October 25). *CHERNOBYL-3 Permanent Shutdown.* Retrieved October 26, 2022, from https://pris.iaea.org/pris/CountryStatistics/ReactorDetails.aspx?current=575

Jian, G., Song, Y., & Zhou, Y. (2006). *Historical Dictionary of the Chinese Cultural Revolution.* Lanham, Maryland: The Scarecrow Press, Inc.

Kabange, S. C. (2017, March 22). *15 of the world's best bungee jumps.* (CNN) Retrieved August 17, 2020, from https://www.cnn.com/travel/article/worlds-15-best-bungee-jumping-sites/index.html

Kaplan, I., McLauglin, J. L., Marvin, B. J., Nelson, H. D., Rowland, E. E., & Whitaker, D. P. (1971). *Area Handbook for the Republic of South Africa.* Washington D.C.: Foreign Area Studies (FAS) of the American University.

Kempe, F. (2011). *Berlin 1961: Kennedy, Khrushchev, and the most dangerous place on Earth.* New York: G.P. Putnam's Sons.

Kershaw, I. (2008). *Hitler: A Biography.* New York: W.W. Norton & Company.

King, G. (1994). *The Last Empress : The Life and Times of Alexandra Feodorovna, Empress of Russia.* New York: Carol Publishing Group.

King, G., & Wilson, P. (2003). *The Fate of the Romanovs.* Hoboken, New Jersey: John Wiley & Sons, Inc.

Kingdom of Navarre. (2014). *San Fermines, Feel the embrace.* Intermedio Comunicacion.

Lallanilla, M. (2013, October 4). *The Dark Side of the Nobel Prizes.* (LiveScience.com) Retrieved February 23, 2022, from https://www.livescience.com/40188-dark-history-alfred-nobel-prizes.html

Lama, T. D. (1999, September 27). *Long Trek to Exile For Tibet's Apostle.* (Time) Retrieved March 27, 2022, from https://web.archive.org/web/20010129054600/http://www.time.com/time/asia/magazine/99/0927/lhasa.html

Lampe, J. R., & Allock, J. B. (2022, August 14). *Yugoslavia.* (Encyclopedia Britannica) Retrieved November 1, 2022, from https://www.britannica.com/place/Yugoslavia-former-federated-nation-1929-2003

Lazarus, E. (1883). *The New Colossus.*

Lejenäs, H. (1989). The Severe Winter in Europe 1941–42: The Large-scale Circulation, Cut-off Lows, and Blocking. *Department of Meteorology, University of Stockholm, Arrhenius Laboratory, S-106 91 Stockholm, Sweden*, 271–281.

Lenin, V. (1935). The Testament of Lenin. *New International*, vol. II, no 1, p. 27.

Lewis, R. (2020, November 19). *Plymouth Rock.* (Encyclopedia Britannica) Retrieved December 14, 2022, from https://www.britannica.com/topic/Plymouth-Rock-United-States-history

Liang, Z., Nathan, A. J., & Link, P. (2002). *The Tiananmen Papers.* New York: PublicAffairs.

Life Magazine. (1948, March 15). Sacred Rivers Receive Gandhi's Ashes. p. 76.

Lincoln, A. (1863, November 19). *The Gettysburg Address*. (Abraham Lincoln Online) Retrieved January 31, 2023, from http://www.abrahamlincolnonline.org/lincoln/speeches/gettysburg.htm

Lindberg, D. C. (1978). *Science in the Middle Ages.* Chicago: The University of Chicago Press.

Lokos, L. (1968). *House Divided: The Life and Legacy of Martin Luther King.* New Rochelle, New York: Arlington House.

Long Bow Group Inc. (1995). *The Gate of Heavenly Peace*. Retrieved September 9, 2021, from https://web.archive.org/web/20120112022914/http:/tsquare.tv/film/transcript.html

Mahapatra, D. (2018, February 5). *How Supreme Court viewed words 'Hindu', 'Hinduism' & 'Hi ..* (The Times of India) Retrieved August 8, 2023, from https://timesofindia.indiatimes.com/india/how-supreme-court-viewed-words-hindu-hinduism-hindutva-in-rulings/articleshow/62782807.cms

Mandela, N. (1994). *Long Walk to Freedom.* London: Abacus.

Marshall Cavendish Corporation. (2011). *Islamic Beliefs, Practices, and Cultures.* Tarrytown, N.Y.: Marshall Cavendish Reference.

Mawdsley, E. (2007). *The Russian Civil War.* New York, N.Y.: Pegasus Books.

McNeil, W. H. (1976). *Plagues and Peoples.* New York: Anchor Books.

Melnik, N. (1986). The message on evacuation of Pripyat.

Mercier, C. (1998). *Hinduism for today.* Oxford: Oxford University Press.

Metz, H. C. (1989). *Jordan: A Country Study - Education.* (U.S. Library of Congress) Retrieved September 22, 2022, from http://countrystudies.us/jordan/43.htm

Meyers, J. (1985). *Hemingway: A Biography.* New York: Harper & Row Publishers.

Mintz, S. (n.d.). *Historical Context: The Constitution and Slavery*. (The Gilder Lehrman Institute of American History) Retrieved January 31, 2023, from https://www.gilderlehrman.org/history-resources/teaching-resource/historical-context-constitution-and-slavery

Montefiore, S. S. (2007). *Young Stalin.* Toronto: McArthur & Company.

mountvernon.org. (2021). *George Washington's Wil*. (Mount Vernon Ladies' Association) Retrieved May 24, 2021, from https://www.mountvernon.org/george-washington/slavery/george-washingtons-will/

mountvernon.org. (2021). *The Death of George Washington*. (Mount Vernon Ladies' Association) Retrieved May 24, 2021, from https://www.mountvernon.org/library/digitalhistory/digital-encyclopedia/article/the-death-of-george-washington/

mountvernon.org. (2021). *Washington's Changing Views on Slavery*. (Mount Vernon Ladies' Association) Retrieved May 24, 2021, from https://www.mountvernon.org/george-washington/slavery/washingtons-changing-views-on-slavery/

Mullin, G. H. (2001). *The Fourteen Dalai Lamas: A Sacred Legacy of Reincarnation.* Santa Fe, New Mexico: Clear Light Publishers.

Murphy, J. (1992). *The Long Road to Gettysburg.* New York: Clarion.

National Park Service. (2021, October 27). *Civil War Facts: 1861-1865*. (U.S. Department of the Interior) Retrieved January 31, 2023, from https://www.nps.gov/civilwar/facts.htm

New World Encyclopedia. (2014, January 14). *Great Purges*. (www.newworldencyclopedia.org) Retrieved June 13, 2022, from https://www.newworldencyclopedia.org/entry/Great_Purges

Nichols, K. D. (1987). *The Road to Trinity.* New York: William Morrow and Company, Inc.

Nicoll, F. (2009). *Shah Jahan.* New Delhi: Penguin Group.

NobelPrize.org. (1998, November 20). *Alfred Nobel's Thoughts about War and Peace*. (NobelPrize.org) Retrieved February 15, 2023, from https://www.nobelprize.org/alfred-nobel/alfred-nobels-thoughts-about-war-and-peace/

Nobelprize.org. (2020, December). *PRIZE AMOUNT AND MARKET VALUE OF INVESTED CAPITAL CONVERTED INTO 2020 YEAR'S MONETARY VALUE.* Retrieved March 1, 2022, from https://www.nobelprize.org/uploads/2018/08/prize-amounts-2021.pdf

Nolen, S. (2013, December 5). *Mandela arrived late to the fight against HIV-AIDS.* (The Globe and Mail) Retrieved December 8, 2022, from https://www.theglobeandmail.com/news/world/nelson-mandela/mandela-arrived-late-to-the-fight-against-hiv-aids/article548193/

Nuclear Energy Agency Organisation for Economic Co-orperation and Development. (2002). *Chernobyl: Assessment of Radiological and Health Impacts.*

O'Connor, T. H. (1993). *Building a Bew Boston: Politics and Urban Renewal, 1950-1970.* Boston: Northeastern University Press.

Olson, C. (2007). *The Many Colors of Hinduism: A Thematic-historical Introduction.* Rutgers University Press.

Orwell, G. (1949). *1984.* New York: Harcourt, Inc.

Pepper, W. F. (2003). *An Act of State: The Execution of Martin Luther King.* London: Verso.

Perkins, C. R. (n.d.). *1947 Partition of India & Pakistan.* (Stanford University) Retrieved September 5, 2022, from https://exhibits.stanford.edu/1947-partition/about/1947-partition-of-india-pakistan

Philbrick, N. (2006). *Mayflower: A Story of Courage, Community, and War.* New York: Penguin.

Pipes, R. (1991). *The Russian Revolution.* New York: Vintage Books.

Pipes, R. (1994). *Russia under the Bolshevik Regime.* New York: Alfred A. Knopf, Inc.

Population Census Data. (2022). *Hindu Muslim Population in India.* Retrieved September 12, 2022, from https://www.census2011.co.in/religion.php#:~:text=All%20India%20Religion%20Census%20Data%202011%20%20,%20%204%20%205%20more%20rows%20

Powers, J. (2004). *History As Propaganda: Tibetan Exiles versus the People's Republic of China.* Oxford: Oxford University Press.

Quan, C. (2021, September 28). *Forbidden City — All You Want to Know (History, Facts, FAQs).* (China Highlights) Retrieved October 1, 2021, from https://www.chinahighlights.com/beijing/forbidden-city/

Raus, E. (2003). *Panzer Operations: The Eastern Front Memoir of General Raus, 1941-1945.* Cambridge, MA: Da Capo Press.

Reiserer, A. (2011, April 8). *NOVARKA AND CHERNOBYL PROJECT MANAGEMENT UNIT CONFIRM COST AND TIME SCHEDULE FOR CHERNOBYL NEW SAFE CONFINEMENT.* (European Bank for Reconstruction and Development) Retrieved October 26, 2022, from https://web.archive.org/web/20110918032131/http:/www.ebrd.com/pages/news/press/2011/110408e.shtml

Renton, A. (2009, September 5). *'Tourism is a curse to us'.* (The Guardian) Retrieved December 2, 2022, from https://www.theguardian.com/world/2009/sep/06/masai-tribesman-tanzania-tourism

Robben Island Mueum. (2022). *Maximum Security Prison.* (robben-island.org.za) Retrieved December 8, 2022, from https://www.robben-island.org.za/maximum-security-prison/

Rotherham, F. (2004, August 23). *Can you Hackett?* (Fairfax Media Business Group) Retrieved August 17, 2020, from https://web.archive.org/web/20110717133251/http://unlimited.co.nz/unlimited.nsf/default/E71409A1DAE3EA24CC256EEC0010D618

Sampson, A. (1999). *Mandela: The Authorised Biography.* London: HarperCollins.

Schock, H., & Sohlman, R. (1929). *The Life of Alfred Nobel.* Surrey: The Windmill Press.

Service, R. (2000). *Lenin: A Biography.* Cambridge, Massachusetts: Harvard University Press.

Service, R. (2004). *Stalin: A Biography.* Macmillan: London.

Shackleton, E. S. (1920). *South: The Story of Shackleton's Last Expedition, 1914-1917.* New York: The Macmillan Company.

Shakya, T. (1999). *The Dragon in the Land of Snows: A History of Modern Tibet since 1947.* London: Pimlico.

Shirer, W. L. (1960). *The Rise and Fall of the Third Reich: A History of Nazi Germany.* New York: Simon and Schuster.

Shomali, Q. (n.d.). *Church of the Nativity: History & Structure.* Bethlehem.

Smithsonian. (n.d.). *The Lyrics.* Retrieved August 17, 2024, from https://amhistory.si.edu/starspangledbanner/the-lyrics.aspx

Söderlind, U. (2013, April 28). *The Nobel Banquets: The First 100 Years.* (Nobelprize.org) Retrieved March 1, 2022, from https://web.archive.org/web/20130428151100/http:/www.nobelprize.org/nobel_prizes/award_ceremonies/menus/soderlind/

South African History Online. (2022, June 1). *History of slavery and early colonisation in South Africa.* Retrieved December 8, 2022, from https://www.sahistory.org.za/article/history-slavery-and-early-colonisation-south-africa

Staelen, P. (2000, October 24). *La Conquête du Cervin.* Retrieved April 6, 2021, from http://www.acorfi.asso.fr/passe/2000-01/20001121.html

Star Spangled Music Foundation. (n.d.). *Additional verse for "The Star-Spangled Banner".* Retrieved August 17, 2024, from https://starspangledmusic.org/lyric/additional-verse-for-the-star-spangled-banner/

Strauss, V., & Southerl, D. (1994, July 17). *HOW MANY DIED? NEW EVIDENCE SUGGESTS FAR HIGHER NUMBERS FOR THE VICTIMS OF MAO ZEDONG'S ERA.* (The Washington Post) Retrieved August 2, 2023, from https://www.washingtonpost.com/archive/politics/1994/07/17/how-many-died-new-evidence-suggests-far-higher-numbers-for-the-victims-of-mao-zedongs-era/01044df5-03dd-49f4-a453-a033c5287bce/

Tames, R. (1972). *Last of the Tsars: The Life and Death of Nicholas and Alexandra.* London: Cox & Wyman Ltd.

Taylor, F. (2006). *The Berlin Wall: A World Divided, 1961-1989.* New York: HarperCollins.

The Art Story. (2022). *Antoni Gaudí - Biography and Legacy.* (The Art Story Foundation) Retrieved February 3, 2022, from THE ART STORY FOUNDATION

The Atomic Energy Commission. (1947). *Manhattan District History, Book VIII - Los Alamos Project (Y), Volume 1 - General.*

The Elders. (2020, July 27). *Masahiro Sasaki: on surviving the atomic bombing of Hiroshima, his sister Sadako and his mission to advance peace.* Retrieved December 7, 2021, from https://theelders.org/news/masahiro-sasaki-surviving-atomic-bombing-hiroshima-his-sister-sadako-and-his-mission-advance

The Nobel Peace Prize. (n.d.). *2013.* (nobelpeaceprize.org) Retrieved February 23, 2022, from https://www.nobelpeaceprize.org/laureates/2013

Twain, M. (1869). *The Innocents Abroad.*

Tyldesley, J. A. (2005). *Egypt: How a Lost Civilization was Rediscovered.* Berkeley: University of California Press.

Tyldesley, J. A. (2012). *Tutankhamen: The Search for an Egyptian King.* New York: Basic Books.

U.S. Department of Energy. (n.d.). *The Trinity Test.* Retrieved February 15, 2023, from https://www.osti.gov/opennet/manhattan-project-history/Events/1945/trinity.htm

Union of South Africa. (1950). *Population Registration Act, Act No. 30 of 1950.*

United Nations Development Programme. (2015). *Jordan Human Development Report 2015: Regional Disparities.* United Nations.

United Nations Educational, Scientific and Cultural Organization . (2022, June 24). *Constitution of the United Nations Educational, Scientific and Cultural Organization* . Retrieved May 5, 2023, from https://www.unesco.org/en/legal-affairs/constitution

United Nations Educational, Scientific and Cultural Organization. (n.d.). *UNESCO in brief.* Retrieved May 8, 2023, from https://www.unesco.org/en/brief

United Nations Scientific Committee on the Effects of Atomic Radiation. (2008). *Sources and Effects of Ionizing Radiation.* New York: United Nations.

United States Census Bureau. (1892-1954). *Statistical Abstract of the United States.*

United States Census Bureau. (n.d.). *QuickFacts: Plymouth town, Plymouth County, Massachusetts; Massachusetts; United States.* Retrieved August 8, 2023, from https://www.census.gov/quickfacts/fact/table/plymouthtownplymouthcountymassachusetts,MA,US/RHI325222#RHI325222

United States Holocaust Memorial Museum. (1942, January 20). *Wannsee Protocol.* Retrieved from https://holocaust.umd.umich.edu/news/uploads/WanseeProtocols.pdf

United States Holocaust Memorial Museum. (n.d.). *German Military Oaths.* Retrieved August 10, 2022, from https://encyclopedia.ushmm.org/content/en/article/german-military-oaths

United States Holocaust Memorial Museum. (n.d.). *Killing Centers: An Overview.* Retrieved from Holocaust Encyclopedia: https://encyclopedia.ushmm.org/content/en/article/killing-centers-an-overview

United States Holocaust Memorial Museum. (n.d.). *Reichstag Fire Decree.* Retrieved August 10, 2022, from https://encyclopedia.ushmm.org/content/en/article/reichstag-fire-decree

United States Nuclear Regulatory Commission. (1993, September 13). *Information Notice No. 93-71: Fire At Chernobyl Unit 2.* Retrieved October 26, 2022, from https://www.nrc.gov/reading-rm/doc-collections/gen-comm/info-notices/1993/in93071.html

USGS. (2015, April 25). *M 7.8 - 67 km NNE of Bharatpur, Nepal.* (Earthquake Hazards Program) Retrieved September 15, 2022, from https://earthquake.usgs.gov/earthquakes/eventpage/us20002926/executive

Veeck, G., Pannell, C. W., Smith, C. J., & Huang, Y. (2007). *China's Geography: Globalization and the Dynamics of Political, Economic, and Social Change.* Lanham: Rowman & Littlefield Publishers.

Vidal, J. (2011, April 19). *Ukraine raises $785m to seal Chernobyl under new 'shell'.* (The Guardian) Retrieved October 26, 2022, from https://www.theguardian.com/environment/2011/apr/19/ukraine-funding-chernobyl-arch

Waldron, A. (1990). *The Great Wall of China: From History to Myth.* Cambridge, Great Britian: Cambridge University Press.

Warth, R. D. (1997). *Nicholas II : The Life and Reign of Russia's Last Monarch.* Westport, CT: Praeger Publishers.

Weber.edu. (n.d.). *Statistics on Slavery.* Retrieved January 31, 2023, from https://faculty.weber.edu/kmackay/statistics_on_slavery.htm

Wells, H. (1914). *The World Set Free.*

Whitney, G. (2006). *Slaveholding Presidents.* (Ask Gleaves) Retrieved from https://scholarworks.gvsu.edu/ask_gleaves/30

Wiencek, H. (2003). *An Imperfect God: George Washington, His Slaves, and the Creation of America.* New York: Farrar, Straus and Giroux.

Wikisource contributors. (2022, October 7). *The Agreement of the Central People's Government and the local government of Tibet on Measures for the Peaceful liberation of Tibet.* (Wikisource) Retrieved October 7, 2022, from https://en.wikisource.org/w/index.php?title=The_Agreement_of_the_Central_People%27s_Government_and_the_local_government_of_Tibet_on_Measures_for_the_Peaceful_liberation_of_Tibet&oldid=11961218

Women's March. (2017, January 16). *Unity Principles*. Retrieved from https://web.archive.org/web/20170125034855/https://www.womensmarch.com/principles/

Wood, F. (2007). *China's First Emperor and his Terracotta Warriors.* New York: St. Martin's Press.

Worldatlas.com. (2022). *WWII Casualties By Country*. Retrieved August 10, 2022, from https://www.worldatlas.com/articles/wwii-casualties-by-country.html

Wright, D. C. (2001). *The history of China.* Westport, Connecticut: Greenwood Press.

Рyp, P. (2009, November 10). *Программа "Время" 28 апреля 1986-го года*. (youtube) Retrieved October 26, 2022, from https://www.youtube.com/watch?v=sC7n_QgJRks

Also by Scott C. Hall

How to Travel the World

100-Day Travel Journal

100-Day Travel Journal for Couples

100-Day Travel Journal for Families

Scott C. Hall is an author and world traveler whose work explores how journeys shape understanding, memory, and meaning. He has traveled to more than 70 countries across all seven continents and believes every destination offers a lesson in perspective. Scott holds a Bachelor of Science in Aerospace Engineering from the University of Kansas and an MBA from Rockhurst University. He lives near Kansas City, Missouri.

Learn more about Scott's travels and books at www.scottchall.com

www.ingramcontent.com/pod-product-compliance
Ingram Content Group UK Ltd.
Pitfield, Milton Keynes, MK11 3LW, UK
UKHW041634190726
13854UKWH00006B/2486